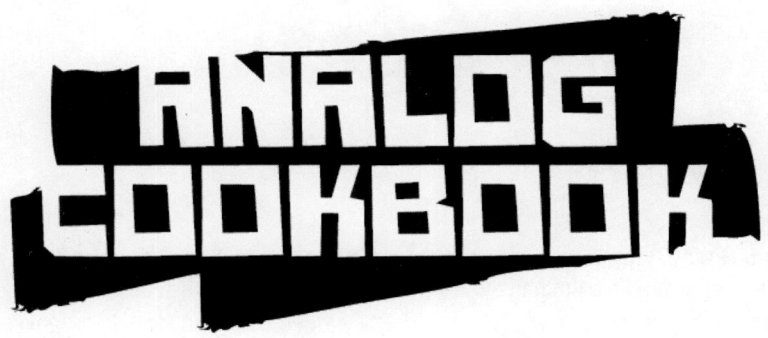

Founder/Editor-in-Chief: Kate E. Hinshaw
Editors: Andi Avery, Hogan Seidel, Gabby Sumney
Cover Design: Hogan Seidel
Interior Design: Kate E. Hinshaw
Analog Cookbook Logo: Sarah Lawrence's Design Emporium
Questions: hello@analogcookbook.com
Published by Analog Cookbook © 2023

Letter From The Editors

Dear Readers,

From Hogan: Why was this theme important to me? I did programming when I still lived in Boston with a Queer local arts organization, and I have been a teacher of experimental film & experimental film history. As an art teacher/programmer who focuses on Queer art history & exp film, I want to continue sharing the works and movements essential to the legacy of Queer art–artists. Artists who have watched as the world has tried to erase them socially, systemically, and politically. Their work inserts the whole body and being, their sexualities and desires, of violence and healing, on many different mediums in radical acts of seeing and being seen.

This is why when we were curating our issue, we began partly to think about the pedagogy of community and learning spaces, the places that keep and extend these legacies. Then we also looked at makers that are exploring themes of erotica in the field of analog art, both looking at emerging, mid-career, and established artists, and how important it is to learn from these radical practices, past and present. How do we create community and safety in exploring these topics of erotica, pornography, sexuality, and explicit imagery? I believe erotica is a powerful tool as it reveals so much about self and nation. It is both personal and reveals larger socio-historical contexts/consequences. It challenges our own learned "norms" and liberates us.

As a young artist, I was, and I can't find a better word for this, liberated when I first saw Dyketactics on screen for the first time. I watched Barbara Hammer in a red convertible drive out to the mountainside in California, strip to nothing with a group of friends, dance, and feed each other. The

From Andi: I saw Dyketactics as a young teenager, during a time when I was constantly searching the world for any information on what it meant to live as a Queer person. Queer representation was so poor at the time, and when it existed it echoed the transphobic/fatphobic/white-centered/male gaze formula for success. And there, buried deep in the avant-garde/experimental section, was Barbara Hammer–playful and free and editing "kinaesthetically," not that I knew what that meant at the time. Truthfully, I still don't know what it means exactly as she meant it. But since going back to school and being prescribed books upon books about the technical process of film editing (Walter Murch, Greg Keast, and the rest), I've found myself wondering why we read about it at all, and if we can't just feel it in our bones–when to make cuts, how to pace them, and how to lead a viewer through the cycle of tension and release that comes from a good edit. In my mind, that's the basis of kinaesthetic editing–the part where my senses guide me through it, and where my body knows what it wants to watch and wants others to see. The part of my art-making practice that relies on listening to what my body wants feels boldly and defiantly erotic.

The part of this issue that fascinates me immensely is the part where we get to ask our contributors over and over–what does it mean for something to be erotic? Why are our bodies drawn to some things, and not to others? And what is, personally, the most intriguing–why are we drawn to things in imagery and art that we don't desire to recreate in our lives, or are not particularly drawn to in our physical erotic experiences? This issue gives our contributors a platform for these exact musings. This issue invites you, our readers, to discover eroticism in whatever our contributing artists offer up as erotic. And we as editors invite you to discover the eroticism in your practice, regardless of whether or not you consider yourself to be a maker of erotic art.

With love and solidarity,

Andi & Hogan
Lead Editors of Analog Erotica

buildings, blast zones, and back rooms. Malic's films have screened in experimental film festivals and Queer bars across the world. His latest film "Living Lessons in the Museum of Order," which was shot at SeaWorld San Diego and the former prison on Alcatraz Island, explores tourism in the age of mass incarceration.

Hogan Seidel is an interdisciplinary media artist living and working in Seattle, WA. Their work has been shown nationally and internationally at festivals such as Onion City, Alchemy, Analogica, Indie Grits, ULTRA Cinema, Revolutions Per Minute, Artifact, Fracto Experimental, and PRISME. They have received funding and support from the Massachusetts Cultural Council, Collective Futures, and the United States Artists Grant.

dark rooms / toxic pleasures, Sally Chessell   **106**
120mm film, darkroom eroticism // Images + Essay

Sally Chessell is an artist concerned with infrastructures of intimacy and works across expanded photographic practice, writing and installation.

Traces, Chantal Partamian & Yara Al Chehayed   **114**
Super 8mm + VHS // Essay

Experimental filmmaker and archivist, Chantal Partamian mainly work with super 8 and found footage. Partamian's work has been presented and awarded at multiple festivals and is distributed by Videographe and GIV.

Untitled (Christ on the Cross), Jamieson Edson   **118**
Yellow polaroid duochrome print // Image

Jamieson Edson is an artist based in Jamaica Plain MA. They graduated with a BFA from Massachusetts College of Art and Design in Studio for Interrelated Media in 2015.

Título 1, Cecilia Romero + Saru Miras   **120**
16mm // Film Stills

Cecilia Romero and Saru Miras are a Queer couple interested in researching new ways of erotica and identity throw analog media.

Screen Kiss (2007-2017), Joanna Byrne   **124**
16mm live film performance with optical and magnetic sound // Stills

Joanna Byrne is a UK-based artist-filmmaker, working with super 8mm and16mm film in a tactile, material way: incorporating found footage, hand-manipulation and physical traces of her body into her films.

In the Age of Community

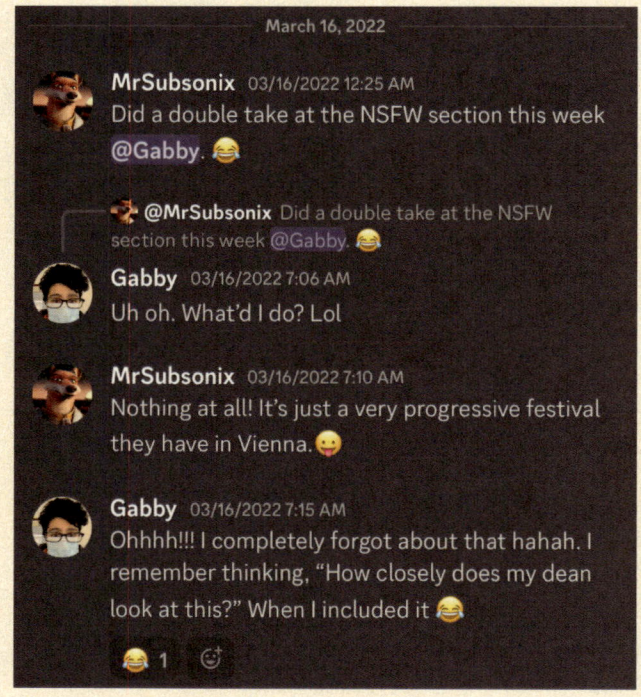

March 16, 2022

MrSubsonix 03/16/2022 12:25 AM
Did a double take at the NSFW section this week @Gabby. 😂

↳ **@MrSubsonix** Did a double take at the NSFW section this week @Gabby. 😂

Gabby 03/16/2022 7:06 AM
Uh oh. What'd I do? Lol

MrSubsonix 03/16/2022 7:10 AM
Nothing at all! It's just a very progressive festival they have in Vienna. 😛

Gabby 03/16/2022 7:15 AM
Ohhhh!!! I completely forgot about that hahah. I remember thinking, "How closely does my dean look at this?" When I included it 😂

😂 1

Standards

The biggest part of my job as the creator and regular compiler of This Week in Experimental is finding places for experimental filmmakers, photographers, artists, and scholars to submit their work. Every week, I comb through a list of websites, my social media feeds, my inbox, and our Google Form looking for open calls, residencies, funds, cool media works, and thought-provoking readings to give our strange little corner of the internet some inspiration and some goal posts. I admit that I don't look too deeply into the Terms & Conditions of every open call I post, which is how I got a funny note from a subscriber on Discord back in March when I included the call to Porn Festival Vienna.

Despite that, I didn't consider how hard it is to find radical places/programmers who are willing to program/curate work that is sexually explicit/pornographic until we started accepting submissions for Analog Erotica, and that's an oversight on my part. I'm not as "from the internet" as someone like my wife, but I am online a fair amount. I see all the same community standards and warnings about posting explicit content as anyone else on social media–Analog Cookbook got an Instagram post pulled in the run-up to this issue because of violating these community standards by including a still from a Barbara Hammer film.

I'm old enough to remember when porn was the point of the Internet. I was a curious teenager in the age of little to no parental controls and anonymous message boards. I was a young adult during the heyday of Tumblr–yes, I know that Tumblr still exists and has successfully held to its weird and unprofitable roots, and I'm very proud of the weirdos who keep that sliver of old-school internet alive. Social media, under the auspices of protecting children from sexually explicit content while maintaining a grip on as much capital as possible, has its so-called Community Standards, which cause flare-up against censorship semi-regularly.

These standards may seem like the price of existing in public space for the most part, but it does have particular costs and consequences for those who make explicitly sexual (or even just nude) content as well as those who engage in sex work to make a living. During lockdown in the states, this conversation came to a head when OnlyFans briefly mulled banning sexually explicit content to have greater access to revenue via major financial institutions. There's a lot to criticize about Web 2.0, but I definitely overlooked this part.

Gabby Follett

Erotica friendly Film Festivals and Screenings

Berlin Porn Film Festival
Brussels Porn Film Festival
Cinekink
Collectif Jeune Cinéma
Excéntrico (Chile)
Failed Films LA
Fish & Chips International Erotic Film Festival
Hacker Porn Film Festival
Hot Bits (USA)
HUMP!
London Fetish Film Festival
MIX NYC (past screening series)
NACHTSCHATTEN BDSM/Fetisch Film Festival
Natural Instincts Porn Festival (Germany)
Porn Festival Vienna
Porny Days - Film Kunst Festival (Switzerland)
PorYes Feminist Porn Award
Post Porn Film Festival Warsaw
Satyrs and Maenads (Greece)
Schamlos! Queer-Feminist Pornography Festival Bern
Scottish Queer International Film Festival
SECS Fest
Sex Worker Film & Arts Festival
Sexuality & Gender Art Festival
The Blue Film Festival at Northwest Film Forum (USA)
Toronto Queer Film Festival
Uncensored (England)

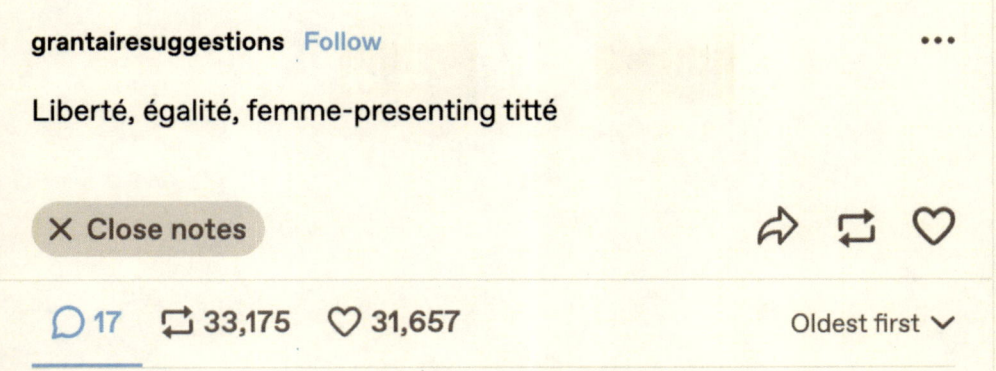

grantairesuggestions Follow

Liberté, égalité, femme-presenting titté

✕ Close notes

↪ ⇄ ♡

💬 17   ⇄ 33,175   ♡ 31,657   Oldest first ⌄

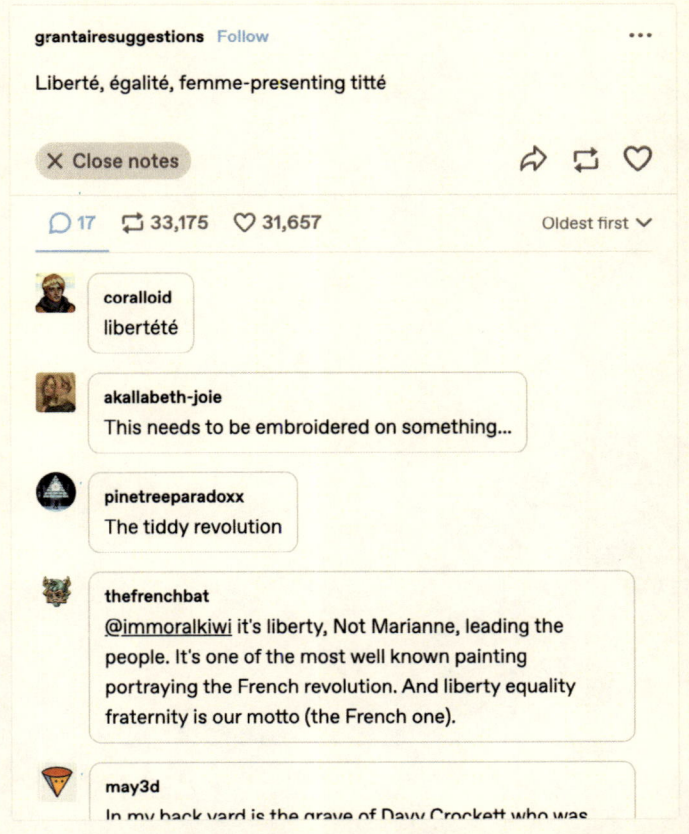

grantairesuggestions Follow

Liberté, égalité, femme-presenting titté

✕ Close notes

↪ ⇄ ♡

💬 17   ⇄ 33,175   ♡ 31,657   Oldest first ⌄

coralloid
libertété

akallabeth-joie
This needs to be embroidered on something...

pinetreeparadoxx
The tiddy revolution

thefrenchbat
@immoralkiwi it's liberty, Not Marianne, leading the people. It's one of the most well known painting portraying the French revolution. And liberty equality fraternity is our motto (the French one).

may3d
In my back yard is the grave of Davy Crockett who was

T4T: A Trans

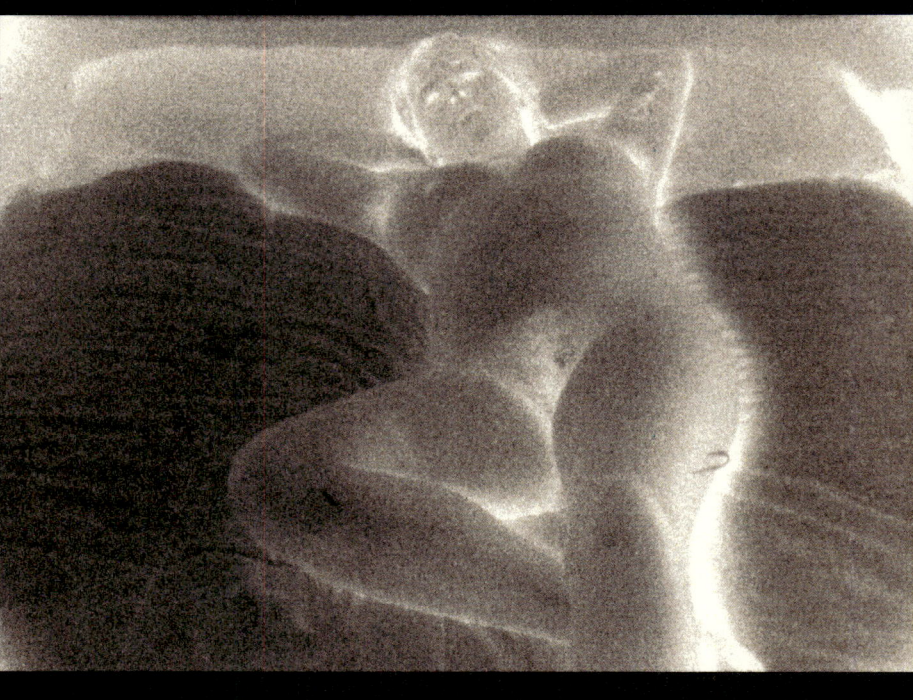

Max
Van Loan

Sexperimental Film

I had the pleasure of reading more than 20 books in 2022, most of them Queer science fiction. Perhaps my favorite has been Meanwhile, Elsewhere, a collection of short science fiction and fantasy stories from trans writers, edited by Cat Fitzpatrick and Casey Plett. I've found that there is plenty of writing by, about, and for trans folks, even within this somewhat niche genre of science fiction and fantasy. But when it comes to the niche cinematic genre of analog experimental film, there are only a few trans filmmakers that come to mind (Autojektor, and Nazlı Dinçel, for instance). Perhaps this is an oversight of my own, so I welcome correction. One type of analog experimental film that I believe has a dearth of trans voices is that of the "sexperimental" film. In the 1960s and 70s experimental filmmakers like Stan Brakhage, Carolee Schneeman, and Barbara Hammer started making films centering around sexuality, performance, and domesticity that included graphic depictions of sexual acts by the filmmakers themselves. Of course, the sex depicted in Brakhage's and Schneemann's films was between heterosexual partners. Partially in response to these types of films, I created T4T in 2021. I wanted to see and celebrate intimacy between trans people, the magical kind of understanding and respect we can show for each other's bodies. In T4T, my partner and I are sharing physical intimacy while nude, but we are not having sex the way that a heteronormative culture would say "counts". But what is sex? And who gets to decide?

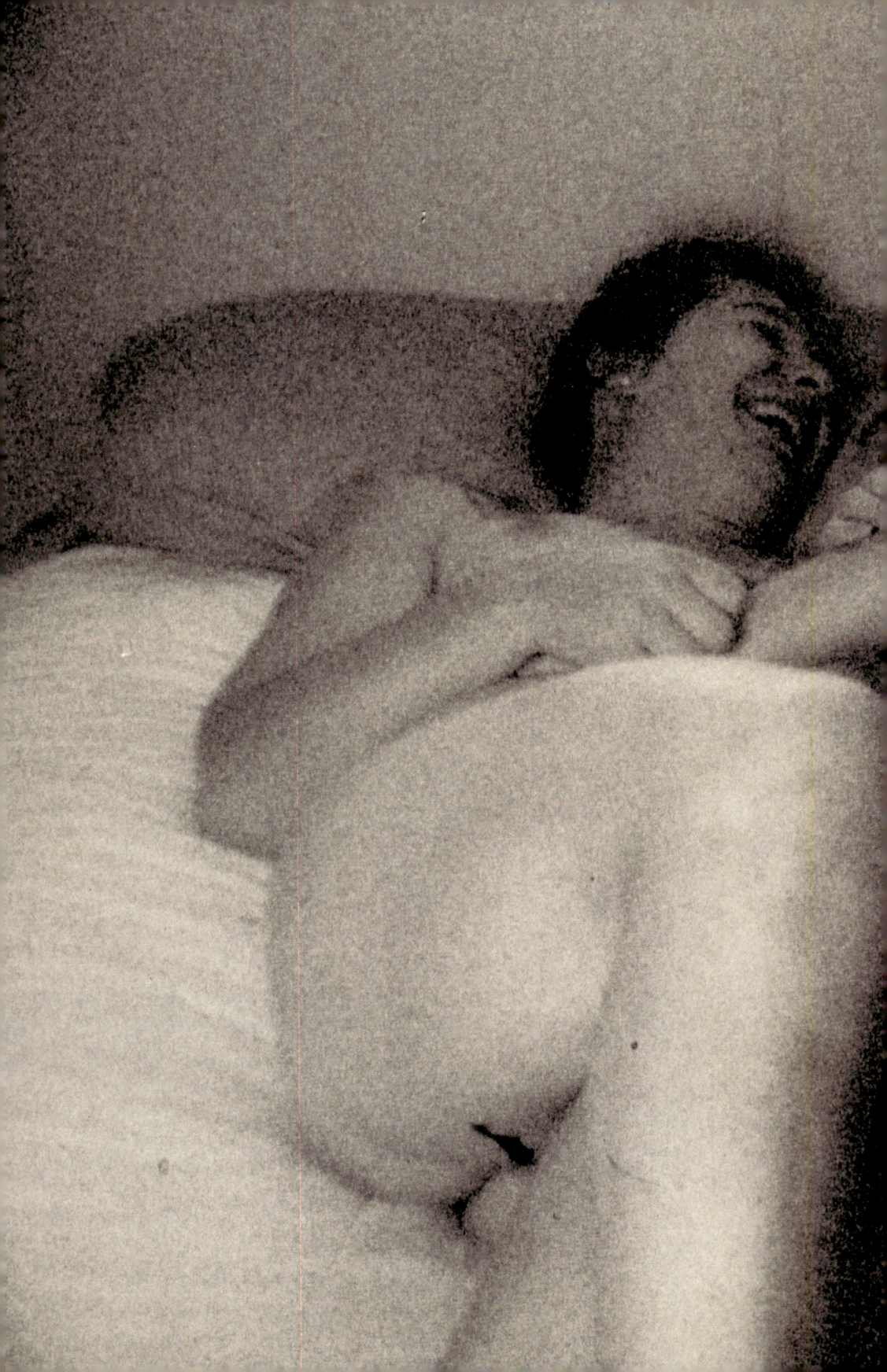

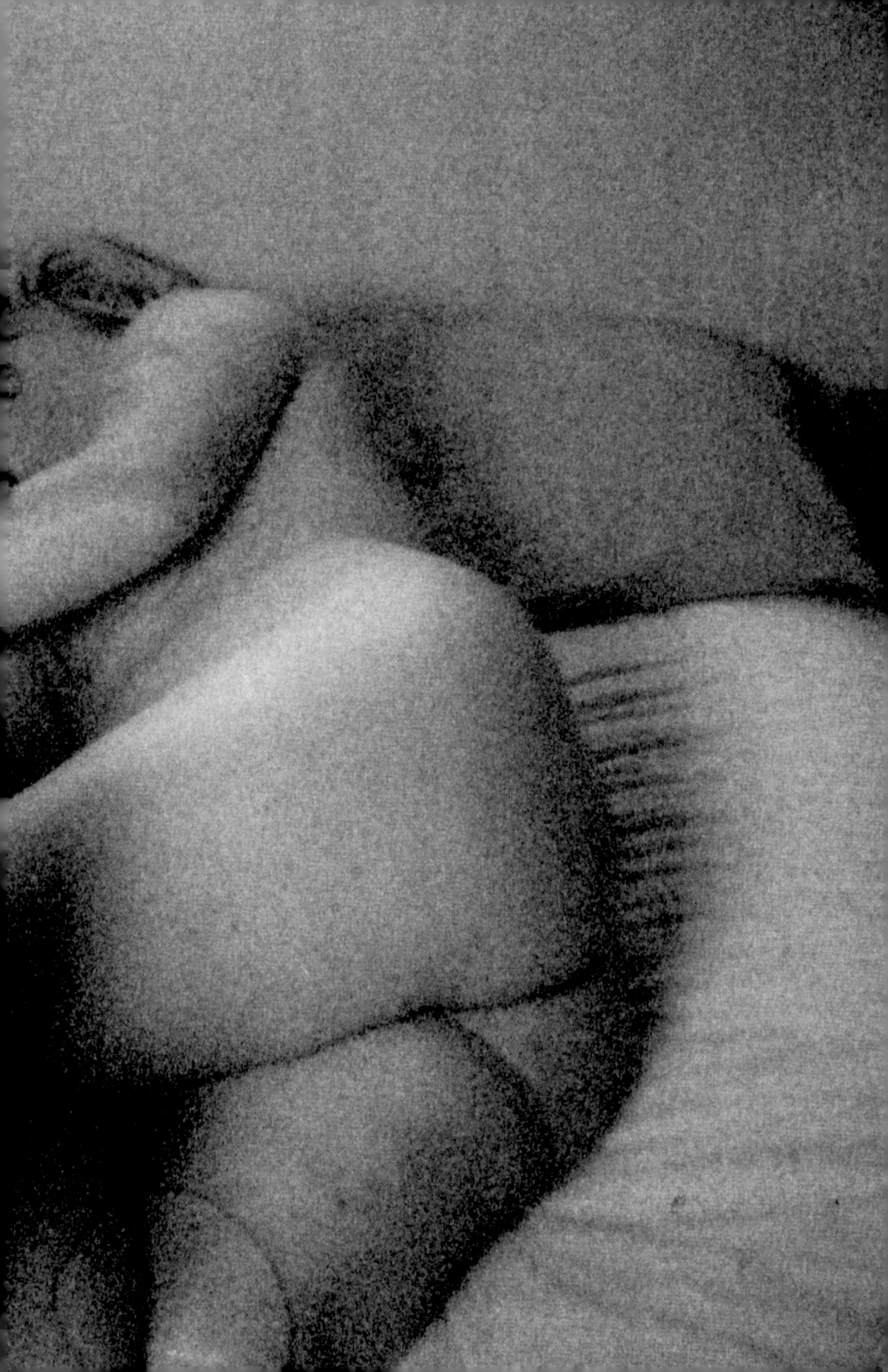

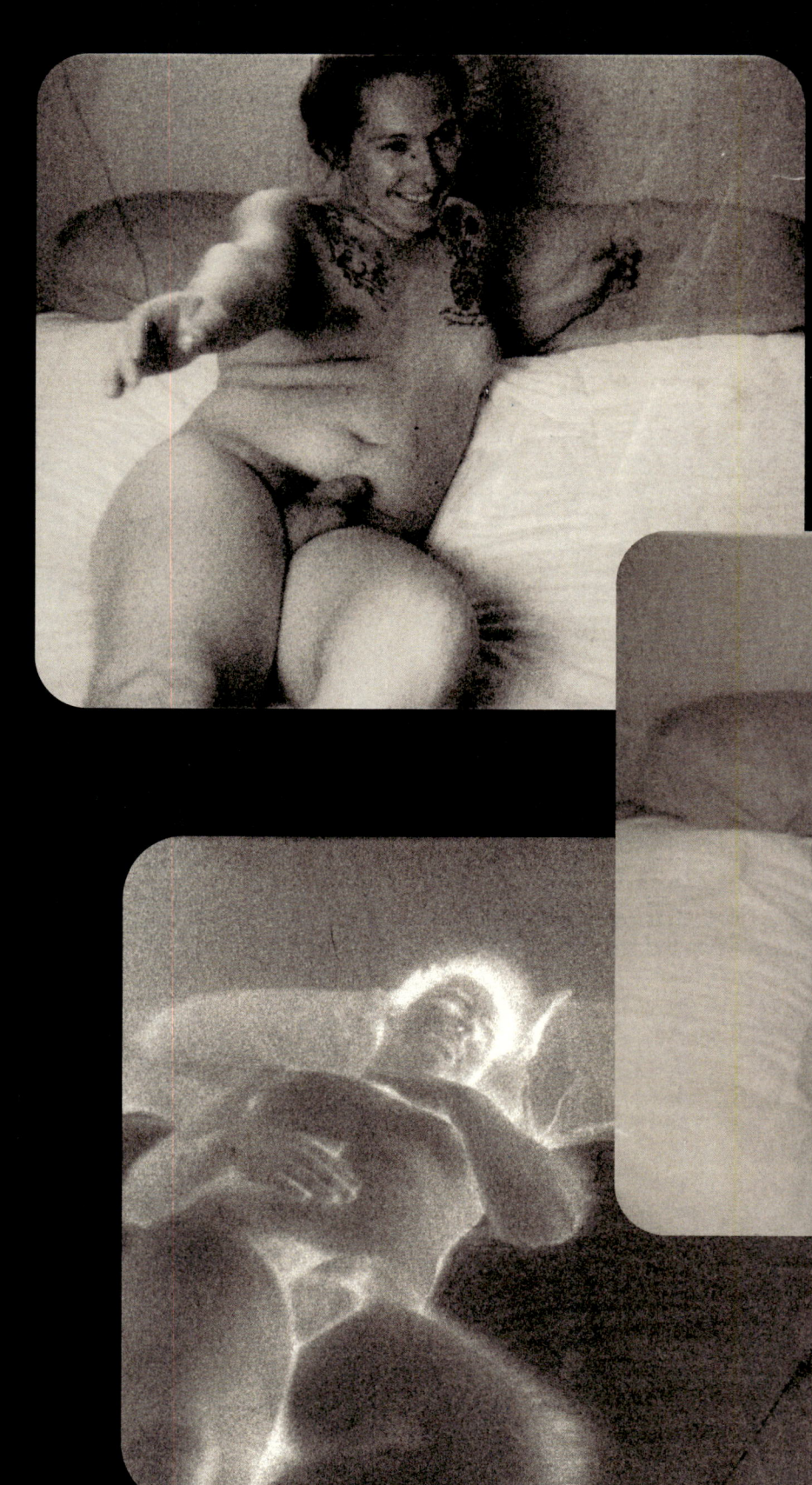

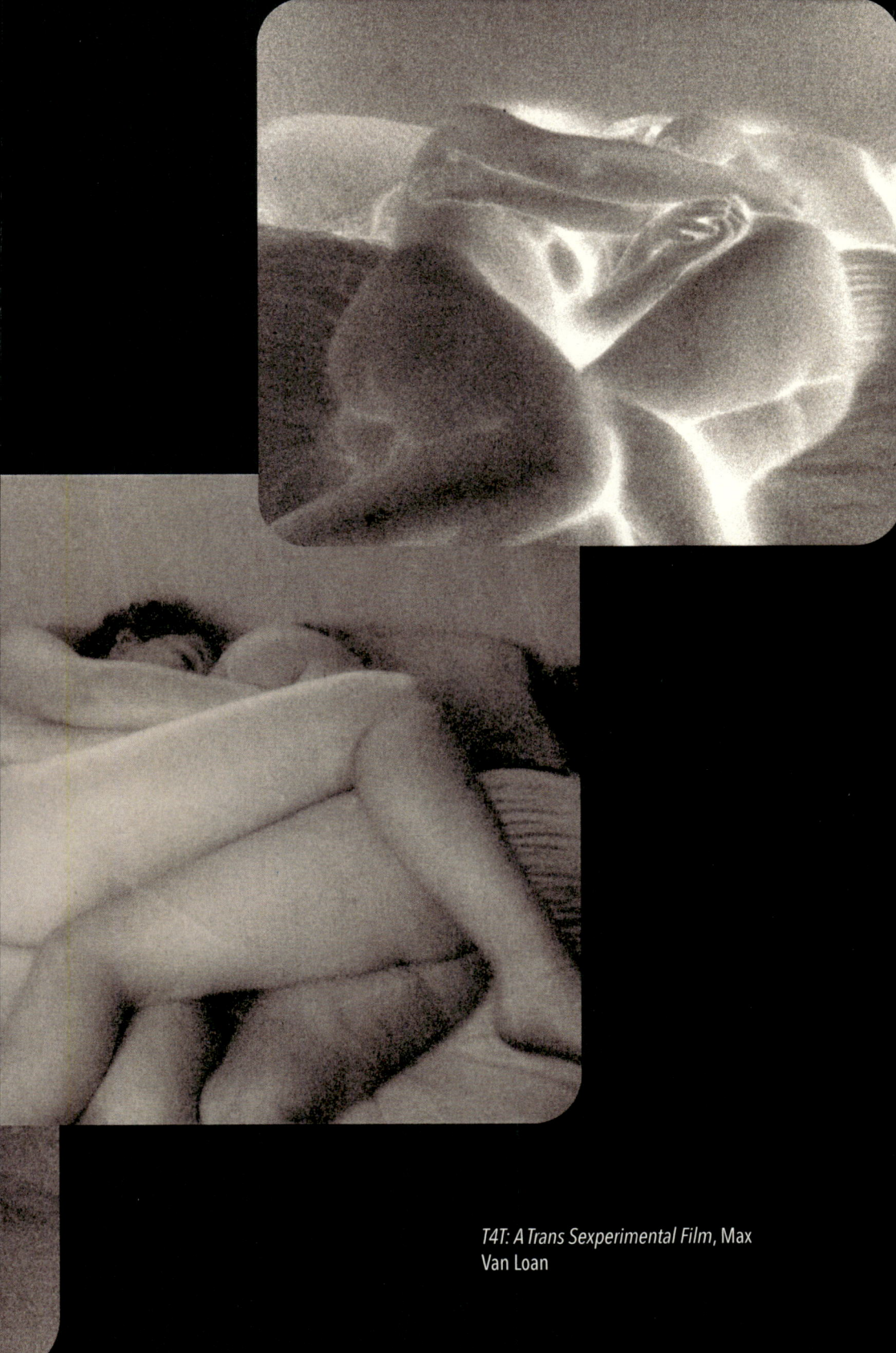

T4T: A Trans Sexperimental Film, Max
Van Loan

Cali M. Banks

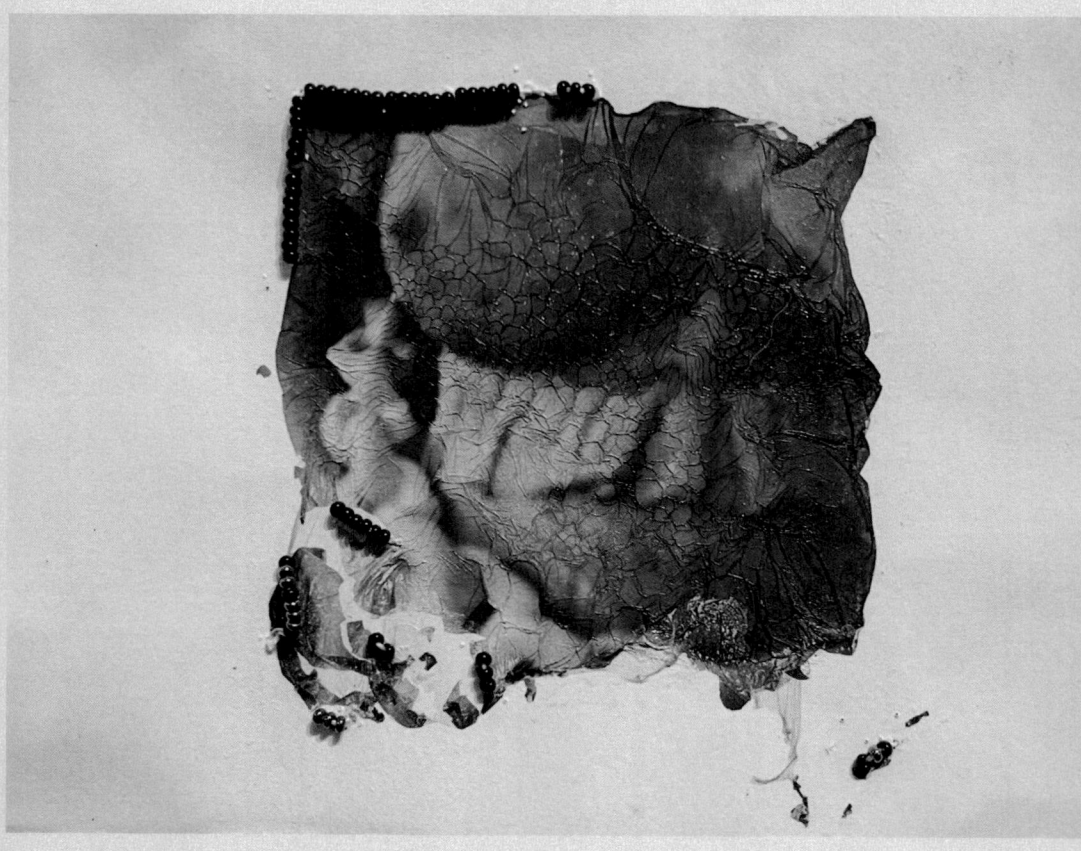

Close Enough To Touch is a series of polaroid emulsion transfers that are hand beaded with traditional indigenous technique. Each image has been captured in Brooklyn, and combines both self-portraiture, still-lives, architecture that is specific to this borough, and symbolism depicting bodies, ritual, and sensuality. Red, black, and white are consistent colors throughout the work as a representation of the Lenape Tribe. Black is indicative of power, strength, aggression, and victory. Red represents happiness and beauty, but also violence and bloodshed. White is indicative of sharing and light. Gold is used to represent value and validation. Each beaded image contains one blue bead, historically known as a "spirit bead" in indigenous beadwork. This is not only a signature in every piece, but also an act of recognition to her maternal grandfather and mother.

In this series you're working with 2-needle indigenous beading. Combined with emulsion lifts it's almost as if you're sewing into skin. Can you tell us about the significance behind the beading, and why these materials are specifically important to this body of work?

My idea was to incorporate breath, tactility, and layers of sensitivity—both physical, emotional, and theoretical, into a series surrounding trauma, chronic illness, and the experiences of women through my personal experiences. The emulsion lifts and beading create a barrier between myself and touch. Through layers of sensitivity, trauma can be imagined as an imprint of the skin. But, through contrasts of soft and sharp elements, there is a reclamation of identity; how my culture is still strong and breathing. I am integrating my indigenous heritage into the paper through beadwork, which was something I fought against for many years. I felt that westernized views of indigenous art always wanted to see my work covered in feathers, beads, buffalo—things that they deemed "indigenous." But, by adding traditional beadwork to my images in my own style, it feels like a sort of reclamation of identity, but also what feels genuine to me. Based on the meaning of colors I mentioned above, I only used beads of those shades.

Can you tell us a bit about your process creating emulsion lifts? Do you have other bodies of work that utilize this technique? Or was it specific to Close Enough?

I started this process about a year ago, after reading through a tutorial in Analog Cookbook! I was in a bit of

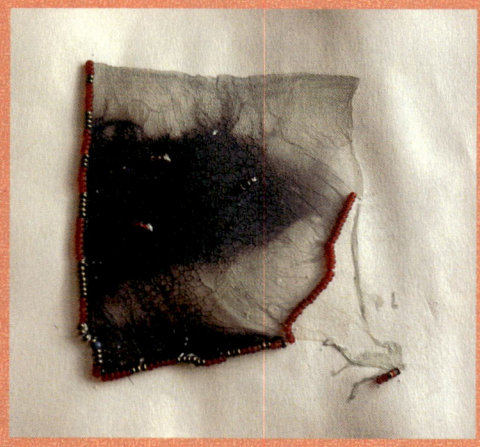

a standstill with my work at that time, and realized I had all of the materials to test it out. I fell in love with how you can manipulate the emulsion to fold over itself or rip. Emulsion lifts tend to be popular in the realm of experimental photography, so I wanted to create work that would set me apart. *Close Enough To Touch* was my first body of work that utilized this technique, but I am in the process of creating more!

How did you come up with the titles for the individual pieces in this series?

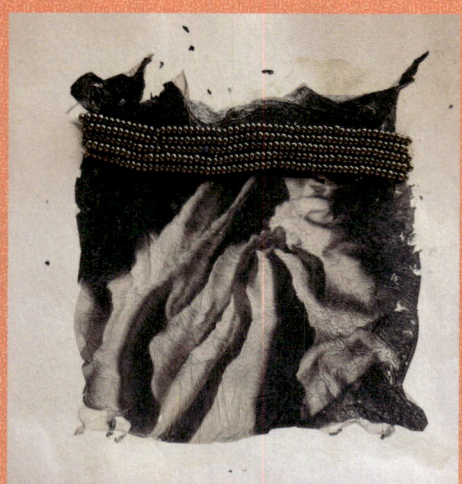

I tend to be a very sarcastic person with a touch of dark and/or dry humor. All of the titles were things men have said to me in the process of a breakup or difficult time in the relationship– which was intense in the moment, but kind of humorous to me now. The titles bring in a sense of sensuality or eroticism, but it's also an inside joke with myself– especially considering how dramatic some of them are.

The work is very personal, did you learn anything about yourself in this process?

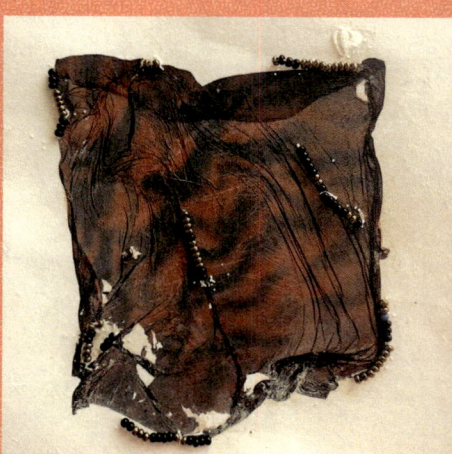

This body of work allowed me to think introspectively, which is something I tend to steer away from. I had to think of how imagery of say, a building, could be representative of my identity, or how colors and the shape the beading took could create different meanings. I also realized that I have gained an immense amount of patience as I've gotten older. The emulsion process itself takes so much patience - from waiting for

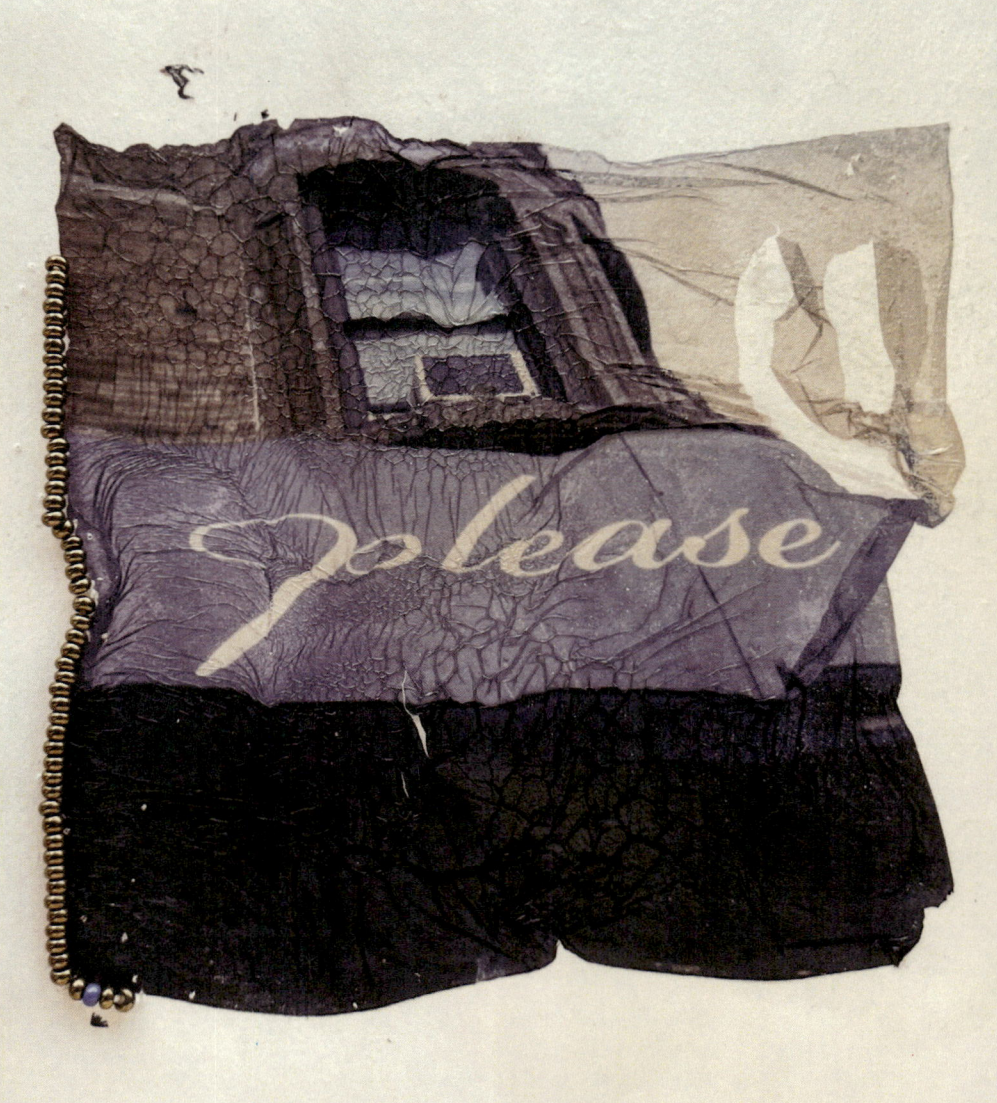

the emulsion to lift in water, to successfully transferring it, to the drying process. But the beading is a whole other ball game. It's not something that can be done fast in any sense, as I am tackling 3-5 beads at a time, and there are hundreds on each image. But, it became a therapeutic process, as the repetitive technique can almost become ritualistic and calming, while being able to connect with ancestors.

I'm so drawn to the images that showcase things that the average person might not necessarily deem "erotic"--the images of the bed, the signage, can you talk about what makes something erotic, or what makes these images erotic to you or in the context of this larger body of work?

I've always been interested in what defines eroticism. Based on who the person is, anything could trigger some sort of arousal - food, scent, imagery. There doesn't need to be full frontal nudity to make someone feel a sense of desire. A bed or sheets can be erotic to some, if you think about what all happens within a bedroom. For example, the piece, "I Haven't Changed My Sheets Since You Left" ... could allude that I wasn't just taking a nap in someone's bed. Flowers could be representative of genitalia, but roses are also a familial ritual. The signage that says please is actually a sex shop in Brooklyn. But, I also am interested in the definition of please. Is someone saying it just to be polite? Are they begging for something? Are they satisfying themselves or others? While these definitions could be thought about innocently, they also can have a more erotic undertone. Like the Rapid Slide image. The signage was a part of a carnival happening on my street, but someone could think of that phrase as relating to a sexual act or secretions from the body. I like to play with double entendre in my work. Also, I personally like to be more subtle, so there are layers of understanding to my work.

24

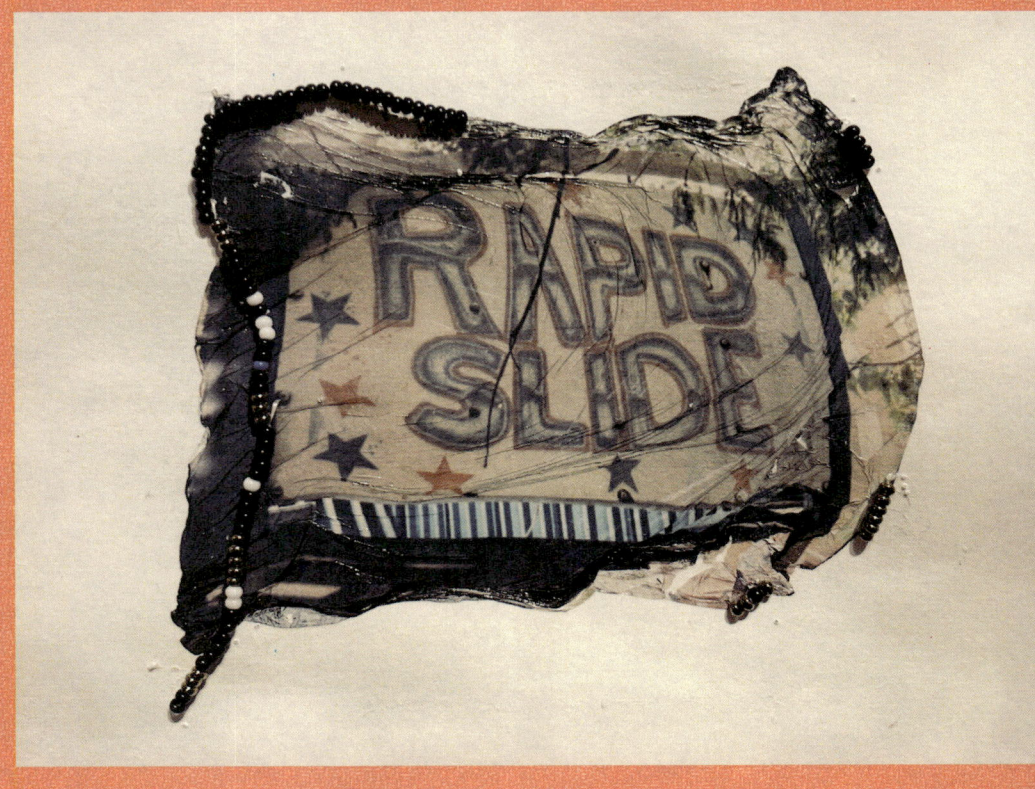

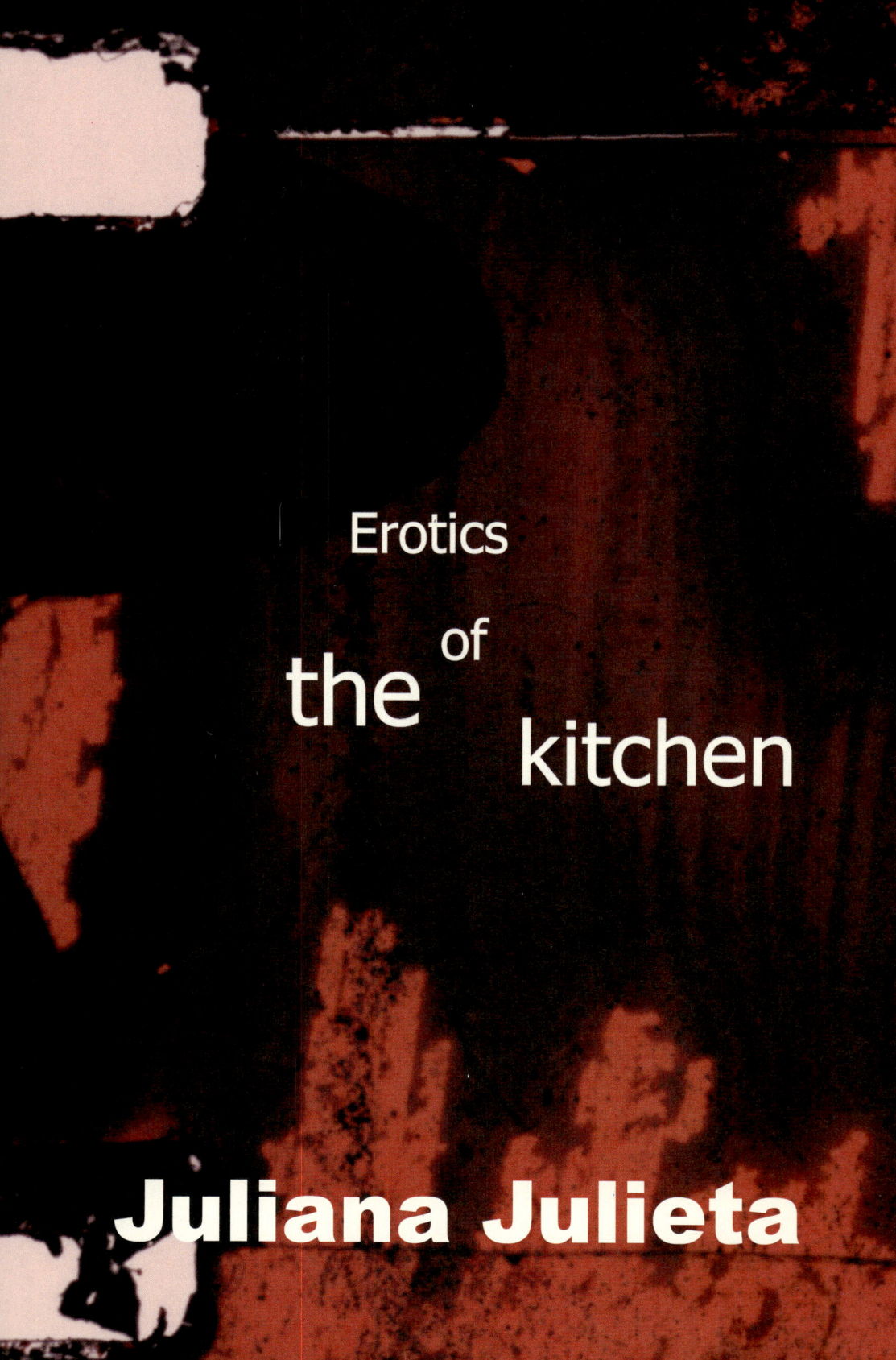

Erotics

of

the

kitchen

Juliana Julieta

What originally got you into analog filmmaking and collage techniques? Or what brought you to working with Mono Aware?

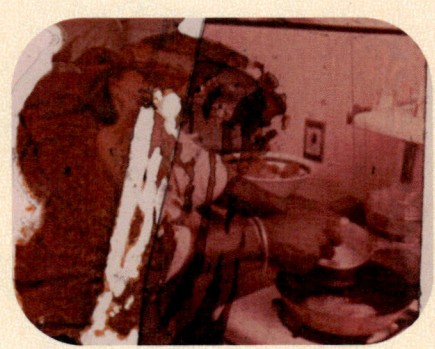

I am very thankful that I've encountered the community of Mono No Aware. I met Steve Cossman in Portugal, when he was helping us build Casa do Xisto (an artistic residence dedicated to cinema and visual arts). I took part in the 1st edition where we learnt how to use the Bolex, shoot, develop (exploring non-toxic caffenol processing). In an exciting intensive week we also planted a cinematic garden and presented our films. I was in love with analog filmmaking, its aesthetic potentialities, and the idea of community building through this common love of film. So I did all that I could to keep learning and had the opportunity to do an artist residence at Mono supported by FLAD.

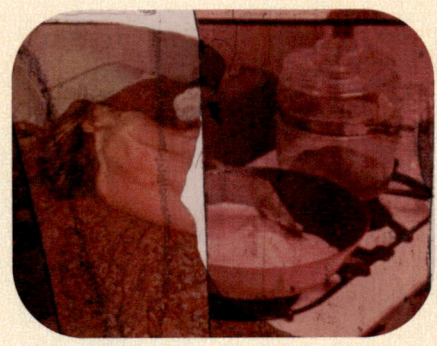

As someone who works primarily in painting, what are your thoughts/ philosophies on collage experimental film that uses additive and subtractive techniques? How do you approach this practice with the eye of a painter?

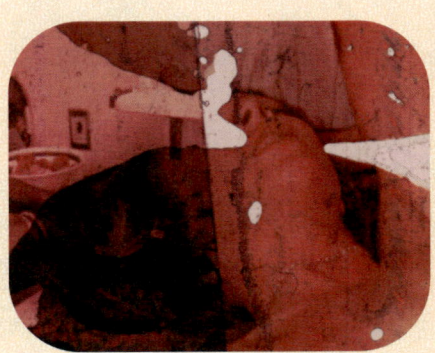

I explore the archival a lot trying to find new relations between heterogeneous fragments. As in painting, collage experimental film can be worked in a very plastic approach. You can boil, bleach, rip it up, paint, overlap and keep building new layers in search of the image you want. For example, cutting the body to pieces and reassembling it in different configurations can be really liberating from the fixed coherent image we are trained and used to see and understand. In painting like in experimental film you can experiment a lot and discover the work in the process of making it, through the medium and its techniques. For example, if you are

27

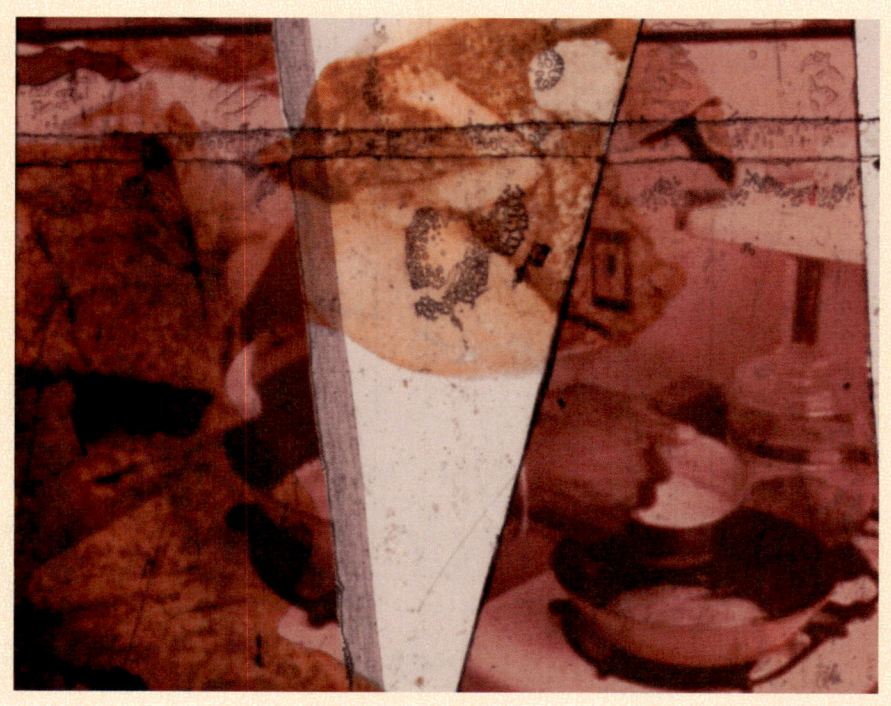

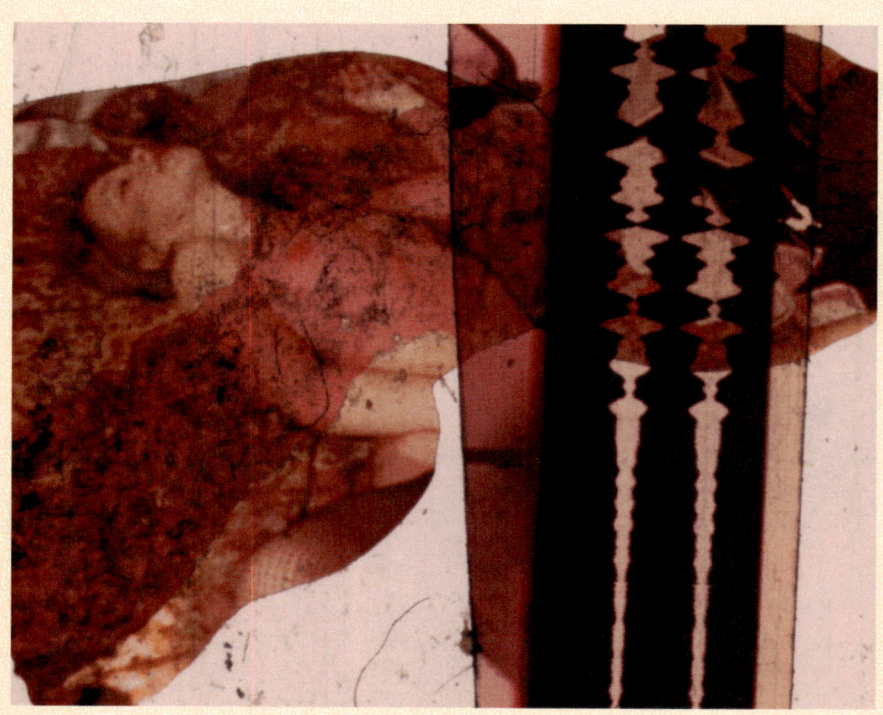

shooting on Bolex, the body of the camera itself can be a creative medium. It's nice to know and explore the particularities of each medium. In my oil painting I believe the materiality of oil is very important to the work produced, the body of the ink, the accidents, the transparency and opacity, painting, whipping, going back and forward. Direct filmmaking is also very rich with plasticity, the materials and techniques can speak as much as the content of the film. The content can be the scratching or the collage. In the surface of film the plastic vocabulary is at play: composition, color, texture, rhythm, mark making, the interplay and succession of shapes, etc. In this piece sometimes you have different temporalities of the same action, like cooking or cutting vegetables and as I was cutting, collaging, and splicing the film I kept thinking for example of Picasso cubist paintings. I am curious to see how the relationship between film and painting can also be the other way around, having my paintings informed by the eye of experimental film.

Tell us about the relationship between preparing food, sex, and the act of collage filmmaking. Why were you attracted to these found footage pieces?

I mean, cooking and sex, it's a very good combo. [Just kidding] I guess my initial intention was to try to give some beauty and different meaning to the porn footage I found. They lacked texture and good taste (in the degustative sense of the expression). I wanted to highlight the movement of hands in both pieces, that's something I'm very fixated on, paying attention to the small ritual gestures of hands performing banal daily tasks. Just that for me has a very erotic charge. As I was saying, in my intention to pay

attention to the gestures of hands, I found these two footages and started collecting fragments where the hands were showing in close-up or were central to the scenes. The hands were massaging, mixing food, cutting, transforming and stimulating other bodies. You see a knife chopping vegetables and the images that flash in a fast cutting pace, bits of pleasure-making glimpsed, the film itself sliced and mixed with other elements to create a new meaning, the film scratched, bleached, torn apart, in a way "cooked" for you to taste. In this approach to direct filmmaking (like preparing food) you can be creative, playing with colors, with forms, smells, flavors, textures and the different states that it can take. Combined with the sexual imagery, through the montage you feel in the ritual part of preparing food an intense rhythm, the calling of multiple senses of the body like the tactile, the smell, the palate or more specifically, the visual texture of all these things. I think rhythm and texture play an essential part in my work, and for me those two dimensions relate a lot with the erotic, not the porn because in porn I understand the texture to be something flat and lacking the sensuality that we feel in erotic works. Those would be less obvious, less illustrative and more intuitive, more felt through the sensations that build up in the body.

What is the relationship between the red hand painted piece that begins/centers the work, and the faded color dye layers of the pink/red found footage? Or the transition from familiar technique of painting to that of collage/splicing/taping?

I was exploring painting directly on film, and seeing how it would feel when the

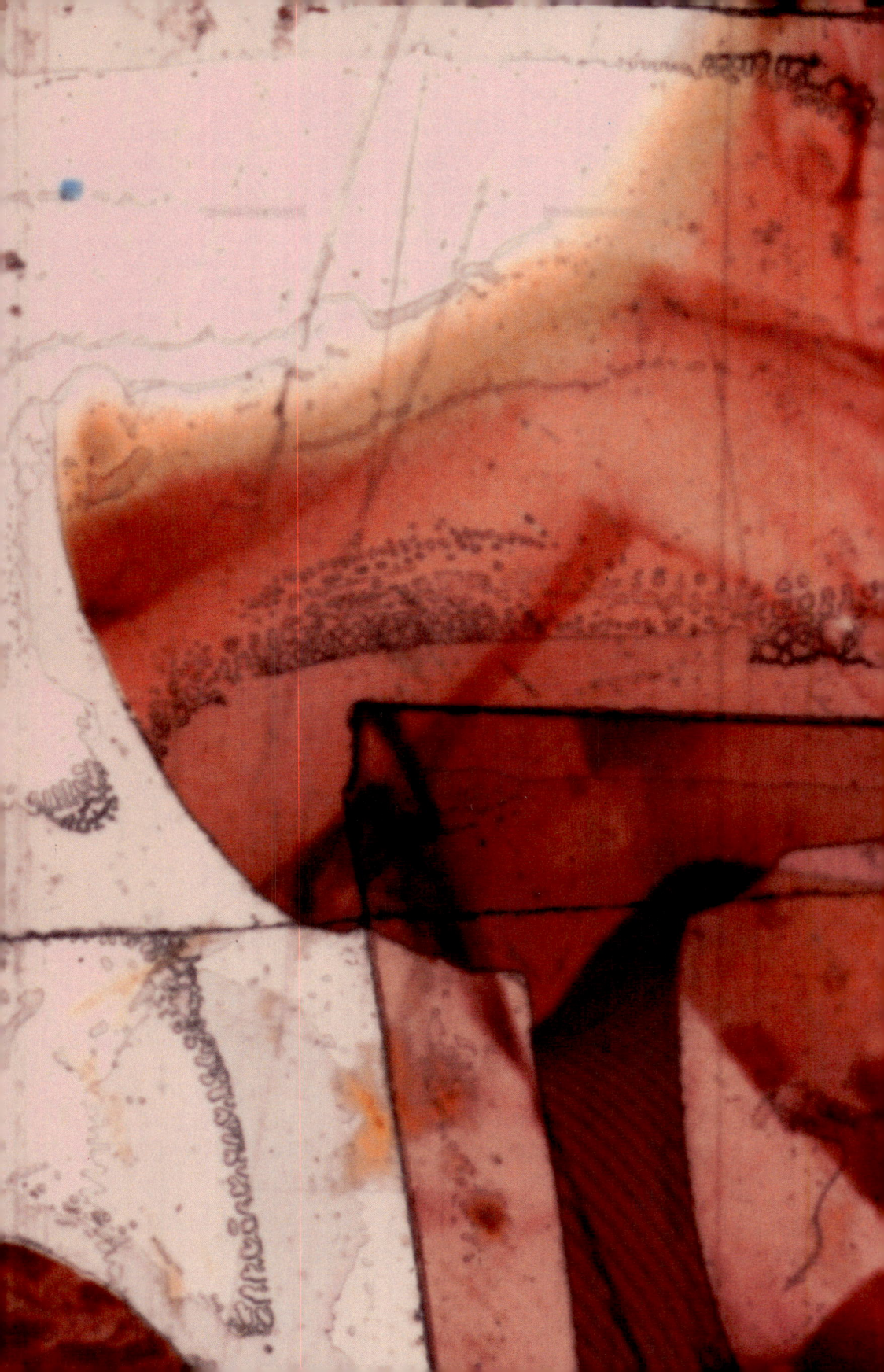

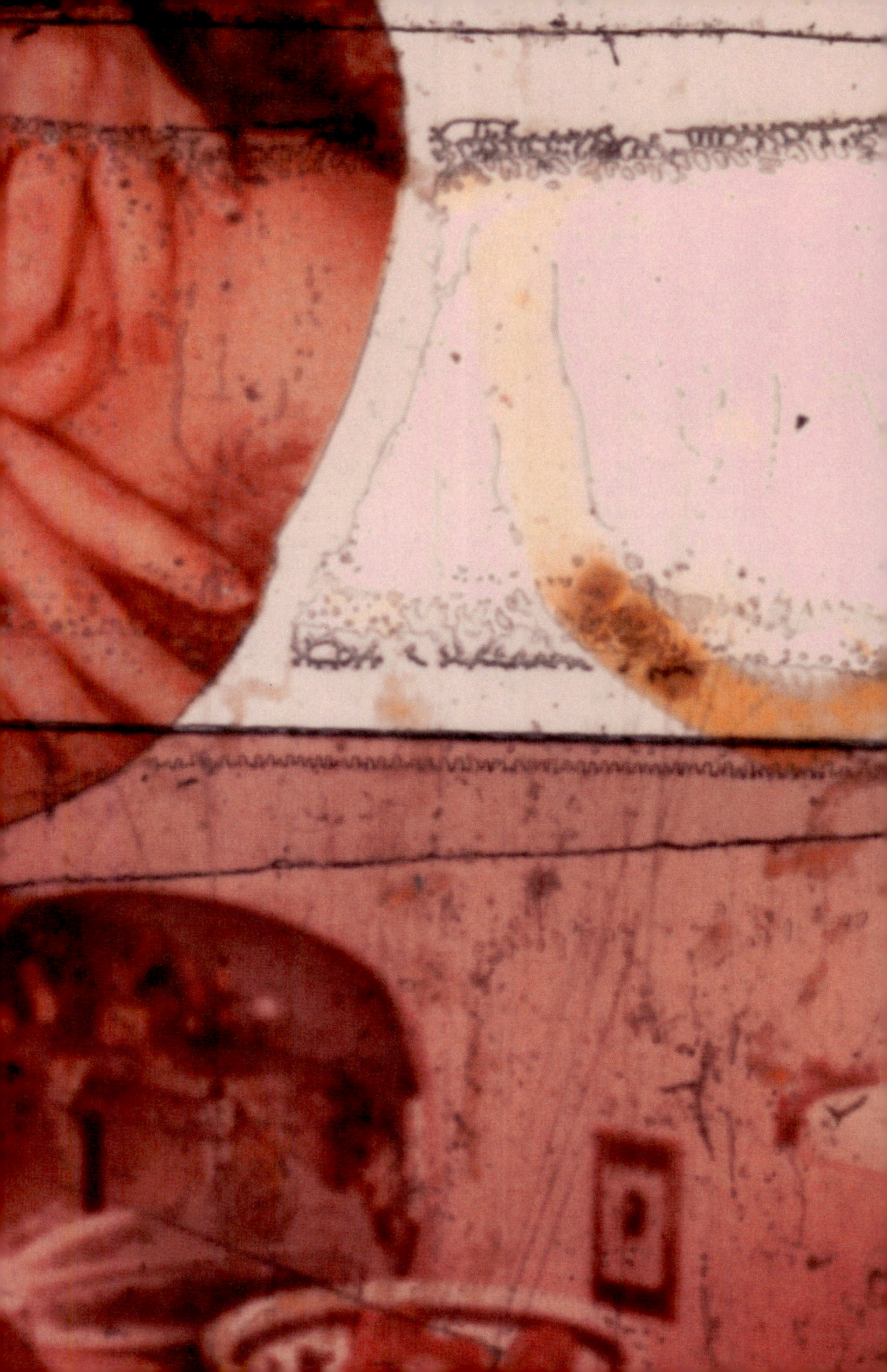

light passes through the transparent surface. Different from the canvas, the texture and different dilutions of the ink can take up a monumental scale when projected and it's very seductive seeing ink like that. I was painting the raw film in red in search of a warm atmosphere, a kind of beauty that I was trying to see if it was possible to give to the porn found footage that I was manipulating. I guess the hand painted piece sets the tone for what you will be about to see next.

One of the goals for my artist residence at Mono was to expand my work as a painter and find ways to explore that in analog filmmaking. Being through shooting, through manipulating found footage, through direct animation (painting, scratching, printing, collaging, etc) or even in the performative possibilities of projecting and presenting the moving image. My paintings are nurtured by my long time love for cinema, and I've always had a concern to try to convey the sensation of movement to the static medium of painting, so this time I wanted to pursue that desire for movement in the cinematic image, keeping a painterly quality to the experience of the succession of images.

Tell us about the silence in this work. As you see the undulation of image and sound track, you are made aware of the noise of kitchen and sex, but we are purposely made to not hear it. Can you talk a little about that?

I guess I felt the film already had a lot of "noise" and that I wanted to make the sequence of the images to generate their own sound. I've listened to the original sound of the films and I was repelled by it, I didn't feel like it had anything

to do with the sensations that I was searching and trying to create. The sound was very distracting and impoverished the image. So I used the sound for its visual expression, adding bits of the undulations here and there as an inherent sound to the image presented.

In this film I think the lack of sound makes you more aware of what you are seeing, and the images go by really fast, you try to follow the fragments of each images as they continue to escape you, changing places, dimensions, techniques—the viewer makes an effort to understand what's really going on but the film refuses any disclosure, beginning and ending abruptly. Like in sex, a logical narrative order is refused and replaced by the engagement in what's happening. The meaning and visual sound is felt in the body and imagination of the viewer through the rhythm and the texture of the images.

Looking at your website, this is your first tactile film. Are you considering continuing with this medium, practice, or techniques? If so, are you currently working on or in the conceptual stage of anything new?

Absolutely. I've been experimenting a lot with different possibilities of making cameraless films, playing with the plasticity of the materials. In my paintings and now in my films I was interested in trying to create what Barbara Hammer called "feeling images," and I think that with the manipulation of film itself I've found new directions to pursue. I've brought some found footage material from Mono No Aware and I'm excited to see what's in there and how I can use it in my future work. And I'm quite excited that we are building a lab in Porto, Tower Lab, and that I'll have the possibility and conditions to continue working on experimental filmmaking back in Portugal.

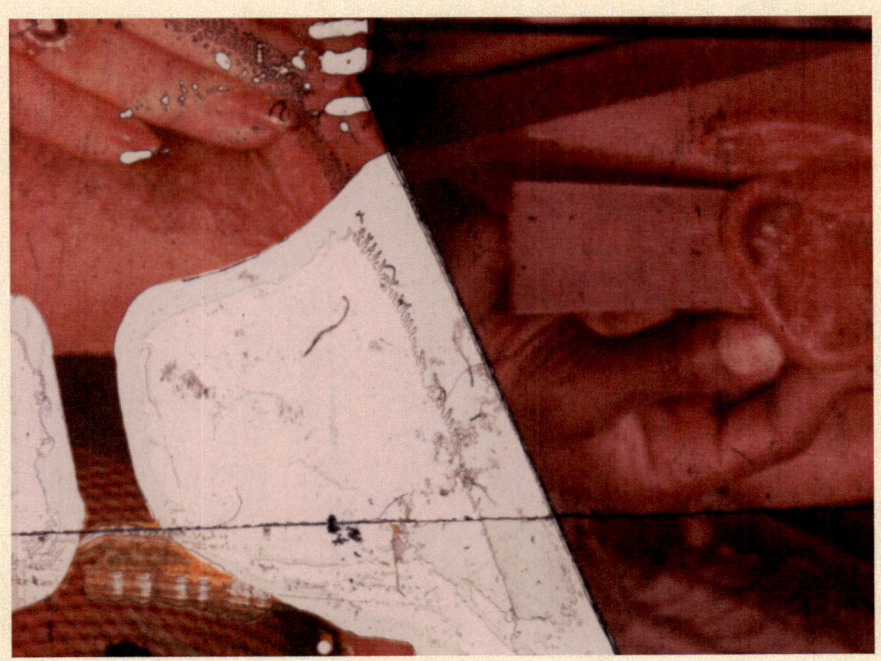

Where do framed bodies go?

What really happens when a nude body finds itself in a film frame? How does such a configuration reveal the somatic essence of one person from the perspective of another? Ever since I started making films 40 years ago, I've been trying to grapple with this complex relationship between the viewer and the viewed. Part of my process as an image maker includes thinking about the dynamic between my own body and those of the people I am observing through my lens. What changes when their clothing comes off? In our visual culture, most of us assume that a nude body is somehow unarmored and thus more vulnerable. Early in my own practice, I decided that I could only come to terms with these issues by taking my own clothes off and allowing myself to be filmed naked as well. This act might have the potential for creating some sort of equilibrium, or perhaps suggest a layer of erotica that I was, honestly, really interested in exploring.

For this issue of Analog Cookbook, the editors asked me to revisit two of my early 16mm films, *Drawn and Quartered* (1986) and *A Biography of Lilith* (1997). They encouraged me to contemplate the impetus for making these films, my intentions during the process I used to shoot them, and how those initial aspirations might have been transformed or subverted by the evolving cultural zeitgeist around sexuality, gender, and pornography. In addition, I wanted to think about the reception the films themselves received either in public theaters during their first years of release or, more recently, through streaming services which allow for private viewing in your own home or elsewhere.

My teenage obsession with the camera started with great Uncle Charlie. He and I would spend hours together looking at the photographs we'd both taken. One afternoon in 1984, when we were sitting side-by-side in Uncle Charlie's study pouring over some travel slides, I announced that I wanted

Lynne Sachs

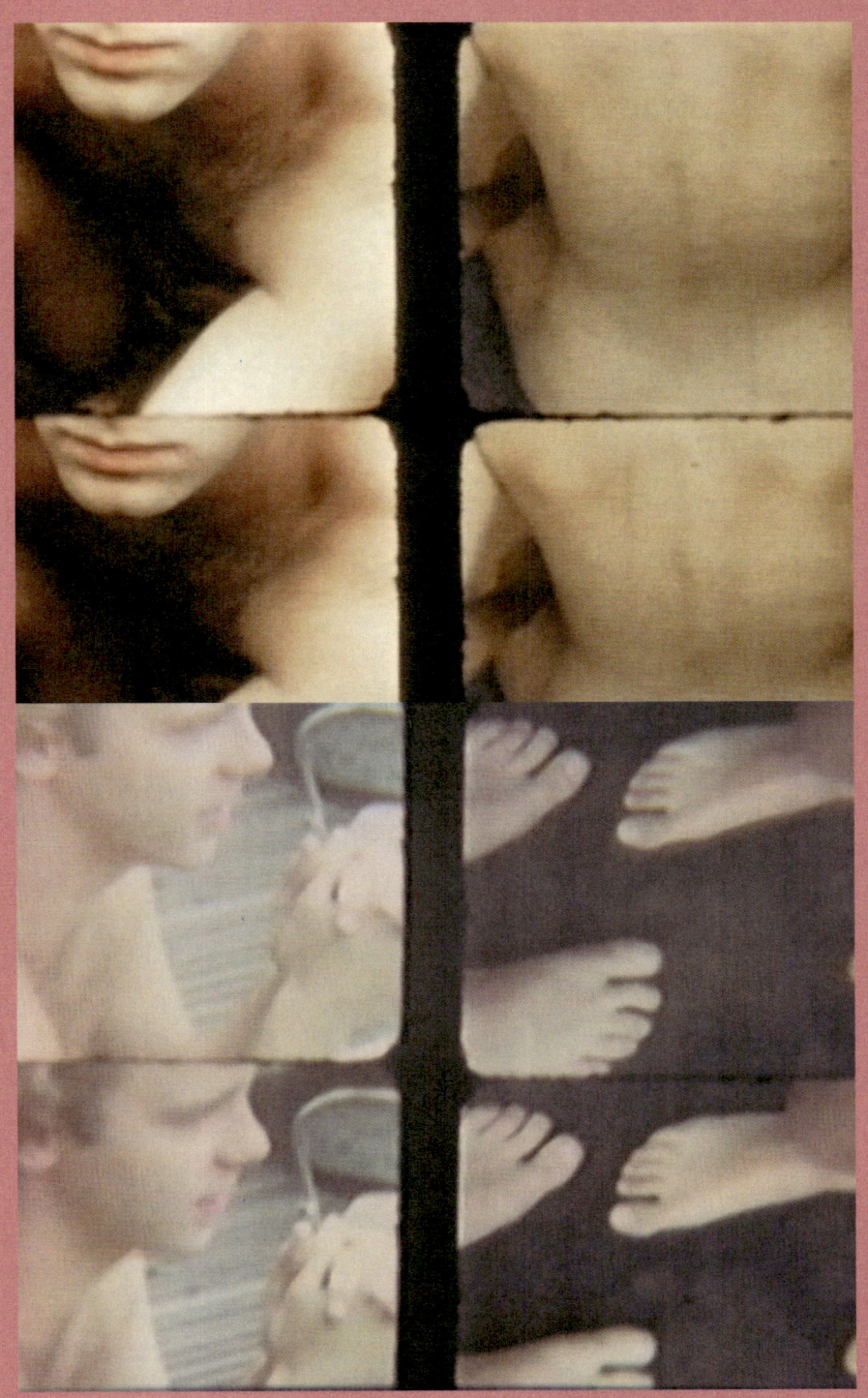

Drawn and Quartered (1987), Lynne Sachs

to be a filmmaker. I was 22 years old. His response was immediate and silent. He got up, pulled an object from a bureau drawer, and handed me a heavy, brown object that looked and felt like a hand grenade. This was the first time I had ever seen a wind-up Regular 8mm Filmo camera. Uncle Charlie explained to me how a 50-foot reel fit into the casing, and that I needed to shoot half the reel one way, then open the camera, flip the reel around and shoot the rest. "After you shoot all three minutes, send the film to a lab to have it processed and split down the middle."

"SPLIT IT DOWN THE MIDDLE?" I thought to myself, "How violent, how intriguing, how corporeal." Strangely enough, I didn't actually use the camera until three years later. By this time, I'd aligned myself with the film avant-garde. Every normal way of doing anything with a camera was anathema. My little movie camera now had an aura I couldn't resist. I convinced my boyfriend, John, to follow me to a rooftop to make a film. Despite having no experience whatsoever with the camera, I'd meticulously planned every shot we would make together. Perhaps I'd been inspired by the organized fluidity of Maya Deren's "Choreography for the Camera." Just as significant, I believe, were the mechanical properties of the camera itself. What would happen if I didn't rip apart the spinal cord of the film?

Once we reached the roof, I surprised John by informing him that we would both have to take off our clothes. I would shoot images of him, and he would shoot images of me. He wasn't happy with the rules, but he accepted them. That must have been the year I first encountered Laura Mulvey's theory of the "male gaze," seen Carolee Schneemann's "Fuses," or pondered

Yvonne Rainer's "Lives of Performers." The artistic practice of being a feminist in the late 1980's was whirling wildly in my mind.

When I took the roll to the lab, I begged them NOT to split the film as they normally would, to leave it all intact after the processing. The resulting 8mm footage was simultaneously thrilling (artistically) and humiliating (personally). There were our two nude bodies on the same screen but also divided by four equilateral frames. I looked at John (fine…); John looked at me (yikes!). Within the parameters of the image gestalt, we are dancing together without ever touching. Our two naked bodies remain totally distinct and apart.

My immediate reaction took me directly to the editing room where I cut out all the frames of my face. I wanted to erase myself from the film. I held these "outttakes" in my hand, breathing a sigh of relief at knowing that my nude body could never be identified. Then I felt strangely ashamed at my own un-hip, modest cowardice. A few days later, I returned to the splicer and "reconstituted" my body by replacing my face, owning up to what I'd made, and, in a way, accepting all of my flab and flaws. This was years before the time of "non-destructive" (digital) editing, so if you were to look closely at the finished film now you would see those cuts (SCARS!!). You would see the mark-making that reveals so much about my apprehension in those days. I premiered *Drawn and Quartered*, my silent four-minute movie, to a packed audience of fellow students at San Francisco State University. Within those few painful minutes, the crowd went from absolute silence to raucous laughter and back to an exquisite quiet. I was shaking. In Medieval Europe, a criminal could be

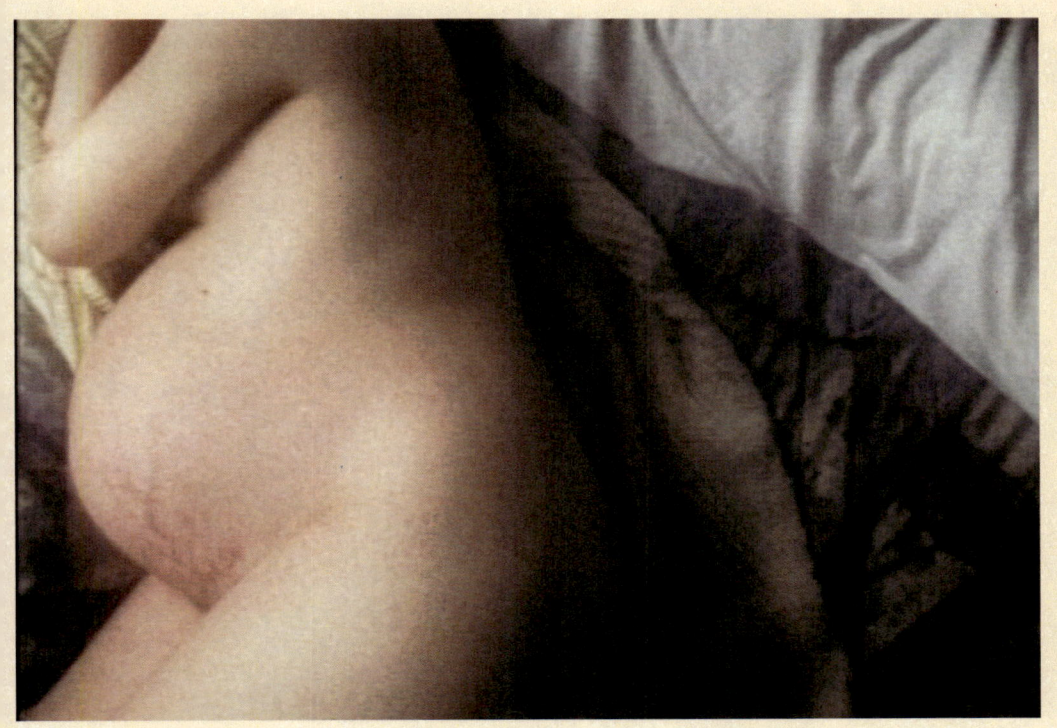

Biography of Lilith (1997), Lynne Sachs

"drawn and quartered" ripped into four parts by heavy ropes pulled by horses. By titling the film with these three words for a form of punishment, I was trying to embrace and contort this violent conceit. In the process, my kinetic imagery of a man and a woman in two separate film frames became a formal site of visualized intercourse. Is my film erotic, sexy, or pornographic? For me, images of the nude body are only categorizable by the eyes and the mind of the beholder.

A year after I completed Drawn and Quartered, I joined a reading group with a group of women experimental filmmakers and curators. We decided to read feminist theory with a focus on the post-structuralist texts that were coming out of France at the time. All the books and articles we chose were written by women who were experimenting with their own modes of writing in order to investigate childhood, the maternal, language, and the body. Each month, we would choose a text by writers like Julia Kristeva, Hélène Cixous, and Luce Irigerary. My

engagement with these texts and the corresponding conversations that happened when were all together was truly profound. Only years later was I able to understand how this communal experience had influenced the writing I did for my films in *The House of Science: a museum of false facts* (1991) and later *A Biography of Lilith* (1997). In 1994, when I was 32 years old, an Orthodox Jewish woman began a conversation with me about the hamsa that I wore around my neck. She offered me an abbreviated history of this palm-shaped amulet about which I knew very little. She recounted the story of Lilith from the Alphabet of Ben Sira, a collection of fantastic tales of kabbalah composed in the Babylonian Empire. She told me that Lilith had been Adam's mythical partner before the time of Eve. More than the expression of an obscure religious narrative, her words were a connection to a part of Judaism I had never known existed. For me, her explanation formed a link to the ancient practices of Jewish mysticism. From that point on, I started to read everything I could find about Lilith. I found traditional religious warnings, anthropological interpretations, and feminist explications. From 1995 to 1997, I gave birth to my two daughters Maya and Noa and made my film *A Biography of Lilith*.

As an artist, filmmaker, and new mother, I soon realized that Lilith's story had already had a profound resonance for me. I grew up up in the American South in a Jewish family generations away from its roots in Germany and Russia. I never heard a word of Yiddish or a single story from the "old world" until I began to read the works of Eli Wiesel, Isaac Singer, Stefan Sweig and Cynthia Ozik. Even farther from my sense of my religious culture was the mythological vision of the cosmos I discovered in Gershom Sholem's Kabbalah and Barbara Black Koltuv's The Book of Lilith.

Lilith was born from the earth, like Adam. From the beginning, she tells Adam she wants to be on top during sex, at least half the time! When he refuses her wishes, Lilith flies (or is thrown) out of the Garden of Eden. She gives birth to demons and remains forever shadowed by her new replacement: Eve born from Adam's rib and far more subservient.

According to the Midrash and texts from other cultures, there are widespread fears of a mythical female demon spirit. Ancient, popular beliefs specifically and emphatically blame Lilith for crib deaths. She is also accused of murdering uncircumcised boys. Men were told to beware of the wild, specter woman who steals semen during wet dreams. I wondered how an ancient mother's fear of this evil persona might have evoked a more internalized terror of something that already existed within her. Like Medusa, the Queen of Sheba, Hester Prynne, the Salem witches, or the anti-abortion legislation of our day, "the battle against the rebel body" articulated by Silvia Federici in her Caliban and the Witch rages on.

In *A Biography of Lilith*, I allowed this myth to infuse my images and sounds. I threw myself into the sensual aspects of the story by writing a series of poems that reflected my experience as a woman meditating on her future. At the Jewish Museum in New York City, I photographed Hebrew childbearing amulets that speak to us of a time in which Jews from Morocco, Spain, and Syria cradled deep-seeded fears of female demons. In the basement of an anthropology museum, I animated the broken shards of a 1600-year-old Lilith incantation bowl once used by women to protect their babies. Inspired by the gestures and evocations of Antonin Artaud's "The Theater of Cruelty", the silent films of Germaine Dulac and Carl Dreyer and the Brazilian Cinema Novo, I wrote a modern-day passion play which includes Shekhina (a feminine manifestation of God), Adam, Lilith, Eve, and a contemporary mother and child. Poetry from the diary that I kept throughout both my pregnancies connects my personal experiences to my research:

In one poem I realize now was deeply affected by my reading of Kristeva's concept of the abject, I evoke the moment when Lilith first speaks to Adam:

Just when I am on my way to becoming, my eyes open and you are there.

Is Eden large enough for the two of us? Wherever I turn, there are branches pulling at my hair. Earth between my toes and under my tongue. I slither and sometimes I use my wings. Earth becomes dirt becomes dirty. Bent knees turn into corners. Am I not right for this world? Before you, I did not know I was I. Now this I is part of my unbecoming.

Later, I imagine a mother

speaking to her newborn child:

You are in your sleep. A smile comes over your face. Lips flutter, flutter, quiver, turn up to touch cheek. I know, am told, have heard – that in the dark, under your cradle, there in the empty space of dust between, lies Lilith, my fear and your danger. She is a cat, a snake, the flame of a burning sword, a feather that tickles at the nape of your neck, broken

glass and nakedness.... I touch your nose and the spell is broken. For a moment your head swishes between ears. To say no, to resist and then to sink into nothing more than a pillow.

My film unravels in fits and starts, like a secret trying to reveal itself. The opening sequence surrounds an image of a haunting Kiki Smith sculpture of a crouching, naked Lilith, followed by grainy black and white images of a scorched landscape and orange jelly fish. Each section is introduced by a quotation from a psalm, an incantation or one of my own poems.

Sometimes I wonder which modality is more personal– the written word or the photograph? In addition to my own poems, I also include 16mm black and white footage of myself nude, just days away from giving birth. I move across the screen as if I am part of a line-up at a police station where an eyewitness is asked to identify a suspect. There is a harsh, clinical quality to the image. Sometimes it is even turned completely upside down, like an object to be observed and discarded. When I look back on *A Biography of Lilith* a quarter century

later, I wonder what my intention must have been. Was I speaking of my own body with disdain or was I wondering how others would react to seeing me on screen without my clothes? Did I feel desexualized by my pregnancy or empowered by it?

Clearly, the invitation to write on my films *Drawn and Quartered* and *A Biography of Lilith* brought up so many memories and reflections for me, from production anecdotes to reassesments of my own assumptions, ones that might have remained static inside me, but have now been stirred. I shot most of my Lilith film in 1995 in Tampa, Florida where I was living and teaching at the time. Since the film included my first foray into directing a quasi-narrative, I put out a casting call in a local indie newspaper and auditioned approximately ten women for the part of Lilith. Most people I knew expected me to "cast" the actor who most resembled 19th century Pre-Raphaelite painter Dante Rosetti's portrait "Lady Lilith." That was never my intention. I am a documentary maker at heart; so, I could only select a performer whose life and point of view I found compelling. I chose the actor

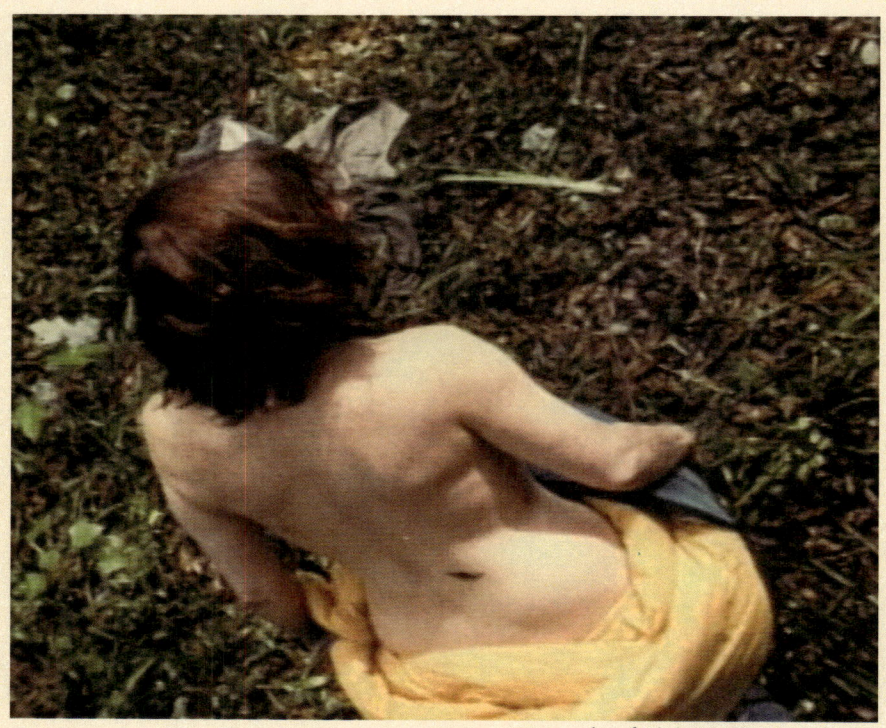

Biography of Lilith (1997), Lynne Sachs

Cherie Wallace who muses in the film on the Lilith myth in the context of her own life which included giving up a baby for adoption and working as a dancer in a bar. I was grateful to her for being so candid and introspective on camera, and for agreeing to appear nude in some of the scenes. She allowed herself to be vulnerable on multiple levels, which for most of us in the field is a priceless quality.

A Biography of Lilith premiered in the fall of 1997 at the Millennium Workshop in New York City. Cherie joined me for the screening. To our surprise, there was a review in a local paper. Sadly, for both of us, the male critic wrote extensively about the fact that I as the director had not provided Cherie with any make-up to wear when she was on camera. He was particularly distracted by the way that her skin appeared on screen. As a feminist filmmaker, I would never have suggested to a person in front of my lens that she wear cover-up foundation. When I read his words, I was indignant. Cherie, in contrast, focused on my failures not only as a director but also a friend. I had not given her the readily available tools to make herself more "attractive." She was infuriated with me for allowing her blemishes to be exposed. After that screening, I don't think I ever saw Cherie again. Ever since that moment of dismay and disappointment, I have asked myself what it means in our field to allow someone to be "exposed" on camera—either psychologically or physically. Did I neglect to provide Cherie, as Lilith, with the armor she needed? What is our responsibility as image makers to the people who help us make our art?

Recently, both of these films have had the occasion to stream. I have been told that *A Biography of Lilith* is the most popular film in my entire 40-year catalog. There is only one reason for this statistic, the streaming service explained to me. It's an obvious algorithm. Nudity. How does this make me feel? Over the last few months, there is a new question that's been coming my way. Just about every person I have asked to perform in my films—clothed or not, has asked me simply "Where will this go?"

Where will their bodies go?

I really do not know.

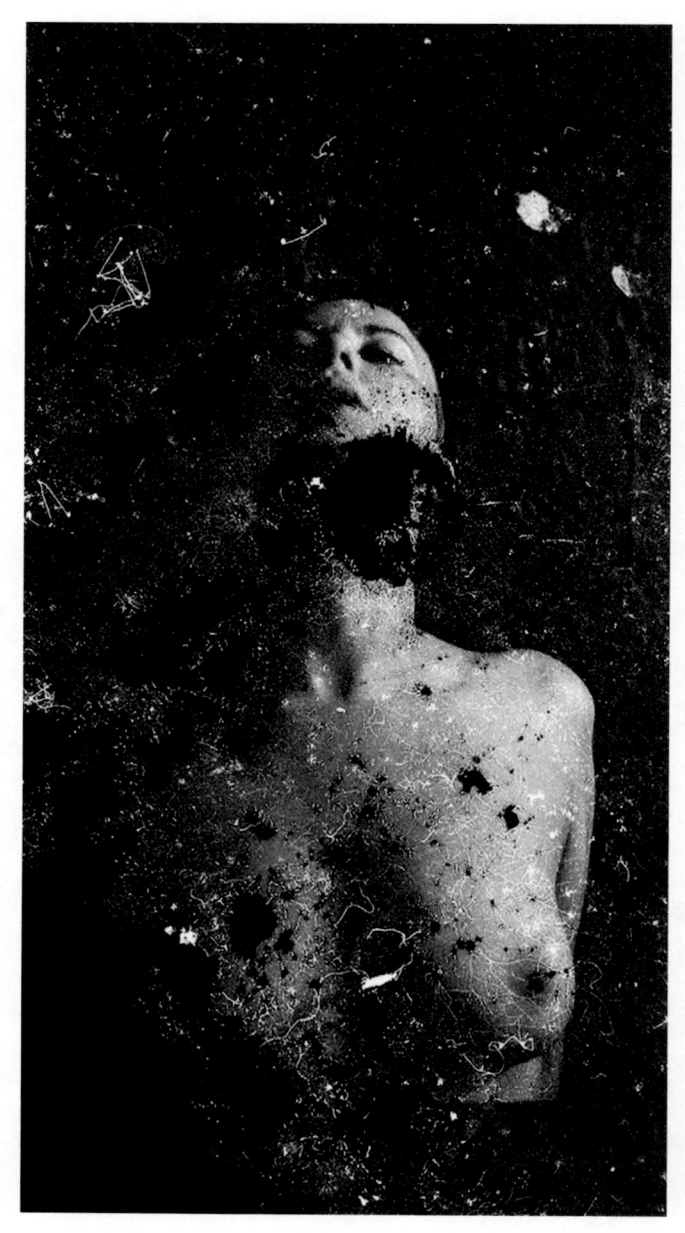

Fire-Proof

Jessica Gerard

To start how did you start out in analog photography. Do you have a background in any other media? What drew you to this medium in the first place?

I started doing photography more than 10 years ago in evening classes, the old-fashioned way, with technical courses in developing and argentic printing. Then I studied in an art school in photo and video and I switched to digital photography. A few years ago I went back to analog photography and did almost just that. I love how analog photography makes room for surprises and how accidents can happen on the end result. I also like the grain of film as well as experimenting with materials.

You explore the theme of resilience in *Fire-Proof*, and draw parallels between the resistance and resiliency of photographic film, the body, and the human psyche. On the flip side, this work also celebrates the fragility of the materials and of the human body. Can you share a little bit about what that means to you?

In my work, I often start from something autobiographical, then I try to make it universal. Here, I wanted to experiment with film while evoking the marks that experiences and time leave on each of us. With the title *Fire-Proof*, I wanted to talk about resilience and resistance rather than damage. I also wanted to pay homage to the witches of the past and those of the present, who are still struggling in our patriarchal society.

Because you're working with destructive processes, does the work continue to flake and decay after you've reached the desired effect? How does that affect your work in a practical, physical regard?

Once I have achieved the desired result, I end the process by rinsing or wiping the film. Sometimes I add material on top, so I also have to wait for it to dry. I store them in plastic sleeves or in boxes.

The images in this series are both self-portraits, and portraits of others. Can you talk a little bit about the differences, if any, in using a subtractive or destructive process on images of yourself versus others?

At first I started with self-portraits to have some photo films to practice on and to do some weathering tests. I liked some of the images, so I decided to keep them. Self-portraits are a special exercise. I had never done one before. I had to learn how to perceive my own image like the others'. It is always more difficult to see yourself in a picture. In the end, I think it's consistent that I'm part of my own series.

On that note, who are your favorite subjects to photograph, and how do you find that your relationship to them (or lack thereof) informs your work?

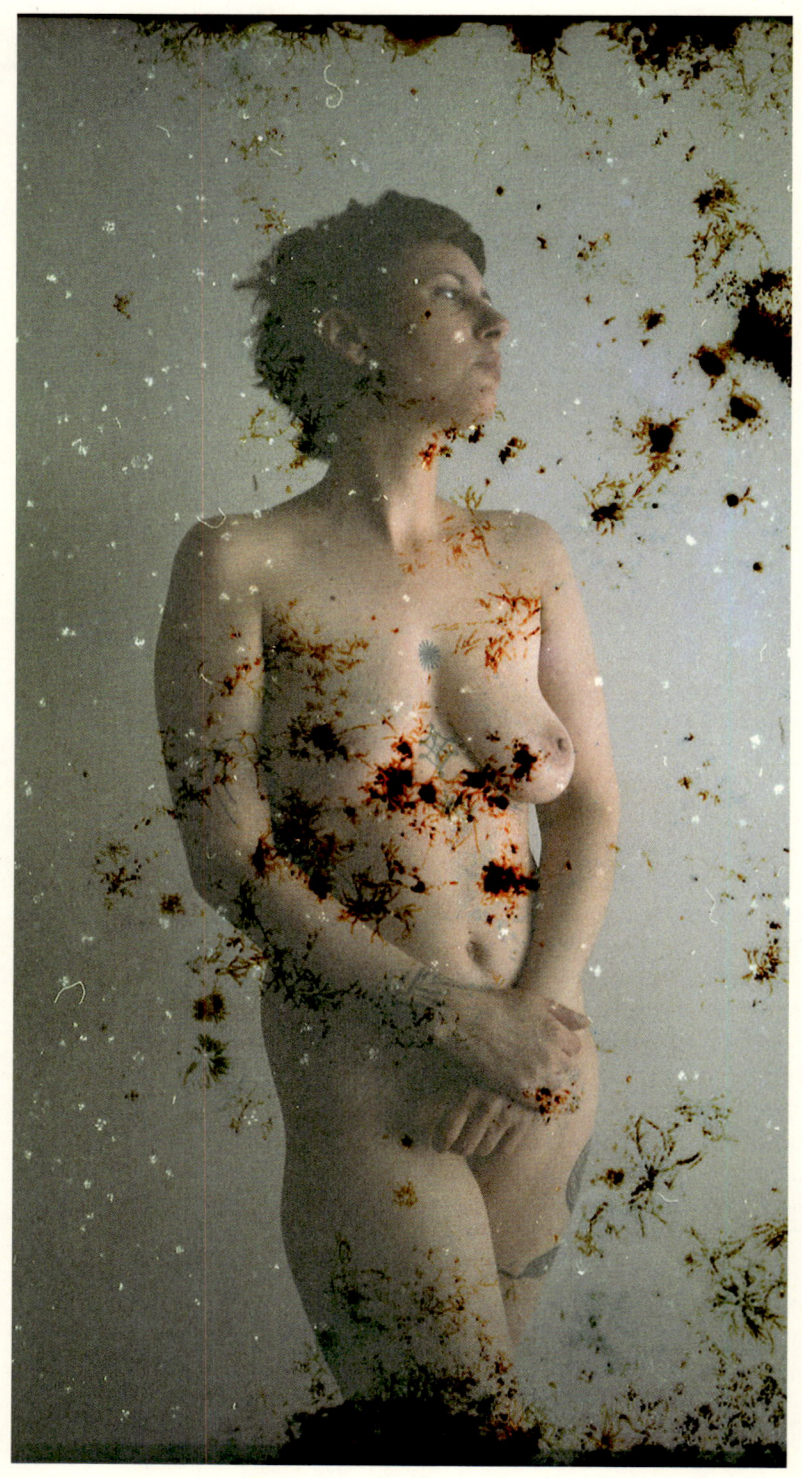

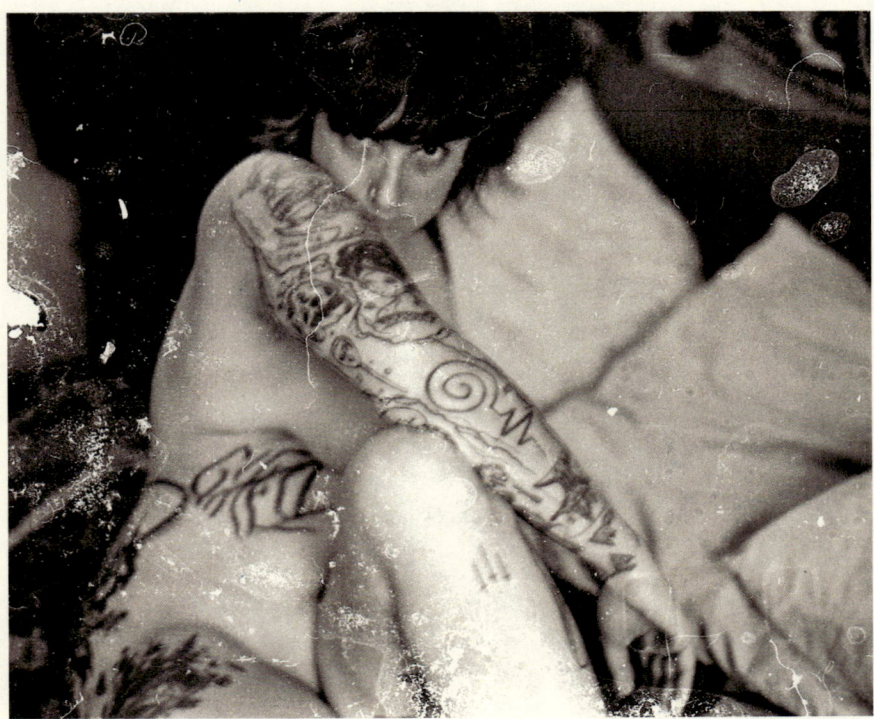

At first I photographed friends and acquaintances. Then I was contacted by women who wanted to try posing naked. I like this type of approach even if it puts more pressure on me. I want them to feel in sync with the image of them that I had captured. I also contacted women in the cabaret and pole dance scene who defend feminist and body positive values.

I don't have any predefined ideas before a photo shoot. It happens with flow and in accordance with the desires of the subject. I also photographed a few men, but for this series I wanted to put women forward.

You only submitted one image that's in color. Is that significant? Is that somewhere you're interested in taking this body of work?

I have done little color photography but would like to do more in the future. Degradation does not work the same on color film because there are 3 layers of emulsion. I would also like to try Polaroid film.

For me, the most erotic aspect of these images is how tactile they are.

Can you speak to why these images fit into the theme of Analog Erotica from your perspective?

It is true that there is something sensual that emerges from the material! These are portraits of naked women as we can see in the so-called erotic photography but with my female gaze, the sensitivity of the models and the alteration of the silver film which brings an additional dimension.

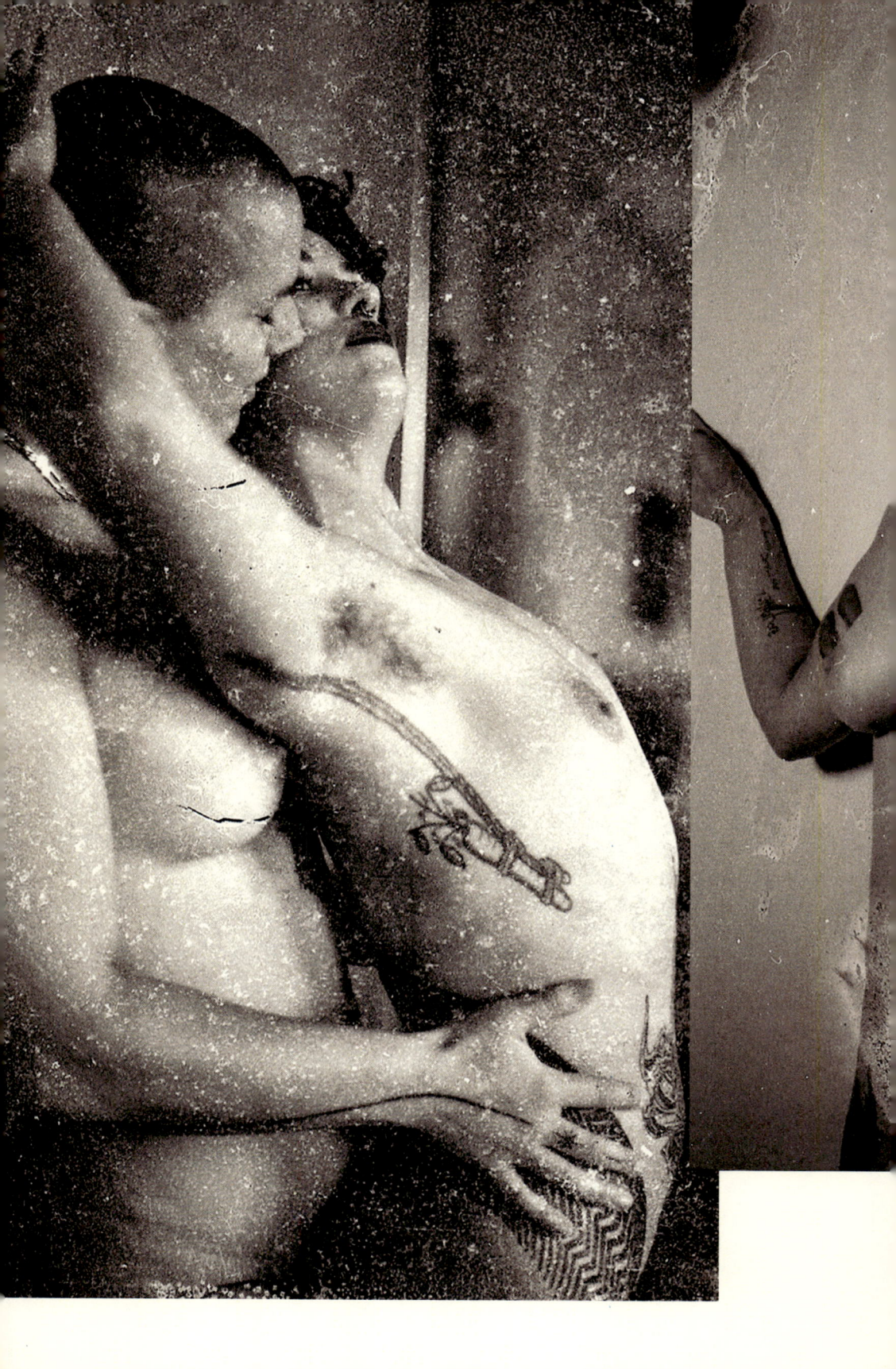

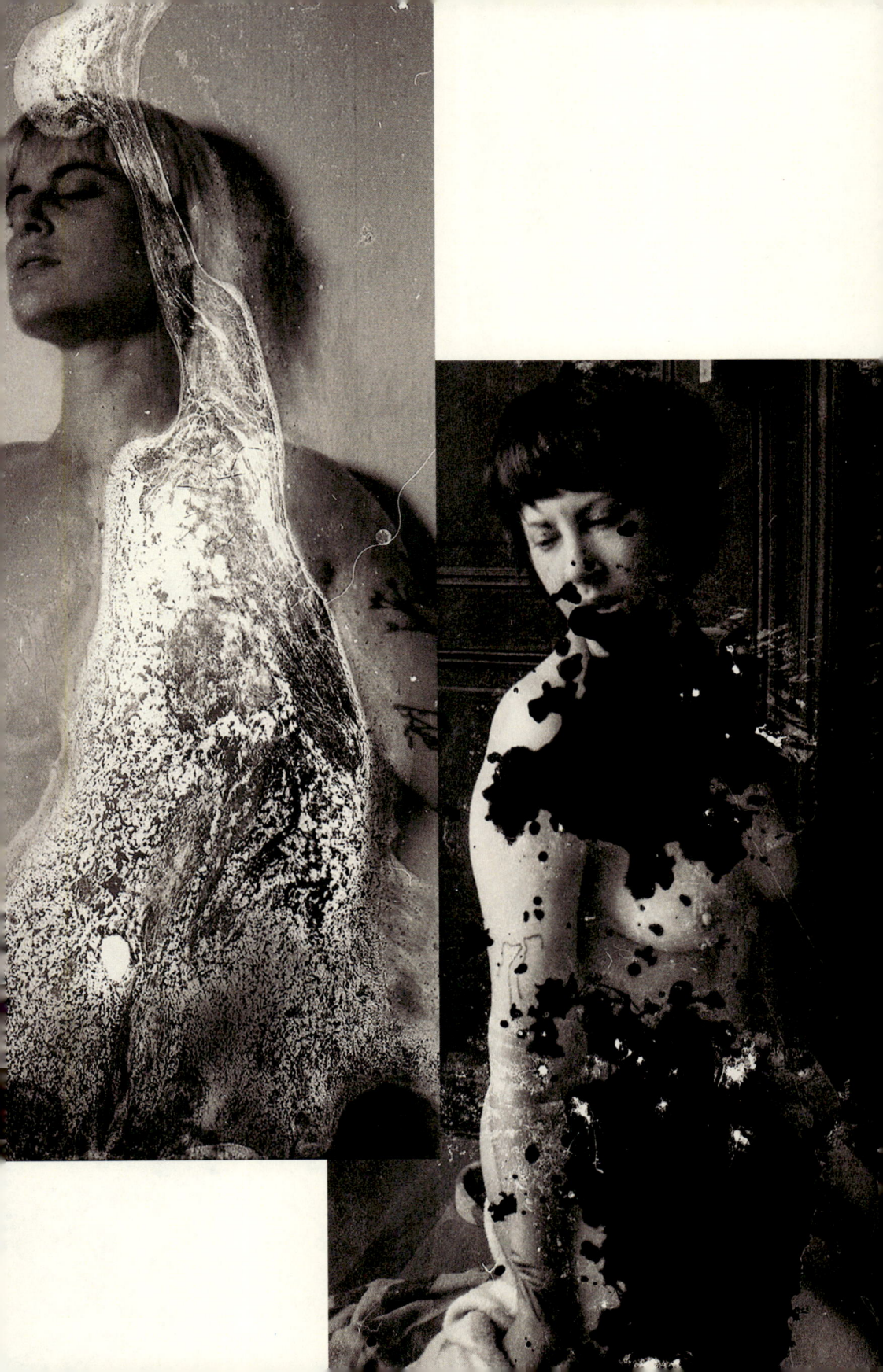

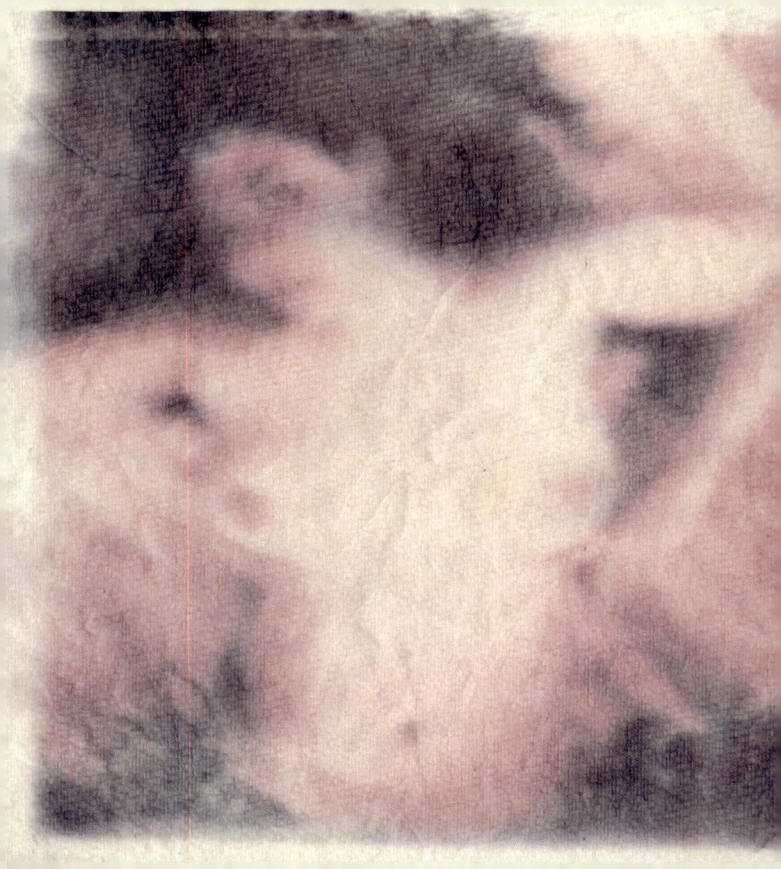

" To photograph one's body is to be brutally aware of being perceived, and the female form in particular is stuck in a hyper-visual world, performing within the confines of a body. This deterministic way of visualizing the female body does not allow for freedom, choice, or true expression. In front of the camera my body feels performative and on display. In my early years of self-imaging, the images would reveal a mirror into the concepts of beauty that I have been conditioned to believe about myself from a young age, by way of media consumption. All of those lessons on femininity, and things I had gleaned over time about actualizing beauty were now being reflected back to me through the lens, and through my way of seeing. **"**

Can you speak to how you chose the title, and how it fits with the work?

This phrase came about years ago, and it was my Instagram handle for a while, before my account was banned due to not following Instagram guidelines. In New York City, it is very common to use the saying "suck my dick" in order to say "fuck you" or something similar to or about someone. People of any gender use this phrase. I speak French and I also wanted to use the phrase but remove the phallic nature of it, so it became "mange ma chatte." Some friends used to even call me mange occasionally during that time.

On your website you share a little bit about the transition of your own self-imaging over time. Can you share a little bit more about that? How did you become conscious of how media consumption shaped your earlier perceptions of yourself?

I have been self-imaging since I was a kid. One of my favorite early self-portraits I took on a beach while on vacation when I was 11 years old. I always was very observant of myself, my view of self, and the ways others view me. As I grew older I continued to make images of myself, but for the most part those images were made on my phone, and they were not taken with the intention of making work. I definitely didn't

consider it my work when I began making images of myself unclothed, or less clothed, which were intended for another, though those photographs are early images of my nude self-portraits. As an image maker I enjoyed creating these images, but the images were more focused on sexual arousal using my body, and I began to feel patriarchy in the room with me. I could feel the way images of attractive women, pornography, and just beauty ideals in general would dictate the types of images I would make. During college I also began to become interested in the ethics of images, the role of systems of oppression in images, and the nature of their subjectivity. I decided I would rather engage my body and self-imaging for my own private pleasure. But I continued to ask questions like "why are these images sexually arousing?" Was it the way I looked, the way my body was held? Which part of patriarchy was telling me to hold my back straight, and open my legs wide? I find that these questions allow for images to encompass all that I've gleaned, they keep patriarchy in mind, and they also encourage my own pleasure to be seen publicly and privately. To see myself mostly.

Have you always worked with film, or is that something relatively new?

I used film as a kid, like disposables at camp. And then in middle school I picked up a B&W film photography course after school. Ever since, film has been a part of my image practice. High school brought me to digital because it was cheap and I was able to share my images easily, which was very important to me during that time. I would make a lot of portraits of my friends and community, as well as videos, and I loved sharing the work with everyone. College brought me back to film exclusively through an understanding of how much

more intentional it makes every image. A lot of care and patience is required, and it also allows for a more unexpected result. A lot of my work is conceptual, so I find a fluid medium to lend to a more human quality within the work.

You mention using wheat paste and stickers to put your work in public spaces. How do you choose where to put your work? What are the drawbacks and benefits, if any, of putting your work in public space?

I find it important to create work outside of technology. Images are so often confined to the small screen of a phone, and I find that to be really damaging to the image and our ability to sit with it, carry it with us, and be present with the work. So making prints has always been very important to me, and I knew that there was something important happening from graffiti writers, and their ability to produce their work freely and publicly. There is so much history of perseverance within graffiti, and the individual's voice and vision is respected and encouraged. I definitely also wanted to join into the street work in order to counter the very male dominated space

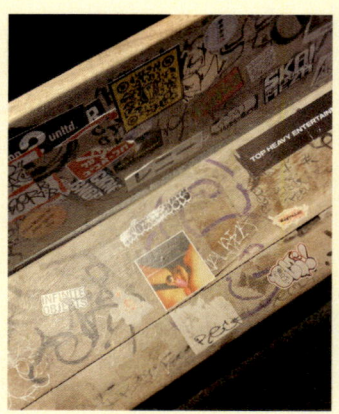

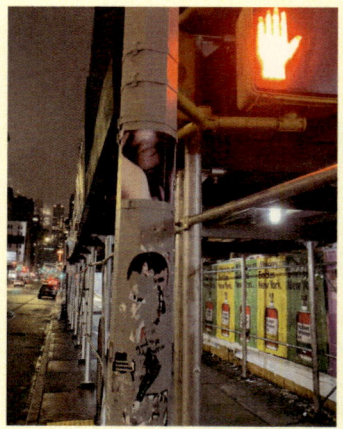

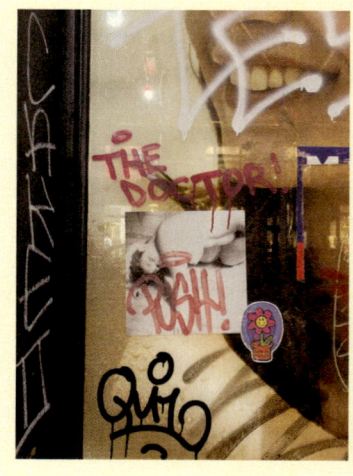

that exists within graffiti.

I have only recently begun my journey into the streets, and where I place my work has been a very important question for me, especially as my work is images of my naked body. I decided early on that, as a white person, I should not post my images up in a neighborhood that is predominantly people of color. This is because my stickers are meant to challenge and to gain freedom from certain oppressive systems in our society, which also are in place to oppress so many other people. And my role in making them and sharing them is to put them in locations where their conversations should exist. So I mostly travel to downtown Manhattan, or midtown to share the work publicly.

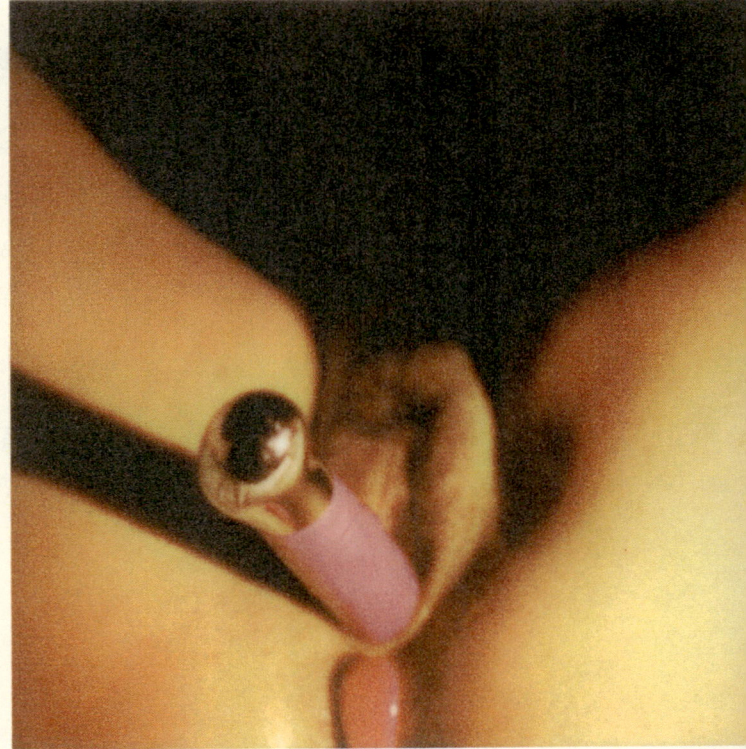

As someone who exhibits publicly, did your practice change at all to adapt to the new ways that people move through the world during the pandemic? As someone whose practice involves self-imaging, did you find that time to be helpful or detrimental to your practice in any way?

Many of my images were produced during the post-

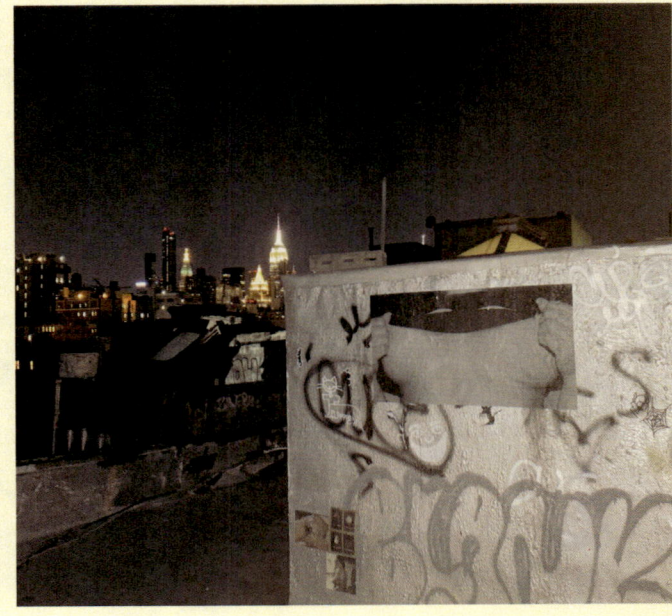

51

Tynan Byrne

" I've been experimenting with polaroids for years now but have only recently begun using them to examine the more intimate aspects of my relationship, my body, and those of friends. In "Sweet straddlers", I exemplify the intimacy of two individuals resting atop one another by being physically close in proximity while harnessing the warmth of lighting present. There's something tender about their posture and the way their body hair blends into each other through the shadows–the sheathing of the penis conveying an internal bashfulness that hints simultaneously at eagerness and hesitation, and a hand emerging from out of frame paused between reaching in or pulling away. "

Sweet Straddlers

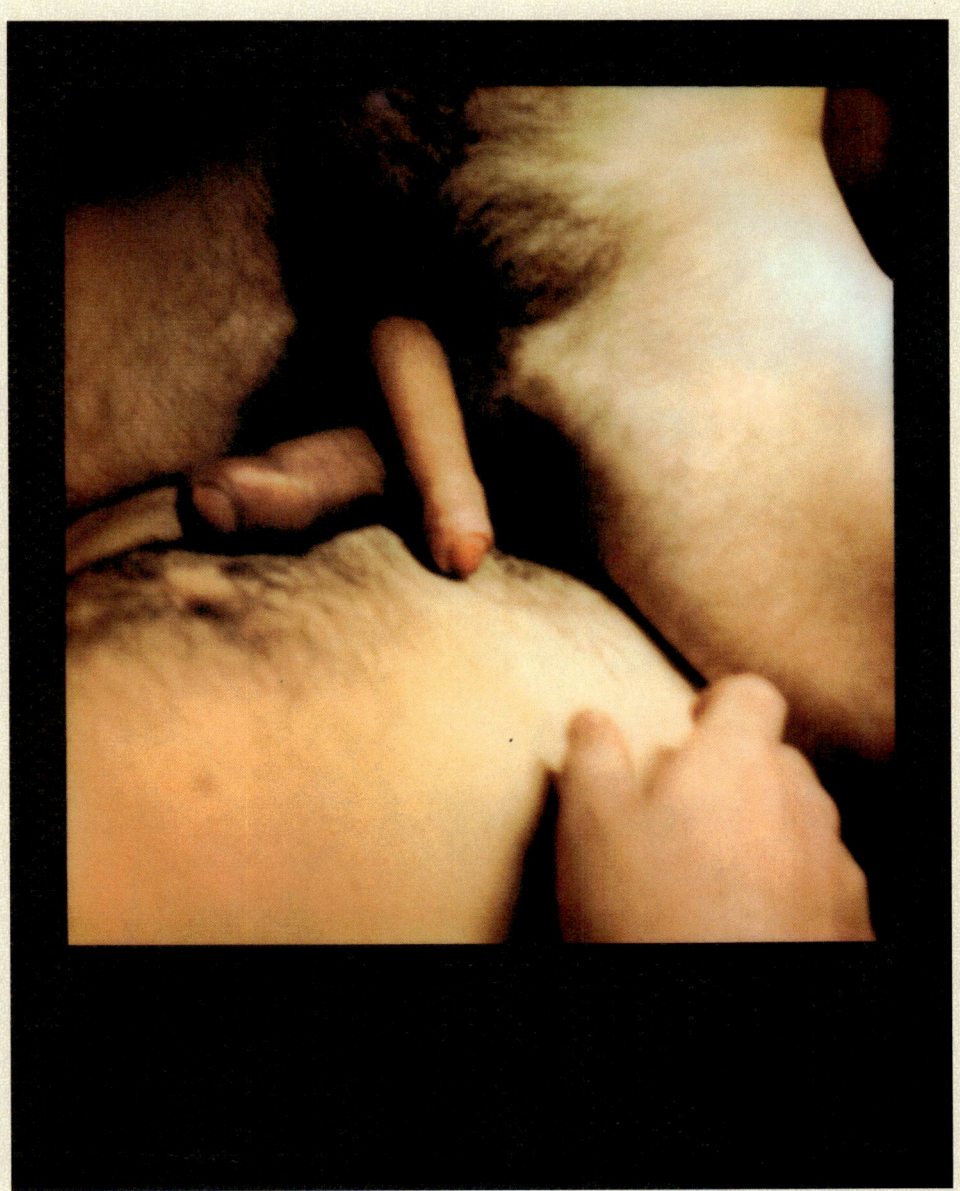

Violence
+ Tenderness

A Conversation
between Kelly
Gallagher & Nazlı
Dinçel

Kelly Gallagher (she/her): First, I want to say I'm obviously, in addition to being your friend, a huge fan of yours. Your films blow me away. Your work inspires me to be more radically vulnerable in my own work, which isn't always easy for me. So many themes come up in your films–the tactile nature and power of intimacy, questions and ethics of filming one's own self and filming others. The power of mark-making and pulling the solitary out into the light, and not just like physical, solitary, intimate acts, but also just quiet and intimate personal conversations, thoughts, memories, etc. What drew you to want to make such powerfully vulnerable work?

Nazlı Dinçel (they/them): When I was a student learning about experimental work, I was always drawn to films that made me feel uncomfortable or that I didn't like. I often found myself thinking about those more than the ones I liked. I guess the work is in the theme of that. I want to challenge myself because I am so uncomfortable in my body. I guess it's just a way of processing the trauma that's also tucked in the pieces. I got into this process where I am putting myself out there and making vulnerable work, but then I feel the duality of that with being seen as narcissistic. So, I get really stuck between this space of wanting to be vulnerable and selfless and share an experience, but then feeling the reality of how that is seen as the subject being myself is intense. Although being your own subject is the most ethical way, or nonviolent way, of making a film– turning the camera towards your own body instead of others.

KG: It's interesting to hear you say fears of narcissism because to me, it's such generous work. It's the opposite of anything that could even be conceived as narcissistic. It's the most radically courageous, brave kind of filmmaking to embark on.

ND: I feel like that happens with any challenging work by AFAB people because we live in a patriarchy. That resistance becomes

grounds for dismissing the filmmaker. I've seen people talk about your work in that way, too. Thinking that could be seen as narcissistic is my own internalized misogyny, I guess.

KG: Yeah, but it's such needed and powerful work. I mean, it truly is. Having been familiar with your work made me feel able to make the film *Slower*. Having been raised so Catholic and pent up and stiff or something, seeing work like yours allowed me to feel safe enough to want to think through things that would have previously felt too difficult to think about.

ND: Does your family watch your work?

KG: Yes, and they're very supportive, which is really beautiful and very special. Their support has always meant a great deal to me. I'm also not trying to actively share my more intimate, deeply diaristic works with them always. Does your family watch your work?

ND: Some of them, but I was going to say, maybe that all has to do with me being an immigrant and not really being connected to my family and being Trans, and in that way having to create my own family and my own community. I'm pretty severed from people who are from my bloodline, but I can see that as also a form of oppression, too. I had to leave my country in order to be able to make this work.

KG: Absolutely, and that comes up in one of your solitary films. I mean, the presence of parents and a grandmother being physically nearby or the moment in *Solitary Acts* when your grandmother opens the bathroom door and is like, "This is a sin, eating in the bathroom." When you include others in your work, does that feel harder than when you're just making work just about yourself, whether it's family or others?

ND: I always talk about this at Q&As or artist talks when the question comes up about consent. I always get consent from my subjects, but also, I feel like, ethically,

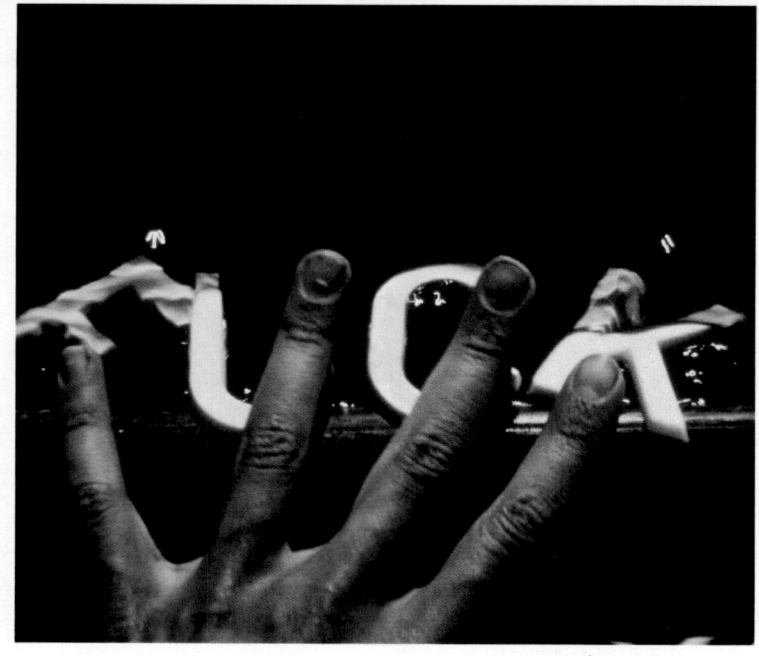

Instructions on How to Make a Film (2018-2019), Nazlı Dinçel

I don't have an issue with objectifying my subjects at all because they've just been white cis men so far, and it doesn't really harm them. I'm like, "Objectify more white men!"

KG (through laughter): That's the film movement.

ND: I wanted to ask you about consent–it's in all three of the films that you shared, but I feel like *We Had Each Other* is also about body autonomy–that's also consent, both sexually and politically. Could you talk about that?

KG: Yeah, you mean getting consent from others to make work with or about them, or do you mean just topics of consent within my own relationships?

ND: Both, I guess, and the

lack of consent of being touched as a female prisoner.

KG: Yes, in *We Had Each Other*, in addition to the sexual and physical violence many of these women survived, they also survived the colonialist, imperialist, and carceral violence of the British government. This is, in part, why I've become a prison abolitionist. Prisons and the carceral state perpetuate physical and sexual violence. I think in these three films I shared with you [*Slower, Do You Want to Go For a Drive?*, and *We Had Each Other*], the issue of consent is being explored in many different ways. Some of my own earliest experiences were unfortunately not always the most consensual, and so consent is something that I've always thought about and valued, and the older I get,

the more I keep ruminating about it and thinking about how I've been affected in my younger years without always having given consent.

ND: Well, yeah, in *Do You Want to Go for a Drive?* There's a rape attempt.

KG: When I think about what we had been talking about earlier, the idea of pulling these difficult things out into the light or like talking about them or exploring them through film (which in turn means then that they're shared with others), there's something powerful in knowing that I'm not alone in these experiences, which also deeply sucks. It really fucking sucks, but it means that I know there's a world of people who are collectively fighting back against this shitty culture and trying to change it for the better. So for me, making these more personal works allows me to meet and connect with other people with shared experiences, and that's a really powerful byproduct of making deeply vulnerable work—finding others that you want to work with to change things, to change culture, to change society. I think in a film like *Slower*, I remember being upset—maybe it was around the MeToo Movement or around that time. I just wanted to engage in the conversation of how harm is experienced. Consent is crucial, but also I wanted to explore the question of whose pleasure is valued in such a misogynistic, patriarchal society; growing up in these heteronormative, straight relationships, it was as if I were being conditioned to understand that the man's pleasure is the end all goal.

ND: Yeah! I don't want you to be offended by this, but when I was watching that, I was like, "Straight sex is so boring!" (Laughs)

KG (Laughing): It definitely can be! It doesn't have to be! Luckily, I found an amazing partner who deeply values my pleasure. But my god, when I was younger and growing up, like, what the fuck? You know? So, it just felt like, in addition to important, necessary conversations of consent that are perpetually

needed and always needed, what do we value in a sexual relationship? Whose pleasure is being seen? Ideally, everyone's pleasure matters. So, it was also just like, "let's talk about good sex, too" because even in consensual sex, if your pleasure is never valued, then, like, that's also harm. That can be harmful in its own way.

ND: You describe it as violent.

KG: Yeah, and I think it is because then you're conditioned to feel like the joy within your own self doesn't matter as much as someone else's. And that's so harmful, I think, and so violent and problematic. Those are some of my interests with the topic of consent, including and beyond consent, that I think are important. *We Had Each Other* is a very different film from [the other two] in that it's about these other women, not myself, and this really mind-blowing powerful, wild, and brilliant way that they thought about using their own bodies to fight back against the torment and torture that they were experiencing by the hands of these colonialist British guards. They were nonconsensually and really violently, perpetually strip-searched, sexually and physically assaulted, etc., and so for them to be able to weaponize their own bodies and figure out this creative

way of resisting the British guards, using their own menstrual blood and excreta, is deeply, deeply moving and inspiring to me.

ND: I love that you can equate that violence to the same violence of someone not giving you an orgasm. It is the same violence. It's just different levels or variations.

KG: To clarify, I believe women fighting for their lives against carceral violence are experiencing the most horrific depths of harm that are unfathomable for many of us. The way I see this conversation building connections around violence, as you mention it, is that I think women's and Transfolks' lives, well-being, and pleasures not being held sacred, protected, and valued by our society has caused so much violence and harm against women and Trans folks globally. I think that work like yours and pulling these more solitary moments, out into the light and discussing them helps us think through: What is the future that we want? How do we get to the place we want to get to where our pleasure is held and seen as a beautiful, sacred, necessary thing?

ND: My body doesn't exist at all since I started transitioning. I'm not getting targeted ads based on gender, and it's been really

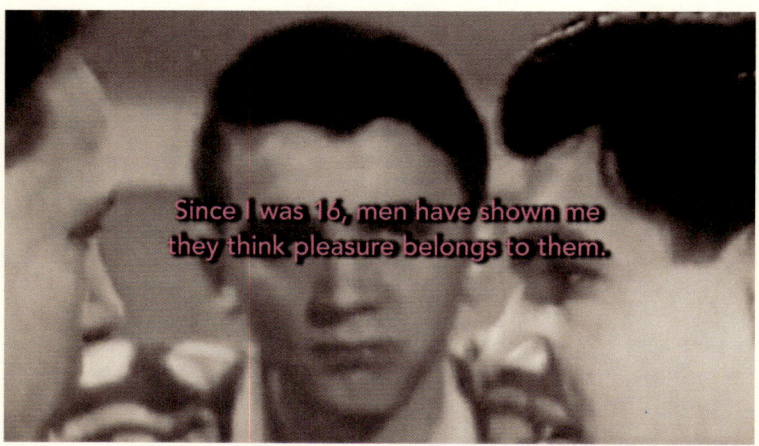

Since I was 16, men have shown me they think pleasure belongs to them.

Slower (2018), Kelly Gallagher

interesting because it makes me feel like I'm invisible in capitalism.

KG: Does that feel like a powerful invisibility or a harmful invisibility?

ND: I'm not sure yet. I feel both, probably. I feel like it is mostly violent, but it's also nice being able to escape targeted ads.

KG: You've been making work for a while now, filming your own body, dealing with the body and the intimate, and I'm wondering, have your feelings changed as you filmed yourself over the years? Have there been changes as you filmed your own body, like throughout the years?

ND: Yeah, I mean, I guess it's never been hard because I work with analog, and there are so many steps to get an image, and because I do all of it by hand, it's a slow process. Or, a slower process than just seeing it right after

filming yourself–and I don't know. It makes me feel like it's someone else, a body that existed in that timeline at some point, even if that was five days ago. Hindsight is 20/20, I guess, with transitioning so late in life, but when I look at my work, it doesn't even feel like it's my body. For example, since starting hormones, I have bottom growth; my genitals don't look the same. My body is turning into something completely different. It's not the body I've filmed anymore. I also haven't made a film in four years, a sabbatical, I guess. I want to make a piece about transitioning, but I don't know what that's going to feel like, and if I'm feeling up to that kind of self-exposure in a Transbody. And it's hard to anticipate, I guess.

KG: Have you enjoyed the sabbatical away from experimental filmmaking?

ND: It's just been anxiety.
KG (laughter): An anxiety sabbatical! You deserve a

restorative sabbatical. Did it feel like the experimental film community was just too toxic?

ND: Yeah. I wanted to ask you that, too. I do want to teach, but I want to be outside academia. It's just the complete opposite of everything I believe in, but then I don't have wealth, so, I don't know, what to do for money. It seems there's just no path for me. That's another reason why I live in the Midwest, it's so affordable. Also, if you are teaching, you're bound to your institution, and the work that you make is tied to that community, too. If it's controversial in any way–not that I think mine or your work is or should be seen as controversial–it creates a weird dynamic within the institution. Because people always want to protect the institution, often for their own benefit or egos. So, if you're making sexually explicit work, then…yeah.

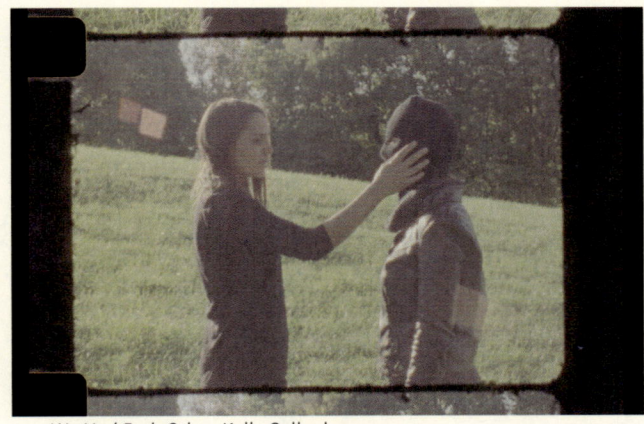

We Had Each Other, Kelly Gallagher

KG: Yeah, I think that what sucks is that as someone myself who teaches at a university, what sucks is that I feel like you, Nazlı Dinçel, are exactly the person that young people should be learning from, and so it's this, like fucked up, sad situation because academia is such a violent place, towards people of color, Trans scholars, folks making more politically radical work, and yet I feel like young filmmakers need to see work like yours. Which is why it's probably, I would assume, taught so much. And yet you yourself feel pushed out of the university space. It's this deeply fucked up problem.

ND: How do you feel about your work, too? Within the university system and in that environment, do you feel like you've been accepted? Or have you ever run into any problems? The imagery of your work is not explicit, but the text is.

KG: Right, right. Yeah, maybe ask me this question again in a couple of years because right now, I'm about to embark on a big film project that looks at histories of solidarity between Irish folks and Palestinians, a pro-Palestinian film that's also prison abolitionist. I feel like I'm just at the start of this project, and a lot of folks have told me, basically, there's no chance in hell of getting work like this supported institutionally. I did get a small grant from my own university towards it already. For me, the way I've survived in this setting is finding other radically political comrades and leaning on each other, and working together to think through how we can best support one another—how we can parasite the resources from the university system and find community with each other. It's a matter of finding your people. I feel like that's just the case throughout life. Like you talked earlier about having to find and make your own family, having to find your people. The university system is one in which there's

so much violence, and one in which there's so much hope. When you look at the students, who are so excited and eager to learn, and you're able to share with them, work like yours, you see how much it means to them, how it inspires them (as it does me). It's something I think I'm just always grappling with and thinking through (academia in general), but it feels like violence that you haven't been hired or sought after because your work is radically political and also visually more explicit.

ND: Do you think that your work is going to have explicit imagery in the Palestinian and Irish films?

KG: Maybe. I mean, I remember when we were at a very big experimental film festival, years ago, I was telling you how–

ND: I love that you're not naming names.

KG (chuckles): We were talking, and I was telling

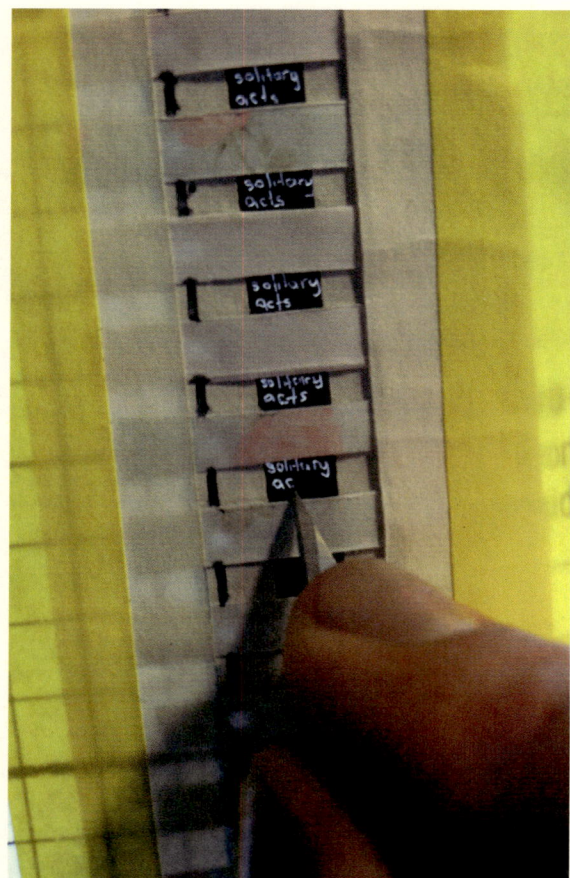

Nazlı Dinçel

and dare to make explicit and difficult work. I guess I'm just grateful about that because, again, a film like *Slower*, which is not visually explicit, but maybe content-wise, might be somewhat explicit. For someone who, like me, grew up so rigid and tense in her own body, I don't know... there's something very empowering and liberating, watching your films. And I wonder if you feel empowered and liberated when you make work like *Solitary Acts* or if that's not what you feel? When you finished a film like one of your *Solitary Acts* films or I also rewatched *Her Silent Seaming*, and *Instructions on How to Make a Film*, which is like, so funny. I love that film. I love all your work, but it was really fun to rewatch that film.

ND: I still laugh when I watch *Solitary Acts #4*. Whenever I'm screening my work, I always project it myself, and it still makes me laugh when Britney Spears comes on. I've never had such a positive relationship with anything I've made, which is so joyful. Pop music and glitter are pretty gay, too. I mean, I do feel powerful watching it, and that's why I think humor is so important. I will generalize, but at the time, I was seeing that when women told their sexual stories in experimental film, it just tended to have this heaviness and intensity. I just

you that I was excited to be there, but I was a little bit bummed because I had made this more politically, explicitly radical film in content (*From Ally to Accomplice*). This was years ago. That one had not gotten into the festival, but one of my more subdued films got in. You just laughed and rolled your eyes, and you were just like, "Of course, Kelly, you know, the more explicit work, didn't get into this festival! That's how it goes." It's just like, filmmakers like you–

ND: I don't know what to do with these compliments!

KG: You'll just have to blush like your hair! [Editor's Note: Nazlı is rocking bright pink hair in this interview.] The more I think about it, filmmakers like you make other filmmakers able to make

also wanted those coming-of-age stories to be joyful and uplifting, and also funny despite the trauma they carry with them. I guess I was trying to fill a space that didn't exist with the work. Wait–what was your question?

KG: I was just talking about the experience as a viewer of watching these films, feeling empowered, and I was curious if you as a maker felt similarly–either while watching them or just if the process of making things felt empowering. It's such a slow process. Your way of working requires so much patience.

ND: It's not unlike animation.

KG (deep exhale into laughter): Yeah. Yeah. I don't know. I was wondering if you could talk about just the act of mark-making.

ND: You mean like scratching?

KG: Yeah! Is that process joyful? Therapeutic? Does it mean something to you in terms of just the physical act of cutting into or sewing into?

ND: It's because I animate text on the film strip. It always felt like another duality because I'm physically scraping my body off the emulsion, creating a word that means something. So, I'm communicating, but only by erasing my own body physically from the frames. I always thought working like that was a funny loop. When I'm doing it, it's very methodical. I go through the entire film, and I mark everything with little tapes, and then after that's done, I scratch. At this point, I know where to place everything physically within the frame. So, everything's streamlined, but it's really intense on my hands. It feels like mindless work, even though it's not. It also makes me feel really connected to craft makers–especially in the context of where I come from and tourism being such a big part of the local income and wealth of a colonized country. This means women are pushed to intricate craft-making, like rug making or things that seem "cultural" to outsiders, which the women in my family have a history with. It's an interesting process, reclaiming that in film work because what I saw when I was being taught experimental film was straight cis men doing the bare minimum of that work and being acknowledged, and women doing that work and not being–not that I mean to be so binary. (laughter)

KG (laughter): Yeah, I've had similar experiences–

ND: With animation, you mean?

KG: Yeah. I'm so interested and engaged in the process itself, and the process feels very cathartic, like you said, that methodical way of working. It's almost just like even when it's exhausting to the hand, I don't know, it's hard to explain except to say it's still really cathartic.

ND: It's meditative.

KG: Meditative! Yeah, and in that way, it's really pleasurable, too. And like so much the content of these films is about pleasure, bodily pleasure, etc. And the way of making is also really pleasurable. Like I wouldn't make films if I didn't enjoy making them.

ND: Do you listen to music or watch something? [Kelly nods] Which one?

KG: All of the above. I love collaborating with people when I get the opportunities and chances to, but it's also just a real joy to work by myself and be able to make movies in my sweatpants while blaring like Mariah Carey. Whatever I'm doing! To create your own, world and thrive there and just do your thing can be really joyful.

ND: I feel like that's erotic, too.

KG: Yeah! Yeah, I think so!

ND: But also, can I have your

61

playlist?

KG: We should share playlists. Absolutely.

ND: I want to go back to *We Had Each Other*. I rewatched it today, and there is something homoerotic about it–especially in scenes of the field, and the caressing of the flowers that juxtaposed with the prison stories. I wrote in my notes: "The use of text is the driving narrative in all the works," and even though the images aren't sexual or explicit, the text provides that context. There's the shot in Slower with the revolver and the text that reads "Eat me." I was like, "Eat me." I was like I wish they did! It would solve the problem! But then there is also the juxtaposition between the imagery and audio of really violent experiences and also the sweet and soft ones between a consensual lover and the rape attempt, for example, in *Do You Want to Go for A Drive*? There is so much back and forth between violence and softness in the text. I guess that is your form of play.

KG: I appreciate you noticing the interplay between violence and tenderness in these different works. I always say my work comes from a place of both love and rage. Not to be like binary to what you were saying earlier, but tenderness and roughness.

I feel like tenderness and violence, you know in my own sexual life or history or whatever, there was such a back and forth between those until I started to realize the power of valuing my own pleasure. It's funny and interesting to hear you talking about–I think you said homoerotic imagery, you know, at some moments, the imagery feels homoerotic in *We Had Each Other*. This other film I made a few years ago about my best friend, called *My Gossip*, it looks at the ways that, historically, friendships between women had been weaponized against them. I think that our society puts all emphasis and the highest value on romantic relationships, but I think that friendship and, even more than that, political camaraderie with others is a realm of relationship that is due, perhaps, the highest of valuing. So, for those women [in *We Had Each Other*], to be able to resist and fight for their own life with others and to do that collectively and to rely on one another the way that those women did–it's EVERYTHING. In reading their letters and learning about them, it felt like the bonds between them were almost otherworldly, just so beyond even comprehension, the love and solidarity between them. I think my attempts to get that on film is where that tenderness, that powerful otherworldly closeness seeps

in. But yeah, you know, tenderness and violence, it's something I feel like I'm swinging back and forth between in a lot of films because, again, coming back to that notion of a lot of my interests coming from a place of both love and rage–rage about the way things have been and are, and love and hope for the way things can be in the future. I think that's where sort of that interplay kind of comes from.

ND: Yeah. I mean, friendships are forever.

KG: It's true. Friendships are forever. Being fresh off of rewatching *Instructions on How to Make a Film*–you know, I work with young people, and I think there's a desire for some folks to make really vulnerable, powerful, beautiful work–and I'm wondering if you've learned things along the way that you would like to share with folks who want to work on making vulnerable work in which maybe they share some like intimate parts of themselves, whether visually/physically/emotionally explicit. Are there ways that you care for yourself in making these works or the things that you think about when you decide what to show, what not to show?

ND: I thought I was going to say that earlier when you said, "does your work make you feel powerful?" It does, but then that's also a catalyst for this four-year-long break because I started noticing that every time someone asked me to share my work or invited me to a screening, I would get triggered. It added up over the years and I feel really burnt out because of it. Showing myself and on top of it, showing my work on analog, which isn't necessarily easy because I want to take care of my prints and make them last as long as possible. So yeah, it put me in this weird cycle of vulnerability where I would feel exhaustion a week later. The only thing I could say is that you can never take back what you share, and that's so important. As far as mental health is concerned, if you're oversharing, maybe there's a reason for that, too. But yeah, I mean: Go to therapy.

KG: Therapy is great!

ND: Go to therapy and take care of your mental health. Make sure that you want to share what you want to share. I don't regret anything because at this point, I have understood the capacity it requires. I've learned it, but it takes a lot. I'm sure that you feel that way, too, with your work. What have you learned?

KG: Caring for yourself is crucial. I agree with this. Therapy is super important,

and in addition to valuing and caring for yourself, which is so important, also caring for each other. This conversation has me honestly thinking about, what are the concrete ways that we can support one another? The experimental film community has so much toxicity and bullshit–

ND (laughs): To put it lightly.

KG: To put it lightly. What could it look like to create community with others and just champion and support their work, check in on them/ on each other, concretely and financially support each other? Folks like you and I work to do that with one another and with people we care about. I'm curious about what it can look like to be a part of a film community that values collective care.

ND: That's what I mean. If you are part of an institution, you are already in that system. Trying to demolish that within the system becomes impossible to do because gatekeeping and oppression is essentially the goal of the institution. How do you have time to yourself, let alone thinking about others, you know? I can't imagine.

KG: I mean, I definitely feel exhausted sometimes. The best way to say it is, there are folks I know who are really trying to think through these big questions: What does it

mean to create a whole new way of relating to one another and supporting one another? And, you know, I feel those moments of genuine care and check in and tenderness in these pathways that we've created outside of neoliberal institutions. I'm thinking of some of the little spaces you and me are part of wherein we're trying to support one another and be there for one another. We know another world is possible and so many of us are working towards that together, but also it takes time.

ND: Right. I've been trying to think of it as we are already creating this kind of space, and I feel like we also need to practice not to criticize ourselves so much because just the fact that we're existing is making a difference. You know? It's slow, but I feel optimistic about it. The impact of the work that we do, that you do is still there.

KG: I really do feel like working with folks like you, appreciating that work, appreciating each other, celebrating the things we're able to do and accomplish, and just being alive together is super important, and I do feel hopeful. I am extremely hopeful for a future in which we continue to keep caring for one another and making spaces outside of the toxic ones we've been handed. Yeah, I feel hopeful.

Art Blah Blah:
A conversation
with Michele
Serchuk
& Midori

By Andi Avery

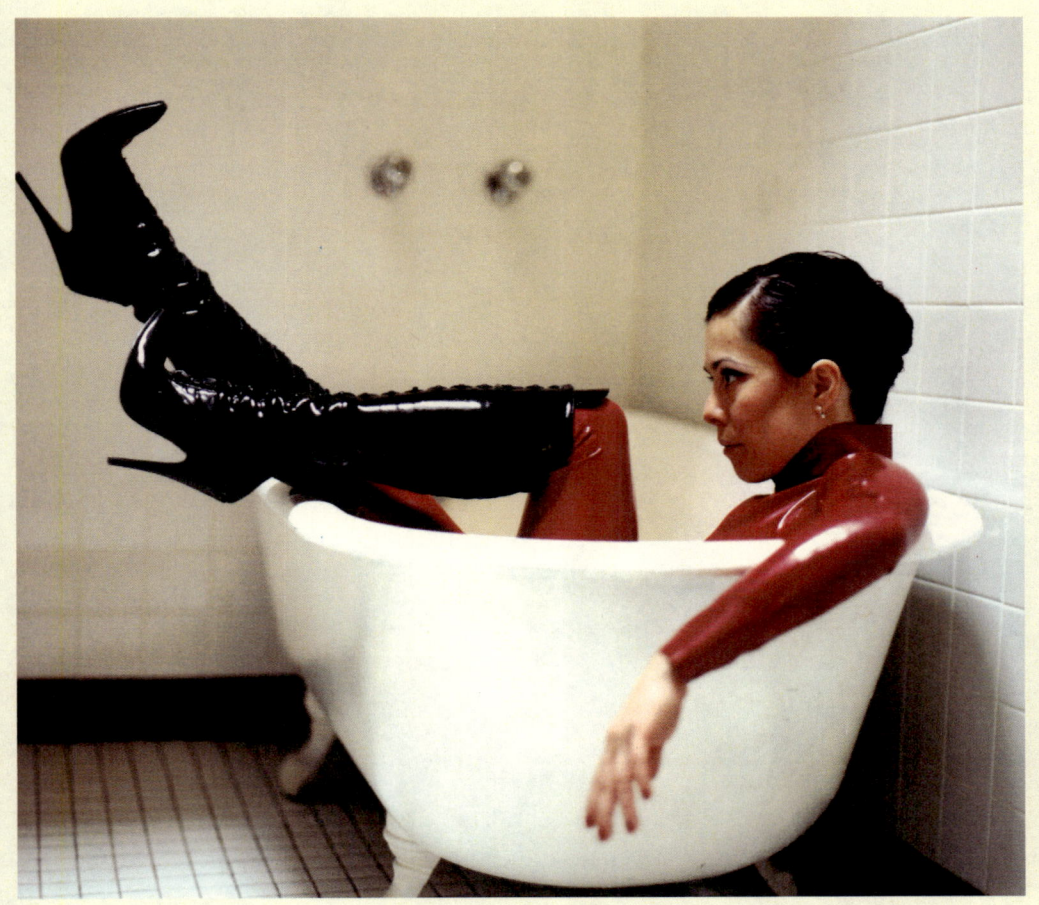

Midori: Tub #16-08 © Michele Serchuk 2002

The photos of Midori are from my series *This Fetish*. Y + X @ the Garage is from my *Ghosts of Desire* series, shot in the Meatpacking District before it was completely sanitized by gentrification.

Andi: Michele, you sent me a write-up about your collaboration with Midori and used the phrase "socially impolite" to describe your work together. I love that phrase. Can we start there?

Michele: Midori used the phrase "socially impolite" when we discussed this interview. I thought right away of the shoot we did in the Body Archive stairwell. I was shooting in this space in the Meatpacking District that is a Sephora now, but at the time it was a garage where they parked the meat trucks. The Body Archive, which was dedicated to body modification and sexual artwork, was upstairs.

There was this raunchy stairwell with a skylight, so we started doing this thing that ended up being glamor junkies, with Midori exploring postures of madness on this hot, sticky, dirty stairwell. And we ended up with lipstick and a powder compact on the stairwell as if it were a needle and a spoon. We

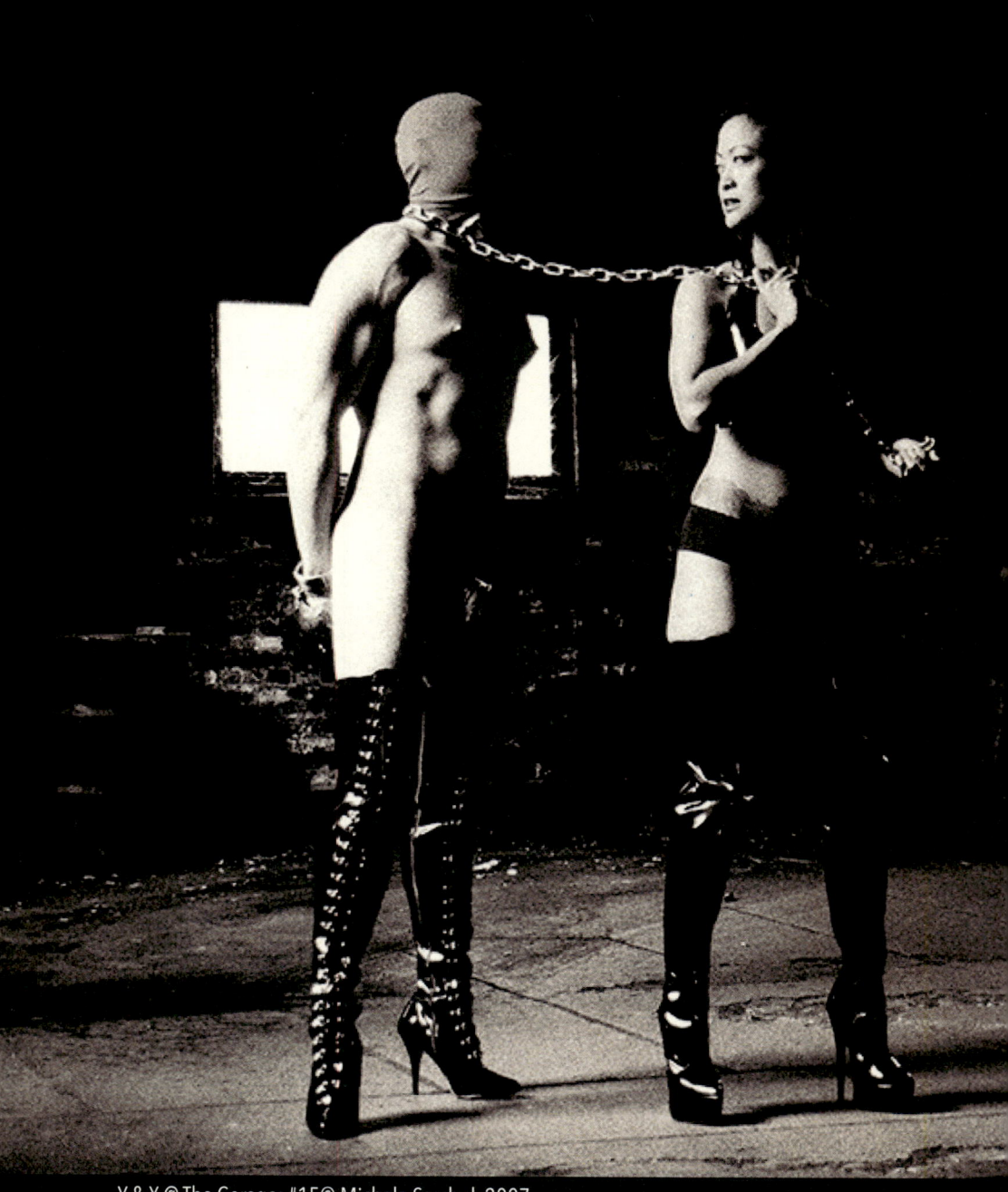

Y & X @ The Garage: #15© Michele Serchuk 2007

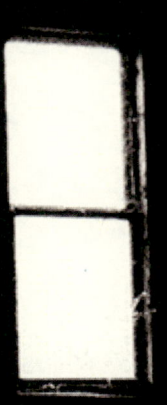

had just spent a weekend at this event where we were playing glamor, and playing dress up–all the stuff that we enjoy and fetishize and take pleasure in. But also looking at it as this construct that can be very negative. And then we started to play with that and just be socially impolite with it.

Andi: You've been collaborating for a while now. Does art making with other people always excite you? Or have you found something just very unique in each other?

Michele: Everybody I work with is unique and different, including Midori. Midori is very collaborative, very creative and very unique, and she gives me a lot to riff off of. I shoot portraits–I'm looking for a personal narrative, for identity. I'm looking for somebody who has something to say and can express it visually to the camera, either physically or with props, whatever. That's the collaboration, right? Midori is especially good at that, and the images that come out of our collaboration show not just that ability on her end but the way our friendship enhances the collaboration.

Midori: In terms of collaborative working, my artistic practice and artist identity just kind of happened–I didn't plan for it. I was doing fun, weird shit with my fun, weird friends in the early nineties club scene in San Francisco. And, you know, I thought Art with a capital A was like the people who went to art school.

Mostly I said yes to stuff like, "Hey, want to do a performance with my 12 foot long boa snake named Daisy?" And, it kind of went like that.

Only recently have I started using the terms like, "I engage in collaborative social practice art because art blah, blah, blah."

Michele: Yeah, I can relate to that.

Midori: Yeah. It makes it sound so important–apparently saying that I do cool shit with fun people needs to be

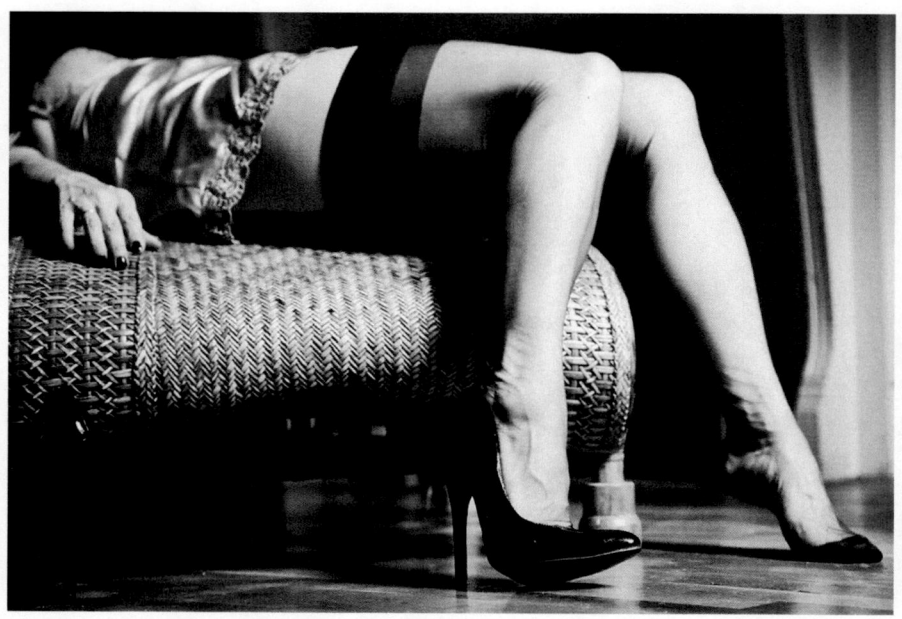

Midori: Legs #34 © Michele Serchuk 2002

said in the other way. So recently my smart art lingo friends have been giving me words to describe the stuff I do. Apparently, I disorient and destabilize the normal perspective, or, in other words, freak people out just a little bit.

Andi: I love that. I also love "art blah blah" as a phrase. I'm the only one on the Analog Cookbook editorial team that is not in academia. They are very good at the words and it can be intimidating.

Michele, when you're photographing someone, do you like to photograph people that you know well? That you don't know at all?

Michele: I have to know something about the person or there's nothing to do except make pretty pictures of pretty shapes. And I'm not really interested in that. I can do it if you pay me to do it. But I really want to make a portrait–a loosely defined portrait. You know, the sexual artwork is portraits, the narrative photography is portraits. They're all about the person. I don't have to know them for a long time, but we have to sit down and have a couple of conversations and I have a structure for how I approach that. But if they don't have anything to say, then we're not a good match.

Midori: It's like negotiation [for a BDSM scene].

Michele: It's exactly like negotiation.

Michele: I taught class at an event that was basically how to put together an erotic photo shoot structure, just like negotiating a scene. And then our friend–well, I found out some time later that he had a class on the opposite, how to go into a scene negotiation the way you would do a photoshoot.

Midori: I'm wondering in that class how many people came wanting to know what kind of camera you use.
Michele: Oh yeah. The couple of times I did it I said, "we will not discuss your technology."

Midori: What?! How could that possibly be?! To be a good photographer, you must have great, expensive equipment!

68

Michele: You must have a tool that you understand how to use.

Midori: That's what the tools say.

Michele: The only way [the equipment] kind of matters in my trajectory is that when I first started shooting again in the nineties, I had a Nikon FM film camera which did not even have a working light meter, and it used manual focus. It's not that having that camera made a certain kind of image, it was that learning that way made me a certain kind of photographer. If I had started off digital with everything automatic, then why would I have bothered to learn any of that? So it helped me see light a particular way.

Shooting on film made me have to select particular moments. It made me have to look for the moment that captured the thing. Whereas digital, I could just throw everything at it and it's in there some place. So in that regard, yes, it mattered, not for the image, but for the artist.

Andi: Michele, do you have any thoughts on your experience shooting analog versus digital? Does it make a difference in relation with your subjects at all?

Michele: Mmm. You know, it's fun being able to look at it and get instant feedback myself as to how the lighting is. I never had the budget when I was shooting film to have a Polaroid back, so I was really shooting blind all the time. So that's kind of nice. But since I started, I would always tell people that we sign a release before we shoot. And their veto is in not giving me something that they don't want out in the world. If you're uncomfortable with anything, anything–just say stop and we'll stop, and we'll do something else. And if we have to stop and go for ice cream, we'll do that, you know? So I try to create a safe space where somebody doesn't have to keep looking at [their images].

And it's much more helpful than having a mirror on set because that makes me crazy. I don't like when somebody is looking in the mirror while I'm photographing them.

Midori: Unless the mirror is part of the thing.

Michele: Yeah. Unless you're going with the mirror.

Midori: There's a great accidental shot you took of me when I was dressing. It was a candid shot getting ready for a shoot.

Michele: Which is fascinating. It's something that I love shooting. Dressing is really personal and sensual and there's a lot of stuff there.

Andi: Excellent segue. What we've learned from our submissions this cycle is that everyone defines erotic as something different. So, what is erotic to to each of you? Broadly or specifically.

Michele: So for me, the erotic is anything that accesses your sexual energy or your erotic identity. How you take pleasure, where you go in your head, how you experience your body. You know, I've talked to photographers who've said "if there isn't a penetration shot, it isn't erotic."

To me, that's just so [a tired sigh]–you know. I show every year at the Seattle Erotic Arts Festival, and the director of the festival once commented that I'm the only one who in some years has nobody naked in my photos. Because it's not always about that.

It's about who you are, and how you experience it. And so if I'm going to photograph it, I have to relate to it on some level. I have to be able to understand what's hot or pleasurable about it for you, or I'm going to miss the moment. I'm not going to be able to capture it.

There are some things where I will just say, "I'm not the right photographer. I'm not going to shoot that because we won't make good images together." So I have to understand it, even if I don't personally find it hot.

I did a shoot with somebody recently that was about puppy fetish, you know, with his headgear and everything. And it's not my thing, but I understand how he enjoys flirting as a puppy. And so that flirtatiousness came into play with me and was erotic. It's not for me, but I got it. And so we were able to do a good shoot.

Midori: Another thing that just popped into my mind is that, for me, erotic also has something that one intentionally hides from society. Wearing a nice dress can be sexy, but it doesn't necessarily hit the mark as erotic. Right? There's some aspect of it that one hides because I was thinking about what's erotic to me, and that can also be disturbing. Like, I find a lot of Francis Bacon's

paintings–a piece of meat hanging, and distorted bodies in self-loathing and homo erotic anguish – to be incredibly erotic. Yeah. So there's a bit of the shadow aspect as well.

Michele: The shadow can be very sexy. It's a great place to explore, and not everybody that I shoot with wants to go there.

You know what I was going to say about that dress? That dress, that itsy bitsy, sexy but not erotic dress, becomes erotic if the person who's wearing it experiences it as something that heightens their sexual experience. And this is why I don't like shooting people dressed up as "edgy" unless they fantasized about it. Putting somebody in latex with fetish shoes and giving them a crop when it's not their thing and they've never fantasized about it is pretty, but not erotic. But even if somebody has never held a crop before in their lives, but they've really thought about it a lot, it can work. So it depends on how you inhabit it.

Midori: And there's a tension, right? Sometimes it's a tiny tension of sharing a secret with the photographer. Or it can be of giant tension like,

"oh, my God, I find Francis Bacon erotic. What is wrong with me?" No, no, it was a Rembrandt. Rembrandt has this painting of a gutted side of beef hanging kind of Christ-like. It's beef, it's a cow carcass, and I sent that as a flirtatious image to somebody.

Michele: And they got it, right?

Midori: Oh, yeah. He's a sick motherfucker.

Michele: Because you know who you're talking to.

Midori: I'm thinking of erotic imagery, even erotic moments in movies, and the tension when there's something that could happen. A straight up penetration shot is not erotic because I know what's happening. There's no mystery. There's no tension. It's like I'm watching David Attenborough narrate the mating habits of Homo Sapiens, you know?

Whereas, like two snails approaching each other and about to have hermaphroditic sex where they bite each other's little slimy dicks off, that's erotic. Because something could happen, you know? There's a great scene by Lauren Bacall in Treasure,

Sierra Madre where she says, "if you need me, Steve, just whistle. You know how to whistle, don't you, Steve? Just put your lips together and blow." And then watching Bogart going, [her eyes bug out]. That's erotic.

Andi: Okay, so of a practical question—working with erotic art obviously requires a lot of trust. What do you think is the most important part in establishing a trust or shared language or whatever it is that makes that kind of connection open up and feel safe between a creator and a subject?

Michele: Well, I mean, I can answer from my perspective, but I'd be interested to hear what Midori needs in order to be able to give. I'm going to ask the same kind of questions that one would ask in negotiating a scene. What's really hot for you? Where's your energy? What do you want to express? What do you definitely want to look at doing in front of the camera? What are you not sure of, but might want to do? And what's absolutely off the table? And you can say stop any time and I'm not going to be mad. There's no art director. There's no editor.

This is personal artwork, and we get to say when

we're done. So I give a lot of agency to the person I'm shooting, and I'm never going to try to seduce them into shooting something they aren't comfortable with. I'm never going to try to push them further. If what they want to do is not enough for me, then I'm not going to do the shoot. Then there's just nothing there for me, you know?

Andi: Is there anything that you would like to add? I mean, I could literally sit here and talk to you all night, but I know that I can't.

Midori: Over the years I have mined my personal discomfort—like the stairwell shoot with madness, the daily performance of the self, of polite and fair and level headed, and all that social nicety. But what's it like to dive into that? I'm drawn to, and fear, the potential for madness – mental illness as well as that kind of metaphysical madness – grief or pain or self doubt. I've done a lot of shooting with Michele around grief, rage, madness, the murderous and predatory, dirty—dirty as in like actual physical dirt, all these are subjects that I,in my ordinary everyday life, try to push away.

Michele: The photo set can

be a safe space to explore. And even in the beginning of my erotic work, you know, I was very aware of the fact that this is an artificial space that we're creating. And as long as it's not something that is so personal and terrifying to you that it must be private, as long as it's something you can say in public, it is a safe space to explore something that is in your heart and in your head, but not in your life. That started off in an erotic context, but that kind of practice still informs the way that I do portraits.

You put on the character, you manifest this thing, and if we're successful, we can show people that this is what this kind of erotic experience is like, or this is what this kind of pain is like. I did a series with Midori that was about the pain within and manifesting it on the body with rope. We did something on racism. We did something on cancer. It's limitless what can be explored.

Andi: I could listen to you talk for a million hours.

Midori: This is our version of art blah blah.

71

Shemale Encounters in 8MM is a breakdown of the ideas that went into the creation and imagery of the short film *Everything is OK | an ASMR to help you sleep at night*, Autojektor, 2021—a discussion on trans identity, fetishisation, and demonising of the other.

Words by Autojektor

Celluloid scars like
human skin,
it ages, it burns,
it can be cut and
stabbed.

The film is tangible and
its physicality is as
much a part of the story
as
the image it holds.

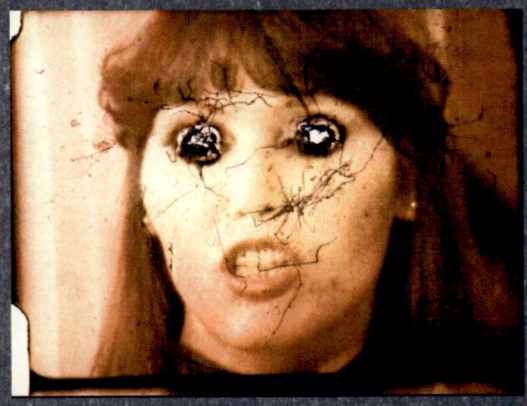

And so, there is a
poignancy to its
destruction,
the victims carry
on oblivious to the
violence.
There is no blood or
gore,
except for the
projector's light that
pours through the open
wounds.

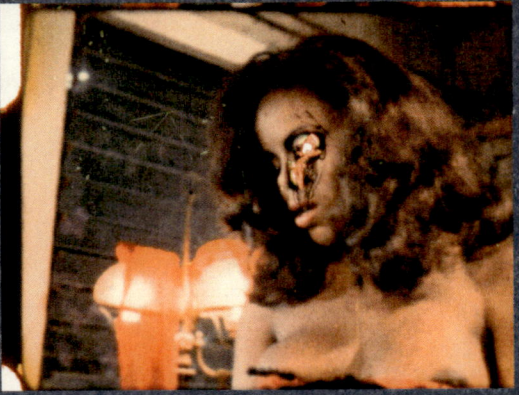

We can understand that
violence has occurred,
but, it is physical
violence that has been
inflicted onto
something
beyond the body.

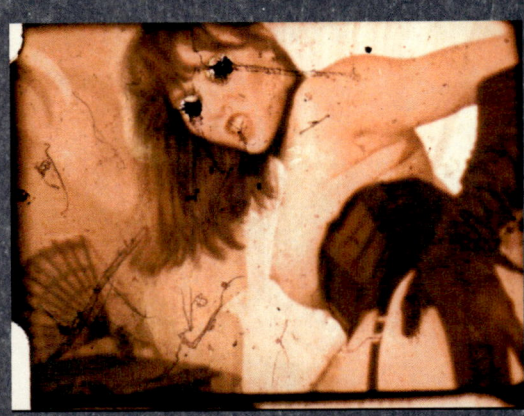

The frame shows a
woman bathed in light.

Sweat glistens on her
breasts, A hand
Gliding down her body
as her fingertips stroke
her soft, supple cock.
She inhales deeply.

A sharp object has torn
through the skin.
A concaved skull.
White voids shine
through the soft holes
where its eyes were.
It's not dead, it is still
breathing.

The frame holds her
tightly.
It cannot leave.
The camera has her as
a goddess, her sex is
unbound by nature.
It belongs to the state.

Her body is fetishized, its
identity is demonized.

Celluloid is as fragile as it
needs to be.

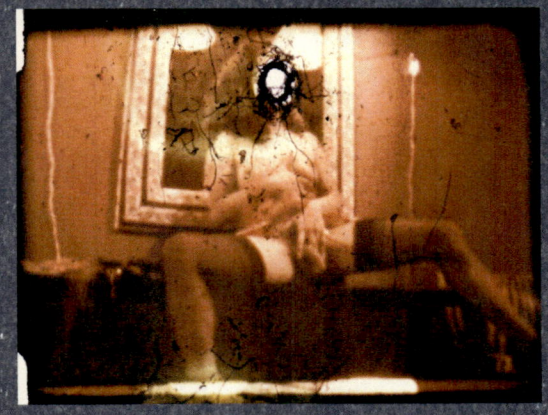

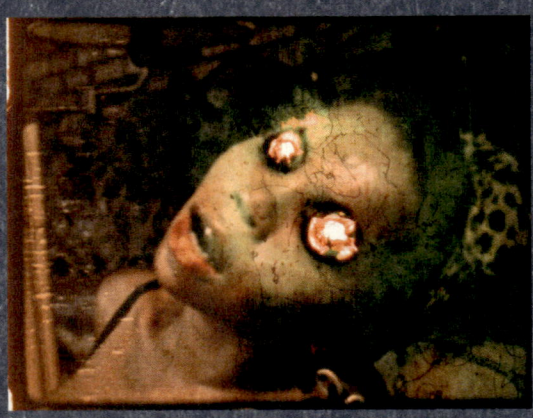

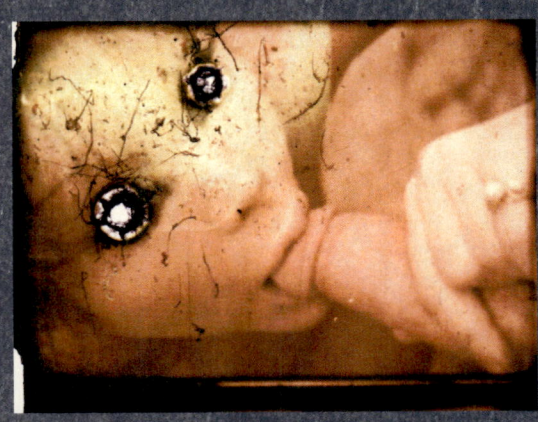

Quack Quack

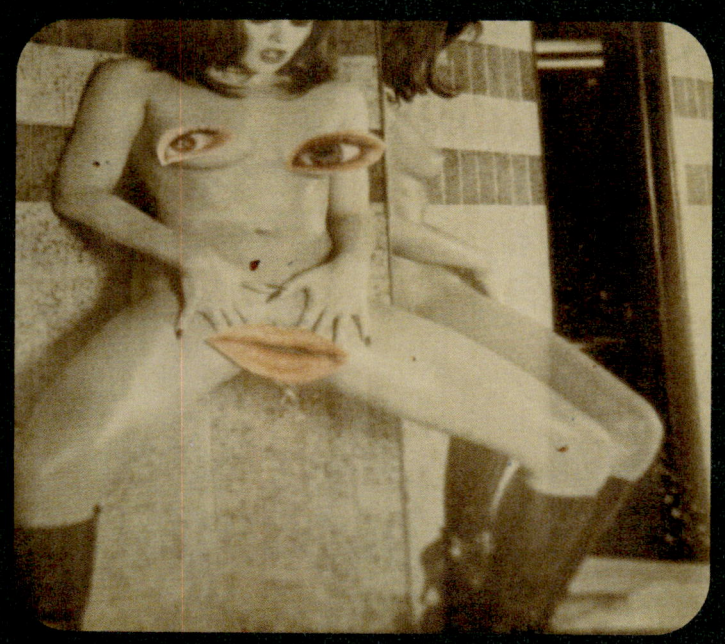

Celina de Leon

Quack Quack is a moving image collage that merges stop motion animation and 16mm analog techniques. Using cut-outs from porn magazines and found footage, the film alludes to the negative effects of female fetishization—particularly of asian women—that feed into incel culture.

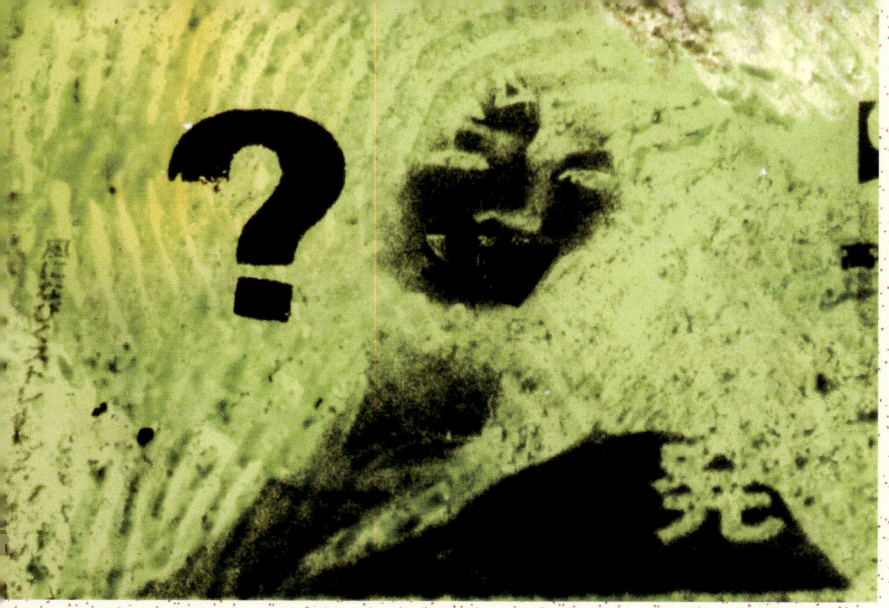

How did you come up with the title *Quack Quack* for your film?

When creating this film, I was thinking a lot about fetishization and incel culture in the media. The film reflects my own experience as a Filipino woman, often feeling ignored or perceived as inferior. I used "quacking" in the film to be an ironic translation of two things, the first being a metaphor to how men understand femmes, and the second being a metaphor to how misogynistic people sound when spewing anti-feminist propaganda online. Titling the film *Quack Quack* was a way to emphasize this loss of communication and worship of empty preaching.

Can you talk a little about the process of sourcing the materials for this piece?

When I started the project, I had no idea what it was going to be about. I had a Bolex, a roll of film, and rainy weather outside. I remembered that I had a bunch of magazine cut-outs I've been collecting over the years and I was immediately drawn to making a stop motion film. My roommate has a collection of vintage porn magazines that I was able to utilize as well. In the case of this film, the materials came before the concept.

What role do these found materials' history play in this film?

The images in the film range from the 70's to the 2000's. Reading through some of the older porn magazines, the misogyny is clear. It's like a slice of history that not only shows differences of the time's styles and looks, but also the time's viewpoints on sex, politics, rent, marriage. Although there's clear signs of sexism within these materials, manipulating these pages now in the 2020's shows that although media has become more PC, violence has only been increasing.

A myriad of techniques are used in this work including mordençage, optical printing, direct animation, contacting printing, stop motion, hand processing, and more. How do you feel these individual techniques working in conversation with one another?

By incorporating all of these techniques, I had to spend a lot more time with the film than I would have if editing digitally. The hand-made nature of the film fostered a closer connection to the materials I was using. Rather than looking up found imagery online, I had to flip through dozens of magazines and cut them out myself. By tangibly splicing and taping the film instead of editing online, every decision I made had more intention behind it. These techniques gave me space to think through the concept of the film. I wouldn't have been able to form those ideas if I hadn't spent all those hours working with the materials and emulsion. Manipulating the film to this extent was necessary in order to flip its original meaning to my own.

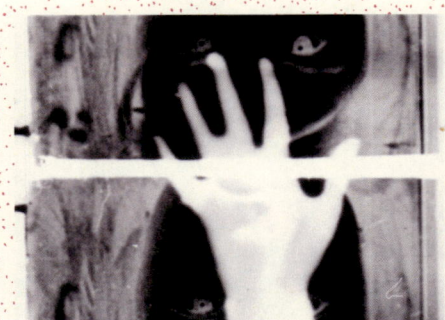

The abstracting of the feminine image seems reminiscent or even in critique or rejection of previous forms of abstraction in representing the feminine body throughout art history (thinking of work in cubism, surrealism, etc). Did any of these makers or forms influence the way you handled these images?

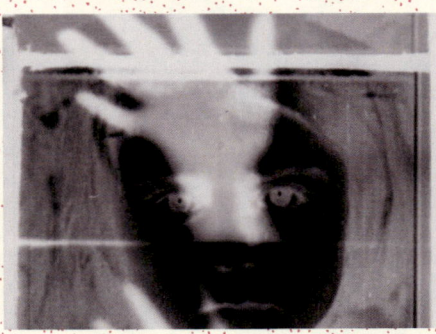

One of my favorite artists/filmmakers is Věra Chytilová. I watch her film *Daisies* (1966) whenever I'm feeling unmotivated or uninspired. She created surreal, feminist films that used humor and absurdism to get her point across. I'm extremely inspired by her style and any other feminist filmmaker that uses absurdism or surrealism. Humor is how I navigate my own frustrations.

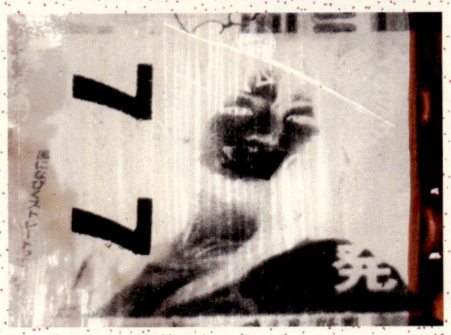

How do you believe your work in conversation or expands on the work of artists like Naomi Uman?

I was thinking a lot about Naomi Uman's film, *Removed,* when making *Quack Quack.* In *Removed,* Uman takes porn reels and uses nail polish remover to erase the female counterpart in each frame. Anyone who works with film can appreciate the time and commitment it takes to do that. Like Uman's film, *Quack Quack* works to critique the media's gaze and fetishization of women. *Quack Quack* and *Removed* both require the destroying of film to get their points across.

You bring up incel culture in your artists statement. A growing community of violent racist, misogynistic, and transmysoginistic young and older heterosexual men. How is

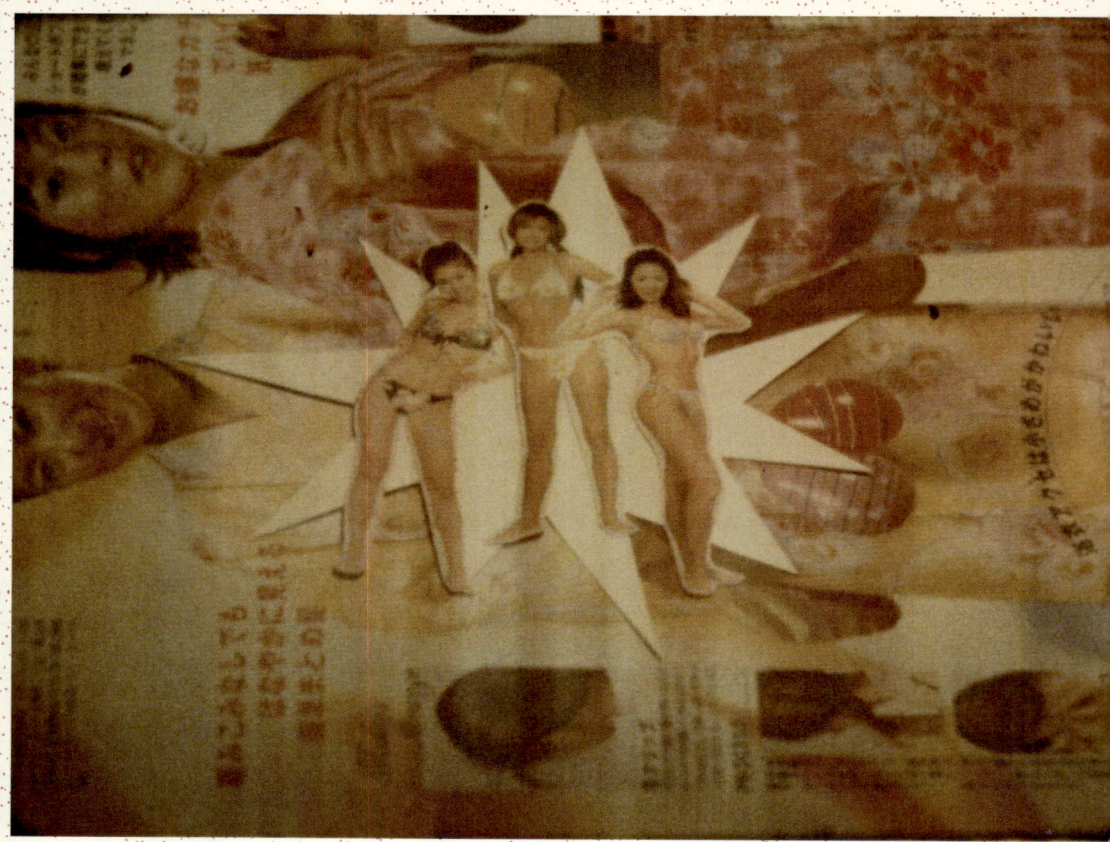

your work addressing these issues of men who blame women and society for their lack of romantic or sexual success? How do you see the fetishization of particularly Asian women feeding into this culture?

Quack Quack was my outlet to vent about violence against women and ongoing gun violence in the states. Instances such as the 2014 Isla Vista Killings or the 2021 Atlanta spa shootings were perpetuated by young men not far off from my own age. By including imagery of "hand-guns" and young children mimicking gun noises on top of female imagery, I'm alluding to the desensitization of this violence. It was important for me to shine a light particularly on Asian fetishization and Asian-hate since I feel these effects myself and these issues have only been more rampant since Covid-19.

Your hands of the maker are very much a prominent part of the film. Both in labor and in abstracting the images we can see. Tell us about that decision.

Although I love making films, I have a dislike toward being on set. By shooting in stop motion and using all analog techniques, it gives me space to work on my own terms with the permission to make mistakes. It also allows me to go in and create something without having a clear plan. I think that's what makes working with my hands so much more personal, allowing the meaning of the film to arise through feeling rather than planning.

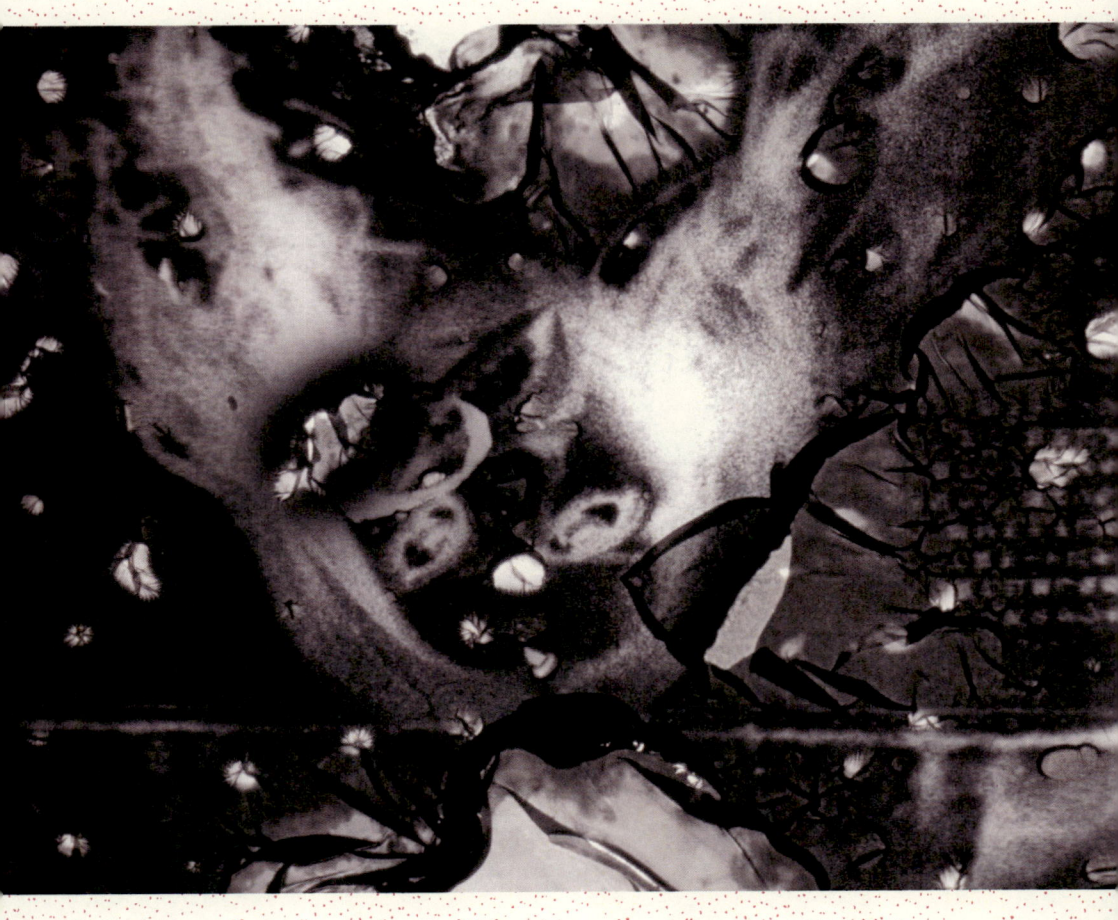

81

Skelehellavision

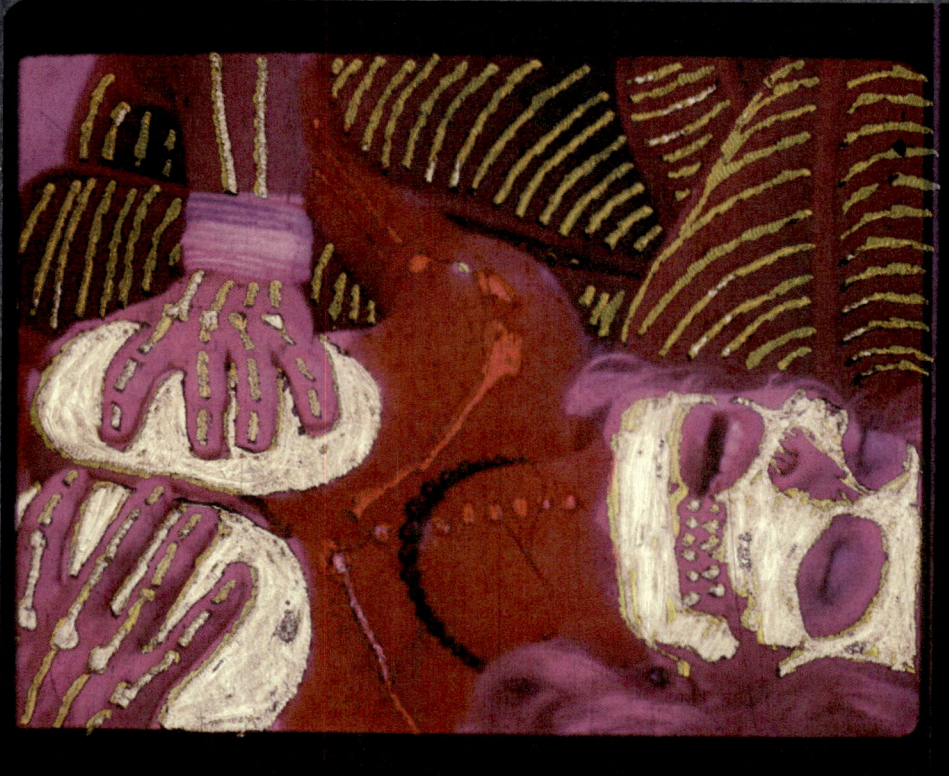

Martha Colburn

A delve into the netherworld, using stop motion animation and found footage 35mm, 8mm and 16mm film.

When thinking about your work, collage animation comes to mind, but Skelehellavision has such remarkable examples of direct animation/removal work. It's also worth noting it's from 2002. Can you talk about what drew you to the Analog Erotica call and this project, in particular?

This film was made more as a cautionary tale, or warning. In the spirit of the illuminated manuscript or a Heironymous Bosch or Brueghel painting, it was made as a kind of flickering moralizing illustration.

There's a lot of depth and control you showcased in the strips you submitted. Can you talk about tools and the labor of love you undertook to make these images?

I cut the film into strips and rolled it up. Then I scratched them on trains and projection booths as I crossed Europe on a 30-screening film tour booked by Jack Stevenson.

So I packed a battery operated mini light table and a scratcher of some kind. This was pre-cell phones, laptops, internet for me. So I had to use a lot of alone time on trains and was not always able to read due to tiredness or distraction. When I got back to my warehouse in Baltimore I re-filmed the strips (using a magnifying glass) to Super 8 mm so I could edit and view the footage. One of the strips is scratched 8mm and that I also transferred to Super 8mm.

You mentioned that you scavenged these films from the Mini-Adult Theater in San Francisco, which according to the San Francisco Theaters blog, closed sometime prior to 2001. Was the theater already defunct when you went

scavenging?

Yes, I had gone there a few times when it was open and saw the most surreal film programming–because it was a 24 hour theater showing only film, they had strange fillers like Jesus walking on the water. I went there because my film distributor from Denmark had sent me an article he wrote about the Mini-Adult. So when it closed I was walking around nearby and either someone told me or I found a junk shop selling stuff from the theater. I worked on this film from 1999 to 2002 because over that time I moved from a stint in San Francisco, to Baltimore to Amsterdam.

You describe the film as, "A delve into the netherworld, using stop motion animation and found footage 35mm, 8mm and 16mm film." Do you see this film as a sex film? A social commentary? A little of both? Or something different?

I don't think it ever demonstrates sex in any normal sense of the word. It kind of deviates into other areas of life and death. I know it was a turning point, where I could not continue to make films that I could not describe, that took a long time to make and had nothing to do with sexuality–because I had moved to Europe and had to get grants to survive. Since making this film I have censored some scenes–even last year! I finally cut the negative so I didn't have to censor the prints.

Lastly, what are you working on now?

I have been making paintings, drawings and collage for the last four years. I made a number of music videos, produced a record and make mini documentaries. My last real film was 2018, *Western Wild* about the controversial German author Karl May.

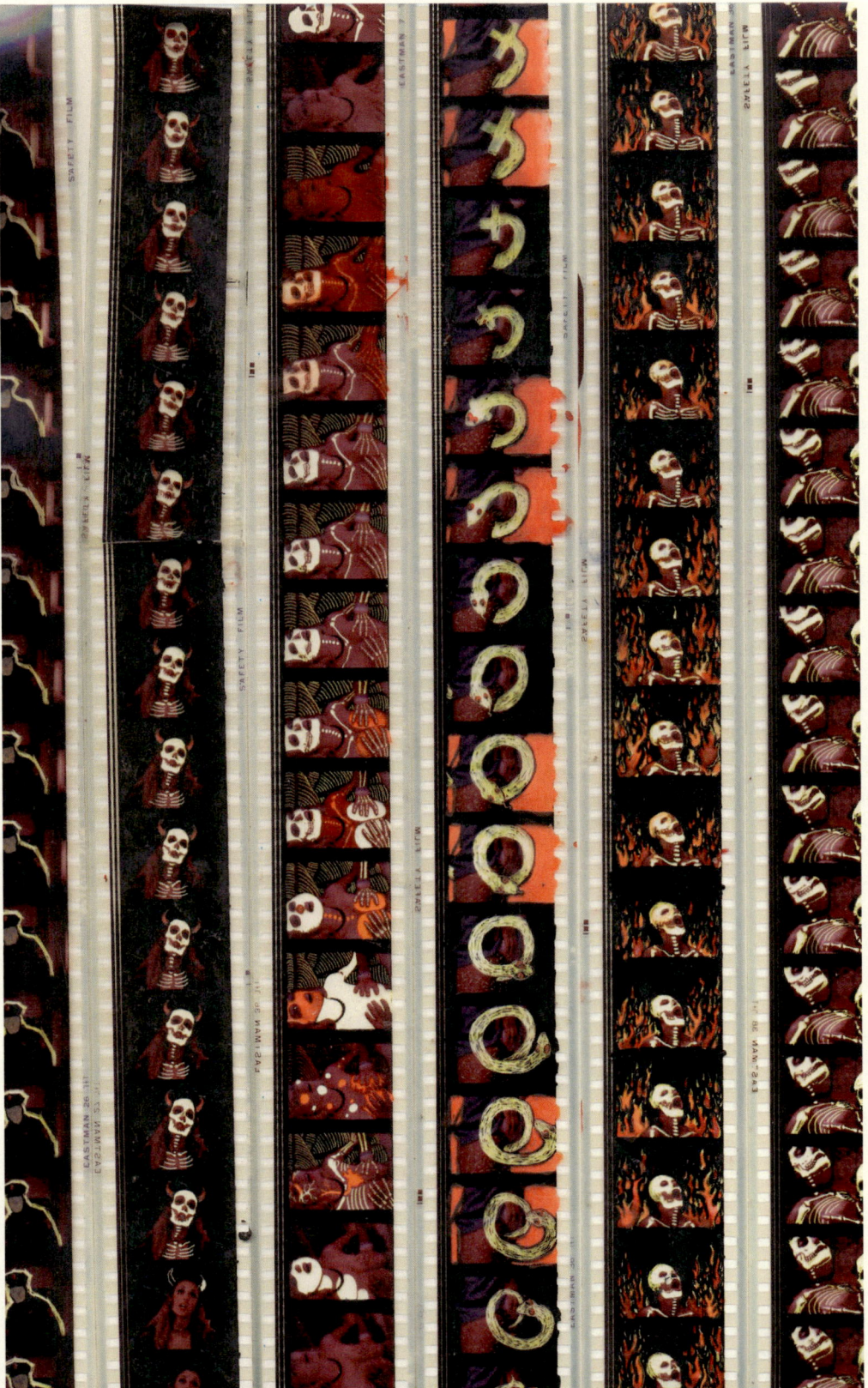

I DON'T KNOW INTIMACY

35mm Stills by

Kmar Douagi

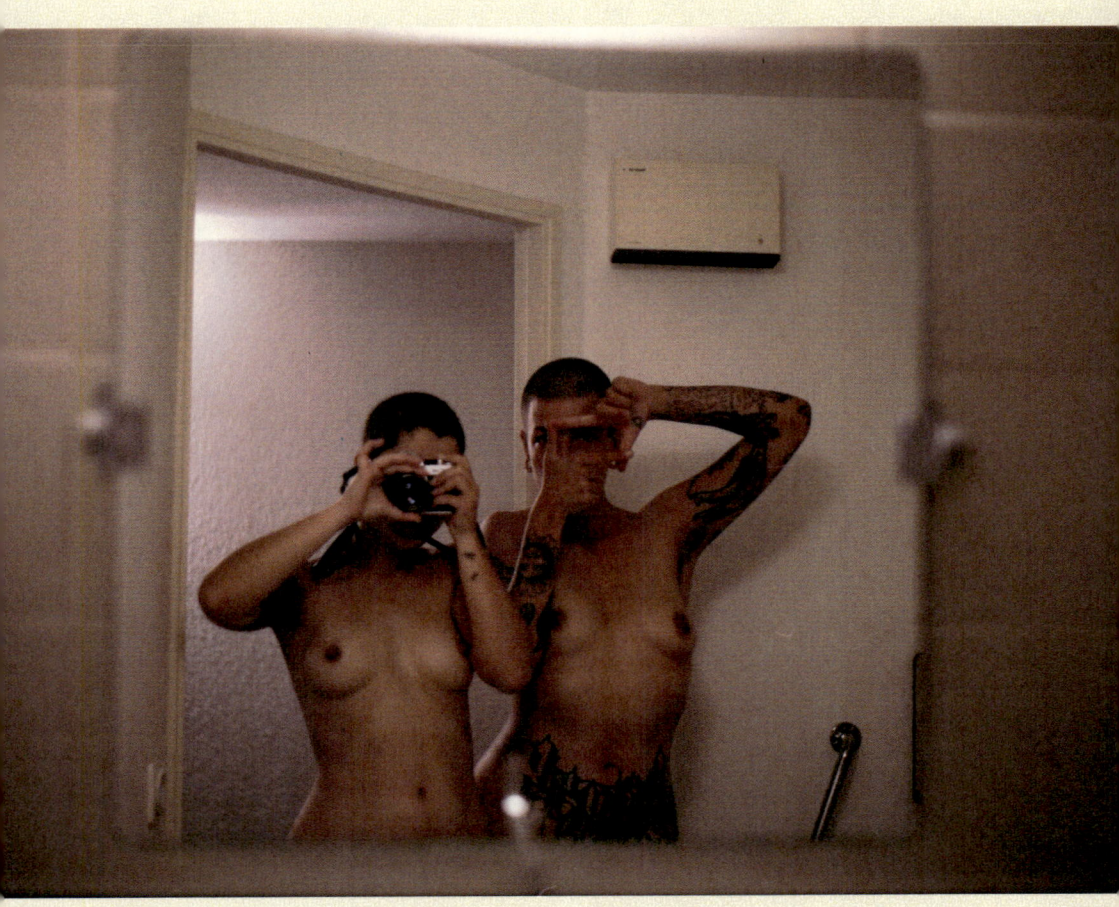

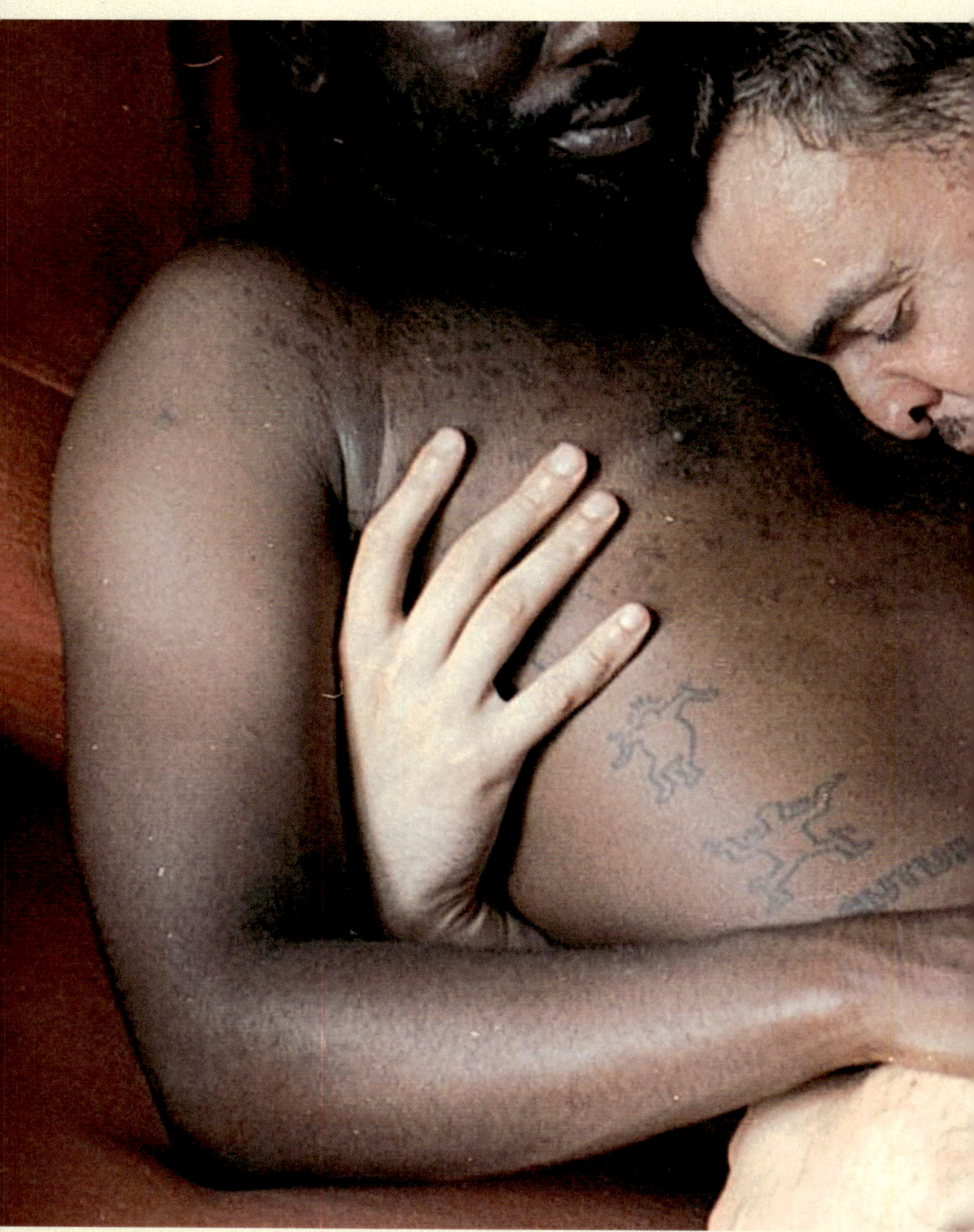

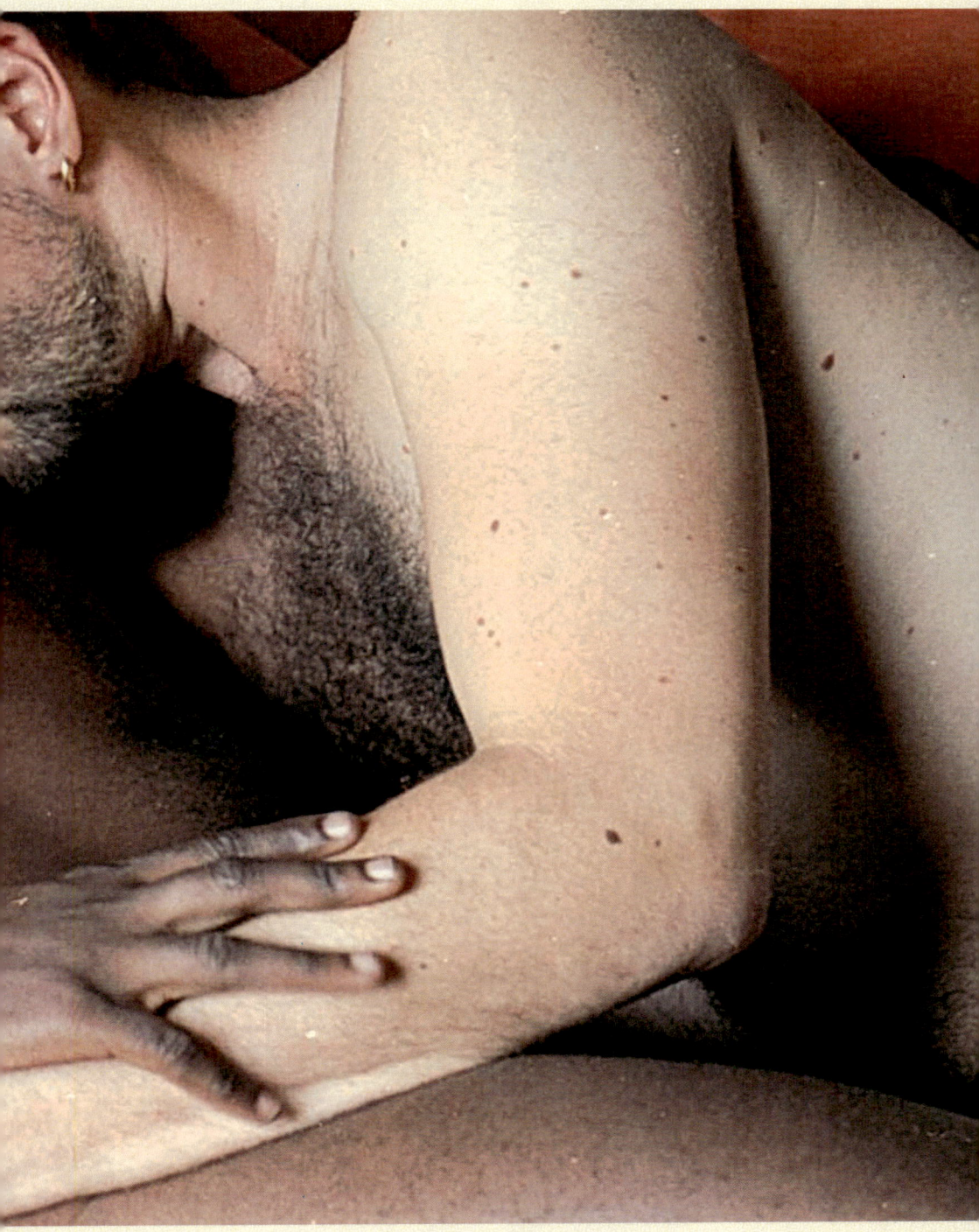

A STORY THAT DOESN'T HAVE TO DO WITH ME

> **"** As I seek to connect with my partner about their research in bioarchaeology, a conversation emerges about survival and what is left behind after death. **"**

Can you talk about the process of making the film-specifically the choice to combine Super 8 with digital video?

As an invisibly disabled Queer femme, I feel I often exist between worlds–history/present, straight/gay, able/disabled, movement/stasis. Collaging digital and analog felt metaphoric and natural. I originally entered my MFA Film/Video program as a dancer who primarily created video for performance installations. I think arriving to filmmaking as a secondary medium without knowing all the rules supported my creativity.

For Super 8mm, the camera didn't feel as voyeuristic as a digital camera. B (my partner) had never used a Super 8mm camera before so that was fun. We experimented with different cameras and the diopter was jammed with one camera. I shot anyway and the footage turned out fuzzy, which I loved. Our bodies disappearing in and out of the background (and one another) created a magical other world. The softness of Super 8mm acted as a protection regarding the audience's gaze. I wanted a gauze or shield from the outside world.

How do you see this work in context with the rest of your practice? Would you say it's an outlier? Or a continuation of ideas you've explored in other films?

Before a story, I had just finished my series of Exit Strategy films. I had a fear that every

Kym McDaniel

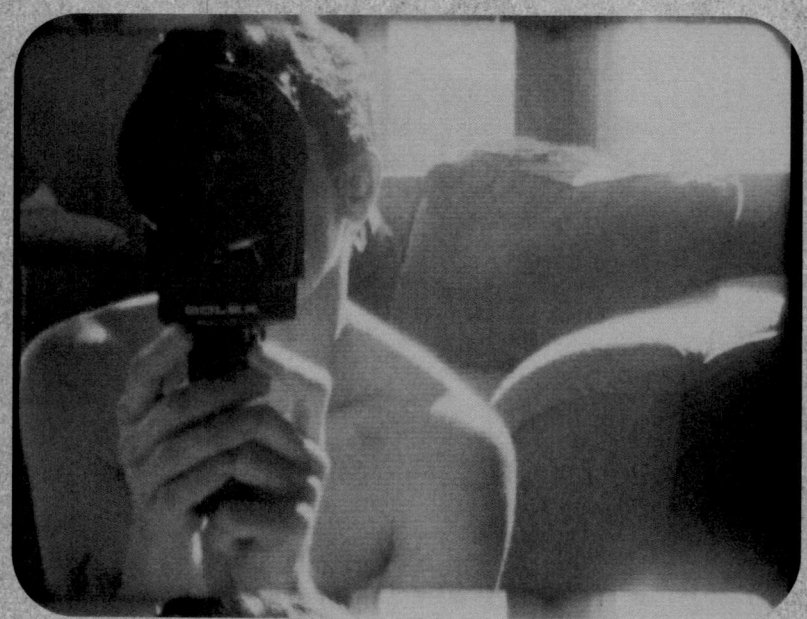

film after that could be considered an Exit Strategy. I was ready to make a film that was different in structure and psychology.

In *Exit Strategy #5*, there is text that reads, "I wonder if I am completely fucked, that I will be alone and in pain forever." I held an idea for many years that I was unlovable, unfuckable, and unwanted. I didn't plan for my next film to be made in a relationship, but I was just so incredibly excited to be in an out Queer relationship and in love. There was pleasure and inspiration inherent in my life. Since my films are always personal, it made sense to me that my Queerness and relationship would become incorporated into my practice.

The film is dedicated to a childhood friend I had growing up. He died in 2021 and the news gutted me. We had grown apart in our adult years but had many childhood memories together. He was the definition of living life Queerly. I hope I honor him in this work.

You're a curator and professor. Can you talk about how those practices inform and challenge your art practice. Balancing these often conflicting demands can be a mixed bag.

Phew. Yeah. It's a lot, right?

When I was making a story, I was teaching Super 8mm in the Cinema Department at

Binghamton University. My interest in Super 8mm for a story was a combination of wanting to better my own pedagogy, as well as being inspired by my student's projects. Some first-time Super 8mm students were producing beautiful footage.

This year, I moved to Salt Lake City to teach as an Assistant Professor in Screendance (Dance Filmmaking) within the School of Dance at the University of Utah. I was a dancer until a head injury in my early 20s. Unable to dance or choreograph, I transitioned to film. Accepting the position here has felt like a welcoming back to dance, as well as a commitment to face my long-ignored grief regarding injury and my dance career. All these complicated feelings feed into my current practice.

The brutal arrival to a "post-COVID" world has been the most challenging demand. I taught online for the 20-21 academic year and maintained a work-life-pain balance I had never experienced before. I have an autoimmune disease that can flare up with excruciating pain. During a flare-up, there's nothing I can do but wait for hours until the pain passes. In Fall 2020, I was taking an online ASL class and one night I took the computer into the bathroom and attended the class laying on the floor. If that class was in person, there was no way I could have attended. But on the floor in the dark, camera off, I could attend. The pandemic opened choices for me. My desire is for my teaching, curation, and artistic practice to provide choices in resistance to that ableist heteronormative world we exist within.

One Queer disabled artist to another: can we talk about your relationship to analog tools given the labor and history of them? What does it mean to you to engage with these tools while living and working

in your body? Do you find parallels with your relationship to dance? Or is it a completely different experience?

I started hand painting clear leader in 2019. I was going through a breakup and used coloring as a method of distraction and meditation. I was combating emotional pain while creating physical pain from the labor. Sometimes the pain, whatever it is, is too great and I lose myself in labor to survive.

Time and space in experimental filmmaking is very different than dance. In dance, you rent studio space per hour, pay dancers for their time, and pay for the performance venue, among other dedications. The whole process regarding time can be very precious. For Super 8mm, I wait for the film to arrive in the mail, shoot on and off to complete the roll, develop or send the footage out, wait, transfer, review the footage and usually don't edit until months later. There is so much space and forgiveness in this timeline. It reminds me of Crip time. When I originally transitioned from dance to film, I was in debilitating pain and my rule was that filmmaking shouldn't cause additional physical pain.

One connection between analog filmmaking and dancemaking is that they are both improvisational practices for me. An improvisation score provides a set of rules for spontaneous interaction to happen. When I shoot Super 8mm, improvisation rules are inherent within the lighting, camera settings, and film stock. Film processing is also an improvisation. I love being surprised by choices made within an improvisation structure.

The thing that really struck me about this work was that it's a collaboration with your partner, which can present a special set of challenges in my experience. There's a moment that you left in the film during the interview, a point of friction where you disagree about how each of you sees their research work–it's a really lovely moment. Can you talk about how you approached this collaboration? Did you always plan to explore your sexual relationship as well as your intellectual and emotional one on screen? Or did that develop during the making?

Thank you. That moment has gotten conflicting feedback!

Since the beginning of our relationship, I've been curious about their research and intimacy with death. On our first date, I asked if they could tell someone had chronic pain after examining their bones. My life revolves around physical pain, and I've always felt very close to death. We are both interested in the body as research, but for different reasons.

Filming together was no problem, getting naked and filming was a lot of fun. Intellectually though, they were quite resistant. I think that is why keeping that moment of conflict in the film was important to me, it was representative of the process. B wanted to know how I was going to treat the case studies we discussed and recorded. I don't really follow a method in the creation process, and as a scientist, I think that was difficult for B. For this film especially, I worked as a collagist and spent about a year gathering images. It was impossible to tell them how everything would tie together because most of the time I did not know myself. I kept saying, "You must trust me!" I wanted

to make the film about pleasure, but in the end, it was about death (oops).

In your response to our theme for the issue, you talked about playfulness and liberation that you gained during these Super 8 sessions and about using short ends of rolls to film each other before and after love making. What did you learn about yourself and your partner through this process? How has it impacted your relationship?

This film has made me realize how trauma had a flattening affect/effect on me. If my brain had a monitor in my early life, there would be no rhythm or spikes in my brain waves, just a flat line. The Exit Strategies represented that lack of rhythm. Each film has a similar tempo, pacing, and delivery. a story is much more rhythmic. I believe my inner life comes out in my work, so a film with more rhythm and movement represents my own inner process of healing and recovery.

My filmmaking work centers vulnerability and I too easily forget vulnerability is not a standard operating mode for people (including B). We have moved across

the country twice in our relationship and gone through difficult life things, sometimes filming is just a reason to play. One of the last rolls we shot, I was like, okay, get naked and just roll around on the bed, I'm going to shine this nightstand light around. After a while I was like, can you roll faster? Faster??? The footage is so funny and bizarre. And strangely sexy?! They have the body of a God! People ask me what I do for fun, and I never have an answer. Next time I'll talk about how my partner and I make naked Super 8mm films.

Last question: what are you working on now?

I enjoy creating work in a series, like chapters in a book. There are two other films that belong in a trilogy with a story that doesn't have to do with me. I am trying to finish them this year…working titles are Biohazard and American Dream. They both include Super 8mm footage, digital, and B. Biohazard is how the medical model of health fails women and Queer people; American Dream is more nebulous. Something about shopping malls, cats, T shots, and surgery.

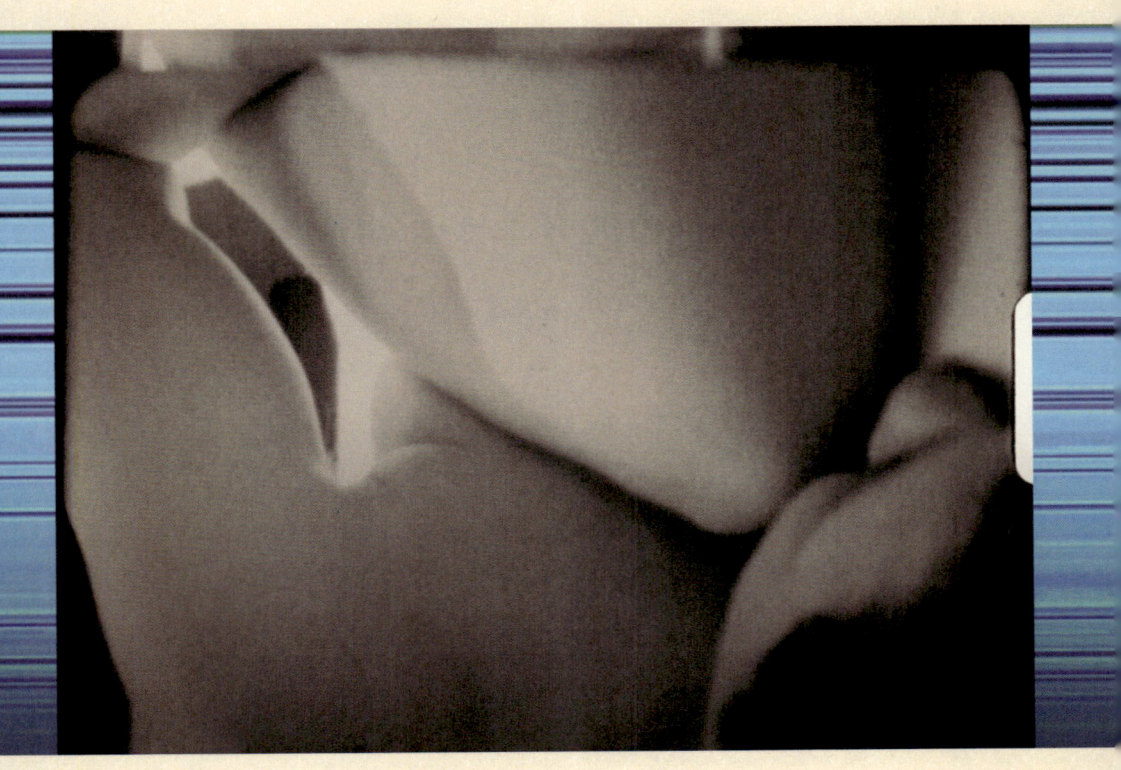

Vaseline, Queer Policing, & Moving Image Legacy

A Conversation between Malic Amalya and Hogan Seidel

Hogan: I already know you and your practice quite intimately now, but would you mind introducing yourself and your practice for Analog Cookbook readers?

Malic: I am an experimental filmmaker, and a white trans fag. I currently live in the Boston area, on occupied land of the Massachusett People, whose name was appropriated by white colonizers.

I primarily work in 16mm film, but not exclusively. My films are nonlinear and often non-narrative. Politically, my work comes from a Queer-feminist framework aligned with prison abolition, decolonization, anti-racism, disability justice, and environmental justice.

I find myself leaning into "nonlinear" more than "experimental." There's something about "nonlinear" that feels maybe more explicit.

Hogan: Experimental has meant a lot of things and in a lot of different contexts in the past where nonlinear feels more like a formal identity. Experimental opens itself up to a lot of assumptions and a whole history of debate. Many of which are exclusively housed within higher education.

Malic: I have a lot of critiques of higher education being racist and classist institutions. I don't think you need to go to college to be an artist and many of my favorite contemporary artists didn't go to college. But for me, college is where I first accessed equipment and studied history and theory.

Hogan: I struggle with this as well. In the US, a lot of the funding and research for arts is done within the higher education institutional level. And for me at least, I love teaching, but it also has been for survival. I need access to these tools. I can't necessarily afford them on my own. I need someone to sort of invest in me, my research and my practice, but also the unintended consequences of institutionalizing artists—you're doing great work, you love your students and teaching, but is this contributing to something harmful? The bottom line for institutions is capital. These institutions do not always have the best interest of you and your students in mind.

Did you learn to work with moving images in college? What drew you to the analog medium?

Malic: The first time I started to think about the different moving image media was as a freshman in college. I went to the School of the Art Institute of Chicago (SAIC) and there was the option of taking video art or 16mm film courses. In my mind, 16mm was to film what architecture is to drawing. I was not interested in measurements or in that type of precision, so I took video art courses and kept my distance from 16mm. It was the late nineties and we're working with VHS, which actually had a linear editing process, much like editing on a Steenbeck.

I ended up transferring to Hampshire. I loved my time at SAIC but when I transferred, it was clear that I was behind academically. So, I focused primarily on film theory and media studies, and didn't take a single studio course.

It wasn't until I got to grad school at the University of Illinois at Chicago that I finally tried working with 16mm film.

Immediately, my analogy of film being methodical, like architecture, was proven false. While you do have to pay attention to many details, I find that the process of reading the light meter, focusing the lens, and then setting the aperture, slows me down enough to be present with the medium.

And, of course, there is the cost of film.
Unlike video, where there is an abundance of tape and now an infinite amount of digital space, with 16mm film, every shot must be carefully considered. Every shot is a commitment.

The manual, hands-on aspects of making 16mm film–loading the Bolex, hand-processing film, editing on a Steenbeck, threading the projector, actually feels more like a fine art practice than digital video making does.

Then there's the way the light goes through the image and the ways that you have these photographic anomalies within the film. Film has a surface, you can draw on it, paint on it, scratch into the surface - it is a tactile, physical medium.

Hogan: Its qualities/ integrities are particular and unique. How does this interact with your meaning making? Maybe we can focus on your film *Vaseline*? One of my new favorites of your works.

Malic: I made *Vaseline* with my boyfriend Nathan Hill. We describe the film as being about a "leather fag eluding the state by recalling his lover bathed in Vaseline." The film is a reference to Jean Genet's novel *The Theif's Journal* and ends with me fucking Nathan and Nathan cumming on a cement wall.

We shot Vaseline in on Tri-X black and white reversal. I had this vision that it was going to be a quick, in-camera edited film. We had a clear plan but by the second shot, I realized that I wanted to have more control over the edit than what an in-camera edited film would allow.

But because we shot two rolls of Tri-X film during our first filming, we decided to continue working with Tri-X. But in order to make a 16mm release print, there was a very long and expensive process of having to make an internegative from the positive reversal, and then cut the internegative and print that.

Hogan: So you lost some of that latitude of Tri-X in that process? I am in love with how high contrast it is.

Malic: Thanks! We were

never unhappy with the high contrast image itself, but the process created a big hassle.

I was working with FotoKem in L.A...Oh, this is relevant to what we're talking about....

Hogan: Tell me about it...

Malic: First, in addition to having to get an internegative made, FotoKem couldn't put the edge code on my digital transfer.

I edited *Vaseline* digitally. Then went back to my workprint and matched the workprint to my digital edit. Then I documented the edge code for the negative cutters at MCAF in Seattle. (I used to work there and I highly recommend them)!

So, finally, the A, B, & C rolls of negative that MCAF had cut were shipped down at FotoKem. FotoKem was in the process of making the answer print when they halted production because one of their workers noticed sexually explicit material in the film print.

After having developed all my rolls, made the internegative, and made a digital transfer, they refused to continue working with me. They sent all my film elements back and I had to figure out what to do.

I ended up working with ColorLab in Maryland. I asked them if they had any issues with working with explicit material and they didn't. I love ColorLab.

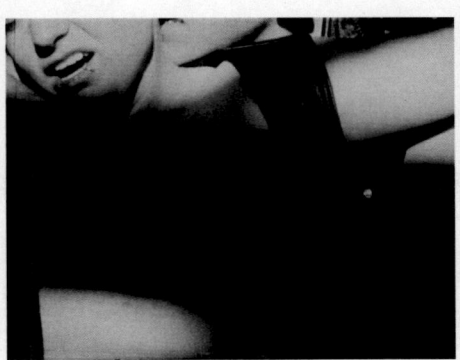

Hogan: Yeah, me too. I have all my prints thus far made at Color Lab.

Malic: I'm so curious, did the other lab type technicians see it before and individually not care, even though it was against their policy? And how much of them refusing to work with us had to do with us being Queer?

Hogan: I'd like to know their past clients. I am sure they have processed, scanned, and printed sexually explicit works.

Malic: I was surprised because they were in LA. I didn't think that LA would be a place of censorship.

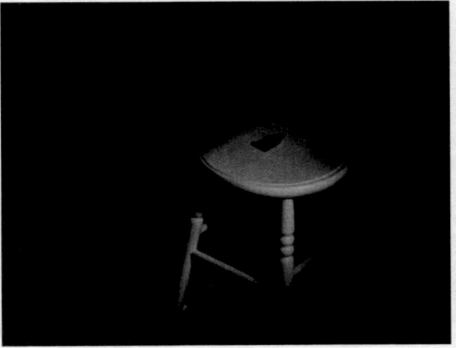

Hogan: I understand being trauma-informed, and alerting people of the work in all spaces where art is shown and made, but there is something about having a policy, whether it is only just enforced for certain bodies, could potentially dictate what people can and can't make. Or, what type of people, can and can't make moving image work..

Malic: There was a feeling when I was in art school that we could make anything. There were no parameters. Nothing was off limits. And, coming from a home where my gender expression was scrutinized, judged, and policed, it felt incredibly liberating.

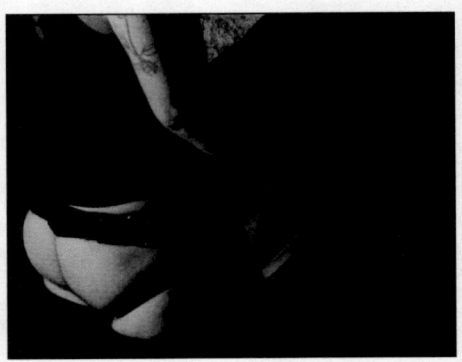

And, at least at Emerson, I feel like students now feel more restricted or like they think that there are these restrictions placed on them. They are even hesitant to use copyrighted music in their films. I literally beg my students not to use that generic copyright free music. I've had Queer and trans students who have been interested in being naked in their films but are afraid it will break some tacit social norm, which feels so different than when I was in art school.

"Vaseline (2016), Malic Amalya and Nathan Nill.

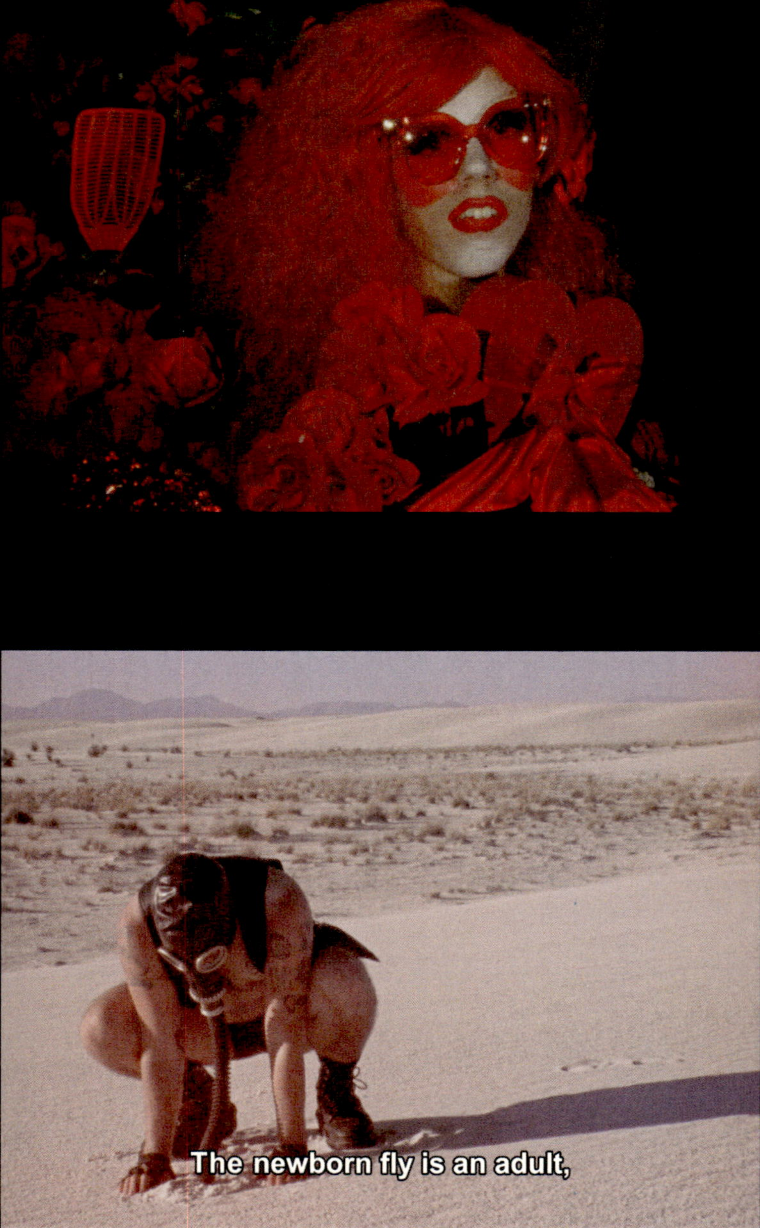

The newborn fly is an adult,

Run! (2020), Malic Amalya

Hogan: It feels different from when I was an undergrad too. It's something we were dealing with in the arts, something we've dealt a lot with in Boston. These spaces that used to be super vulnerable–people realized there are a lot of terrible things that happen because of this vulnerability. Teachers take advantage of their power and vulnerability to abuse students. While we're trying to create safe spaces in higher education and get these terrible and predatory humans out of these institutions, we have lost something. I think the loss is worth it in the larger picture of getting these predators out and keeping students safe, but I have seen new faculty afraid to even show work with nudity or sexuality. That comes at the erasure of a lot of Queer makers.

Can we talk about radical vulnerability while also being safe and accountable? Like, can we do that? Not police each other and our bodies, be able to be super vulnerable, but also set new standards for how we have community and respect for each other? I hope we can get there.

I am happy that Colorlab was able to make this print.

I just think about how many pieces are lost due to this censorship, in the classroom and in the lab space.

Malic: I never considered that a lab wouldn't print my film.

I was furious. And also very determined to get my film printed. I probably would have shipped to Europe if I needed to. But that's a privilege. That would have cost a lot more; it's not something everyone could afford.

Hogan: The US has some purity issues, but even looking at where *Vaseline* was shown, it was shown a lot abroad. I always find my work that deals with radical ideas relating to body and gender or is sexually explicit, always programmed more outside the US.

Malic: Definitely. *Vaseline* has screened more in programs where curators intentionally sought the film out.

There's always this question in the back of my mind: Is it too Queer for experimental festivals? We definitely discussed cutting out the scene of Nathan cumming. I'm glad we didn't.

But when I think of the

origins of experimental cinema, there's so many Queer filmmakers.

Hogan: Speaking of the history of Queer artists and experimental or nonlinear filmmakers, what makers have inspired you, or whose shoulders you stand on as an artist, or are of a legacy of radical practice?

Malic: As a young videomaker, Sadie Benning was my absolute favorite artist. It was so incredible to see this Queer, Riot Grrrl aesthetic in video art. Jennifer Reeder, who I worked with in undergrad and grad school, showed me their work when I was just 17.

In grad school, I loved Chantal Akerman.

Hogan: I may be projecting because I've seen *Song for Rent, After Jack Smith and RUN!*, but is Jack Smith on that list? I know a lot of us have complicated experiences with his work.

Malic: On one hand, visually, Jack Smith creates these Queer utopias. I think that we still, as filmmakers, as Queer filmmakers, have a lot to learn from the way Jack Smith composes his films–the density of props and costumes, the layers of bodies, the choreography of movement. It all feels effortless on his part - like a documentation of being Queer. In my mind, visually, his films are the fantasy of how me and my Queer friends look every day.

At the same time, I have a lot of discomfort with his work. In *Flaming Creatures*, there is this rape scene. I always feel so confused. How can we laud Jack Smith as a Queer icon while such a huge part of the film is this woman being sexually assaulted?

I find that scene horrifying but then I question myself. Am I misreading it? Because Flaming Creatures is a non-narrative film made with consenting performers, should we read the scene as a consensual BDSM fantasy? Or, are we afraid to critique misogyny and rape culture within our Queer art icons cause we have so few of them and their work feels so precious?

In 2018, the San Francisco Cinematheque asked me to curate a program in honor of the new San Francisco Transgender Tenderloin District, where their offices are located. I was doing research and Canyon Cinema graciously gave me a number of Jack Smith's

screeners, including his 1969 film, *Song for Rent*.

At the time, I was working on my film *RUN!*, which was in many ways a response to Trump's military ban and to mainstream LGBTQ+ movements that see inclusion in the military as a step towards equality. I was filming at these military sites in New Mexico, where the first nuclear bomb was developed and tested. And I was working with this question of how ideologies of war structure landscapes, community rituals, cinematic technology, entomology and bug spray, pandemic management, and how we think about LGBTQ liberation.

Then in Jack Smith's *Song for Rent*, he is in drag under a gigantic American flag with the song God Bless America looping. Jack's character, who is dressed in bright red from head-to-toe and using a wheelchair, is based on the Kennedy matriarch, Rose Kennedy.

I was so uncomfortable with the film because I didn't know how to read it. I was wondering if Jack Smith was aligning 4th of July celebrations with camp? Was he indulging in US patriotism?

And I was uncomfortable with my own reaction. I don't want to ask art to spoon feed me the artist's political position. If you can read an artwork in a few seconds, it's either political propaganda (which has a time and a place in my heart) or is bad art.

Then I felt obsessed with my discomfort with the film's ambiguity. I started to strategize about how I could get curators to screen *Song for Rent before RUN!*. Then I was like, "Oh, I can just recreate it" and make my remake an intro to *RUN!*. Eventually, I decided to have my remake as its own film and to intersperse footage into *RUN!*, so they are two individual pieces.

I was actually quite nervous about how *Song for Rent, After Jack Smith* was going to be received. It was made and played at a few festivals during Trump's presidency and I wasn't sure if there was a place for ambiguous art when it came to the topic of US imperialism.

One moment of solace for me is that in both the original and in my remake, there is a part where Jack Smith is waving this toilet brush, that's very dingy and clearly used, under the American flag. I've

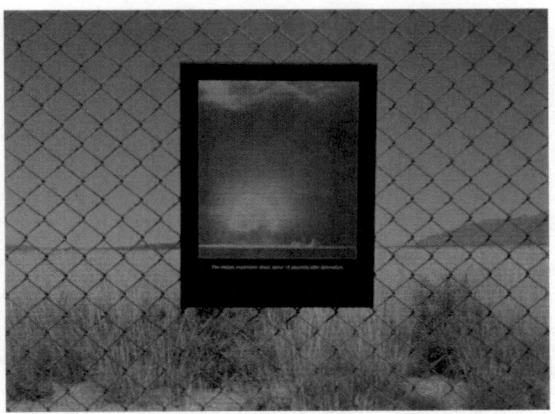

Run! (2020), Malic Amalya

latched onto this as the clear articulation of critique.

Hogan: Can you talk a bit more about the characters in *RUN!*? How you used this recreation as your critique for exploring these themes of US imperialism and Queer liberation.

Malic: In *RUN!*, there are three recurring trans characters. Jade Theriault is in full drag as Jack Smith. "Barbara Bush" (Rae Raucci) wears a black leather dress and has these long black leather gloves. And there's a leather fly character—played by me—who wears a black leather shorts, a bar vest, and fingerless gloves, as well as a gas mask. While it isn't an erotic film, per se, it felt critical to me to interrogate white supremacy, state violence, and questions of Queer liberation within a Queer visual culture

that represents Queer sexuality and gender self-determinism.

Hogan: And if I can go back to your film *Vaseline*. That is such a powerful film, where sex is liberation. Where sex can liberate this "leather fag" from this world of policing and surveillance. How do you see erotica imagery being used as a tool or how do you see it a vehicle for change?

Malic: In the Bay there's a Queer direct action collective called Gay Shame. One of their actions that I went to was a protest of a prison-themed pride party hosted by Kink.com. While the event was happening, Gay Shame projected, "Pro-Sex, Anti-Prison, Queers for Abolition" onto the outside of the San Francisco Armory, Kink's studio and party venue. In conversation

about the event, Eric Stanley, an organizer for Gay Shame, explained that prisons don't just police gender, they actually create categories of gender.

What Gay Shame and other anti-racist prison abolitionists have illuminated for me is that, yes, Queer liberation is sex positivity, kink positivity, gender self-determinism, and a culture of consent. AND, we can't live in a pro-sex, pro-Queer, pro-gender self-determination culture without prison abolition.

Nathan and I started making Vaseline within the first year of our long distance relationship. Something that shaped our relationship during the first few years is that a few days after our first date in Chicago, Nathan got arrested for shoplifting in Florida. Nathan ended up being stuck in Florida, at his friend's mom's house, for three months. Then he was on probation in Chicago for the next year and a half.

While Nathan was waiting to find out if he was going to have to go to prison and for how long (Florida has extremely harsh punishments for shoplifting and, apparently, very tight security), we were texting and talking on the phone a lot. At one point I sent him this passage from *The Thief's Journal* by Jean Genet:

"Lying on the table, it was a banner telling the invisible legions of my triumph over the police. I was in a cell. I knew that all night long my tube of vaseline would be exposed to the scorn- the contrary of a Perpetual Adoration-of a group of strong, handsome, husky police men. So strong that if the weakest of them barely squeezed his fingers together, there would shoot forth, first with a slight fart, brief and dirty, a ribbon of gum which would continue to emerge in a ridiculous silence. Nevertheless, I was sure that this puny and most humble object would hold its own against them; by its mere presence it would be able to exasperate all the police in the world; it would draw down upon itself contempt, hatred, white and

dumb rages."

-Jean Genet, *The Thief's Journal* (1949)

When Nathan got back to Chicago, I went to visit him and he took me to the Sky Factory, these clusters of abandoned silos just south of Pilsen [a neighborhood in Chicago].

I had actually lived near the Sky Factory when I was in grad school and every time I would bike by them, I would stare longingly. But I didn't dare go explore them by myself.

So, internally, I was freaking out that this babe who I was crushing on so hard was taking me to the Sky Factory–a spot I had always wanted to go to. It was a place he and his friends went to regularly. As we were walking around, I knew I wanted to make a film there with him.

As Nathan and I were talking about making a film together, we returned to the Genet passage and the history of Queers being policed and the connections of Queer liberation, publicly and privately defying gender norms, cruising, public sex, and prison abolition.

I want to pause for a moment to say that it's important for both Nathan and I to acknowledge our white privilege. *Vasline* isn't trying to cover all aspects of the prison industrial complex. We want our film to be in solidarity with prison abolition efforts, especially ones that examine how prisons are white supremacist institutions. Our film is a small act of resistance, specifically about Nathan's experiences and how it impacted our relationship.

Hogan: It's an artifact of a moment between lovers, right?

Malic: Yeah, in many ways *Vaseline* chronicles the beginning of our relationship. There were three different weekends of filming. In the first rolls, there is clearly infatuation and desire but it's reserved. The next time we film we are passionately making out on camera. Then in the last rolls, we are actually fucking.

One thing that was really important to us is that we shot the entire films ourselves. Even when we're both in the shot, we had like one of those bulbs that you squeeze to make the camera run.

Hogan: The air shutter releases?

Malic: Yes! Nathan was stepping his foot on the bulb to activate the camera while we were fucking. And this bulb is very similar to an enema bulb in many ways.

Hogan: I have once or twice made that visual connection.

Malic: (laughs) Running the camera became part of the act of fucking.

Hogan: The vulnerability is liberating and seeing yourself represented in the way that feels beautiful to you both. And then also the possibility of creating a liberatory experience for other people who view this work.

Malic: Right! There's so many ways that non-normative desires, sexuality, and genders are policed, minimized, invalidated, obscured, and erased.

We're in this moment where trans visibility has become very heightened. For me, as a person in my early 40s, I've had the privilege of being part of incredibly supportive and creative Queer communities for the past twenty years. Yet, trans people—particularly trans youth and particularly trans women, girls, and femmes are being relentlessly targeted by anti-trans policies. And violence towards trans people, particularly trans women of color, has increased at an alarming rate.

Again, *Vaseline* doesn't address all of these issues. It's one short film about Nathan and I's relationship.

As I said before, Nathan and I started *Vaseline* in the first year of our relationship. As a trans person, it can be hard to escape feelings of gender dysphoria, especially in regards to my sexuality. For me, the film is a conjuring of trans fag sexuality. At the risk of being too vulnerable, it was literally a way to negate my gender dysphoria, especially as I was navigating spaces that are predominantly comprised of cis-gay men.

An essential part of the film are these objects or visual markers that symbolize Queerness and/or Queer sexuality in the right context. For example, a tube of Vaseline in a medicine cabinet is for healing chapped skin but in the pocket of a person caught loitering in the dark, as in *The Thief's Journal*, it's a symbol of public, gay sex.

I wanted my chest surgery scars to function in a similar way. A suture scar indicates that someone had surgery, which is kind of mundane—many people have surgery, but in a certain shape on a chest, it becomes a record of gender-affirming top surgery. I didn't want to over emphasize my scars, but I wanted them to be visible for anyone who might be looking for representations of themselves or of their lovers.

Hogan: It's just fascinating to think about the relationship of the policing of Queer bodies that happened as you say with history, and especially film history. I always think of how Jonas Mekas was arrested for showing Jack Smith in the 60s.

Your film, *Vaseline*, was also being sort of censored by this Film lab, but then it also came back to be shown at Anthology Film Archive. There's something kind of radical about that, but at the same time, even after decency laws were abolished, now 80 years later we are still seeing censorship and the policing of Queer and Trans bodies rear its ugly head.

dark rooms | toxic pleasures

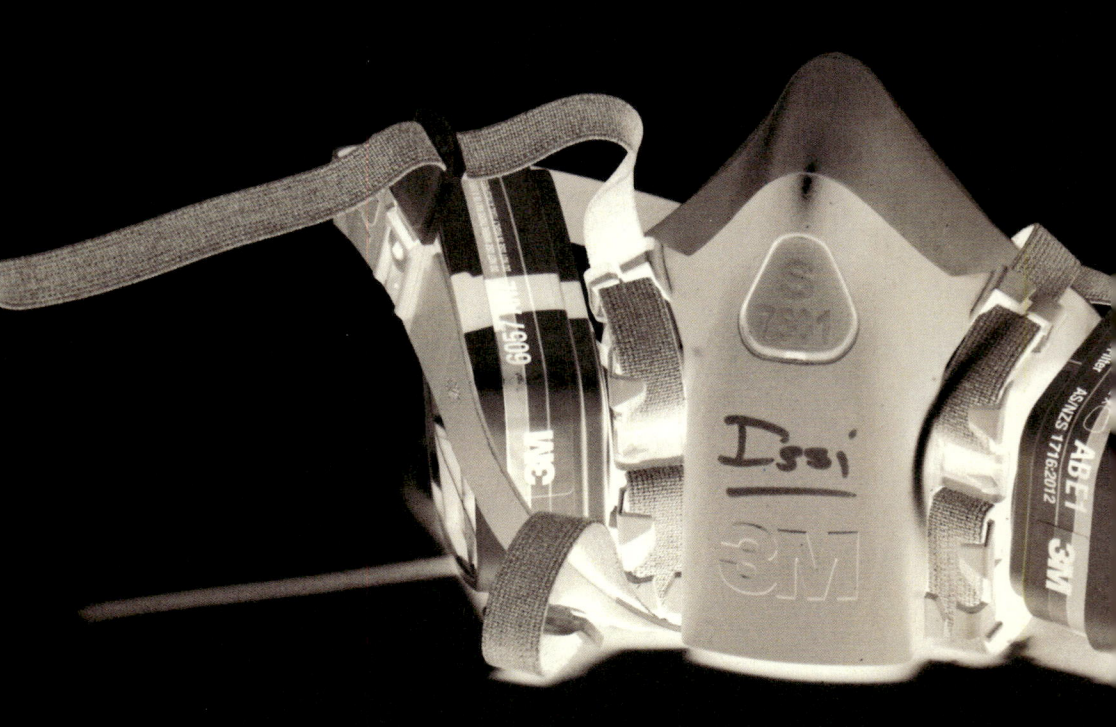

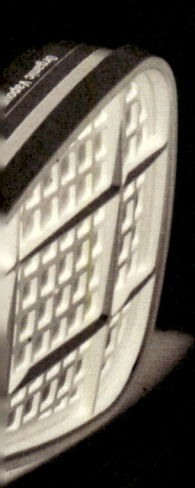

The black and white darkroom gurgles and moans. The ventilator whistles a wind through the velvet curtain and extracts the lingering fix in the air. Wet lubricates the drains laced with the smell of rubber gloves and plastic aprons. Under red lights the apparatus lie potent. An image latent or manifest, its relations of production made messy. **What can be more analog than touch?** Its continuously variable physical quantity reminding the body of its edges and its openings.

Darkrooms promise labor and pleasure (if it's your thing), risk and reward. Play safe or play dirty, the toys are at your disposal. It's fetish, pretty straight up, because this is the house the master built – all **guncotton, gelatin, silver and pulp.** Less a closet, more a cinema for projections. In the big daddy mainframe of modernist dreams, I stray with ambivalent desires, seepage and glitch. Less fantasy more specter. For these toxic pleasures will make you uneasy if you breathe in too hard or stay too long.

Sally Chessell

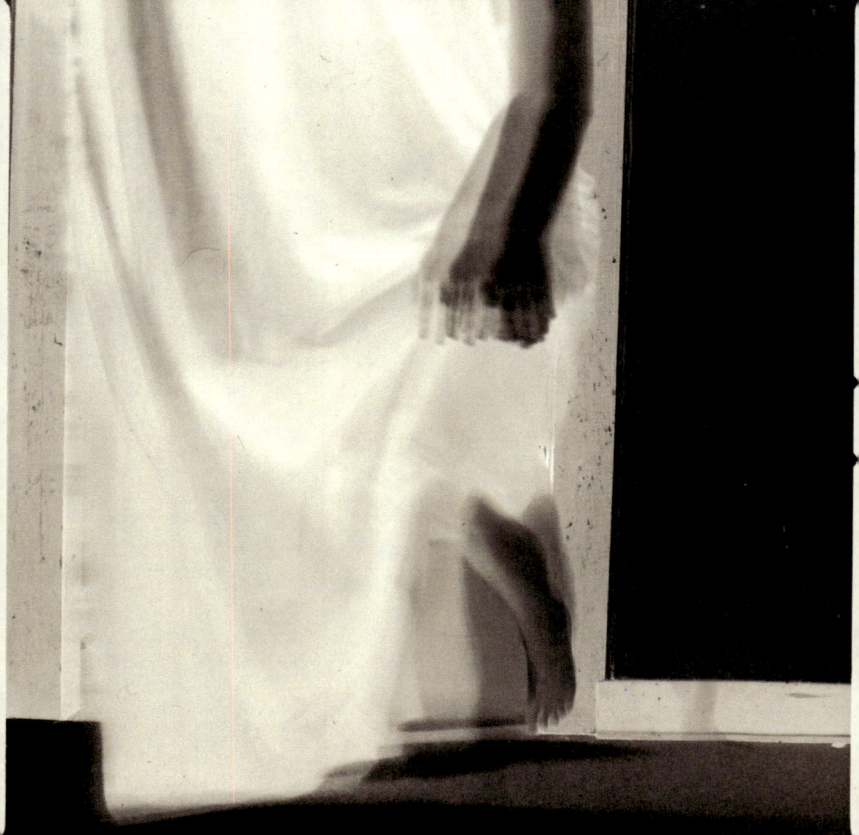

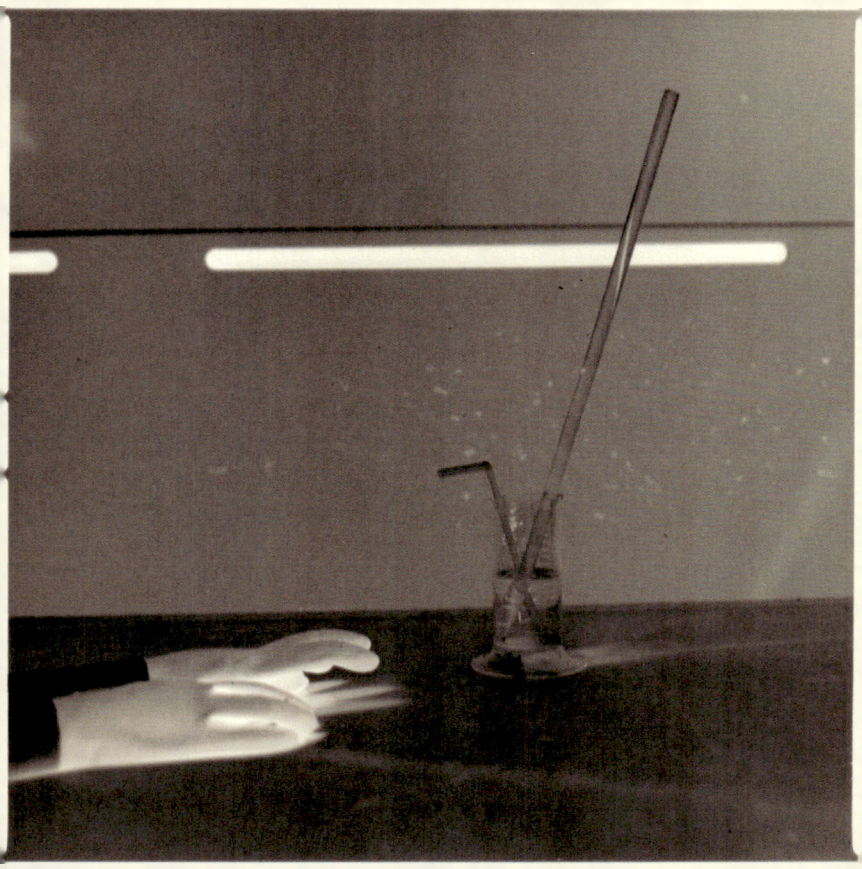

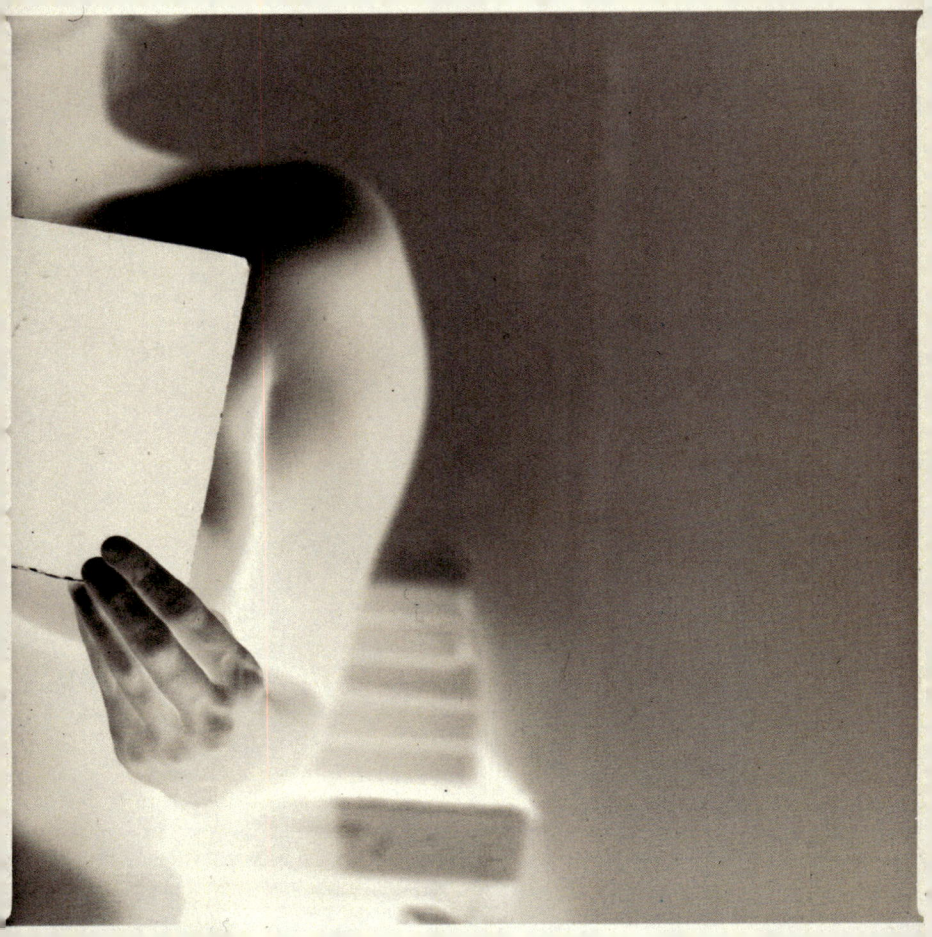

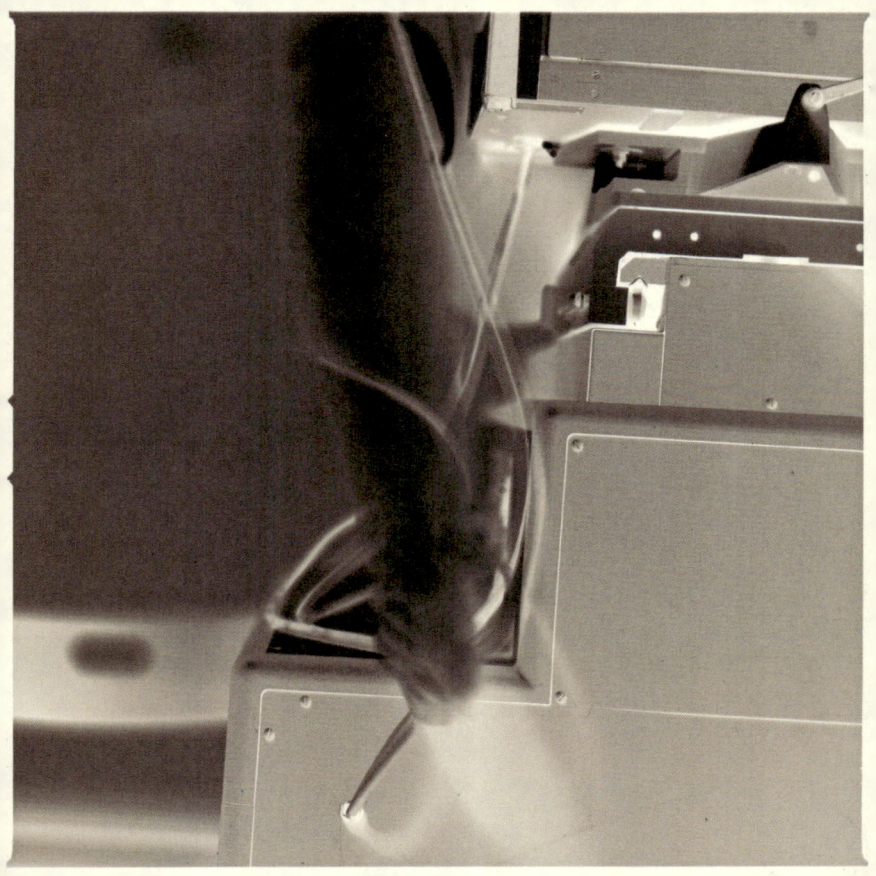

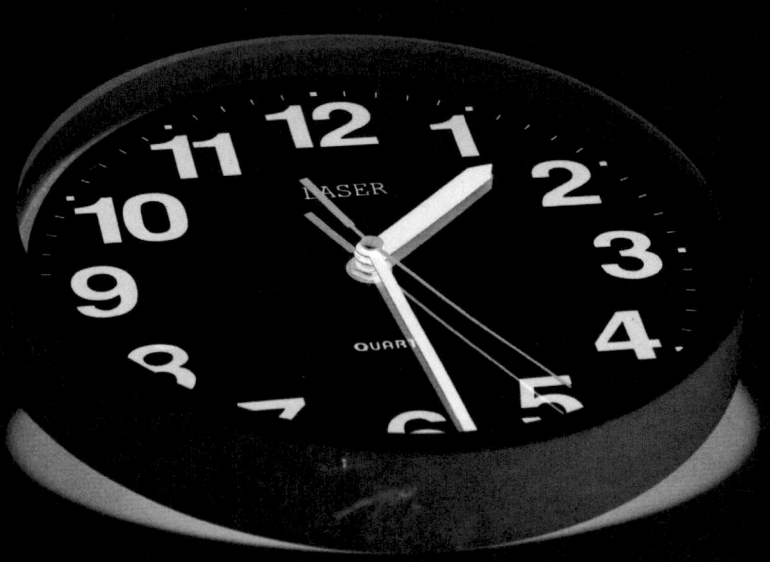

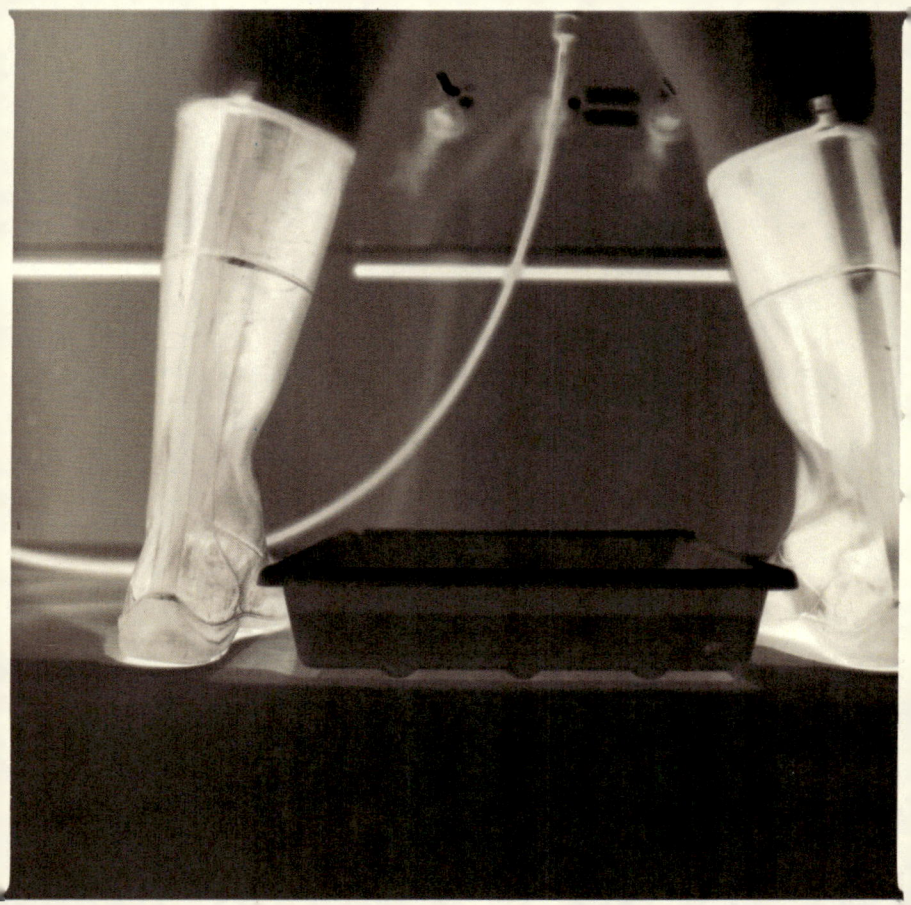

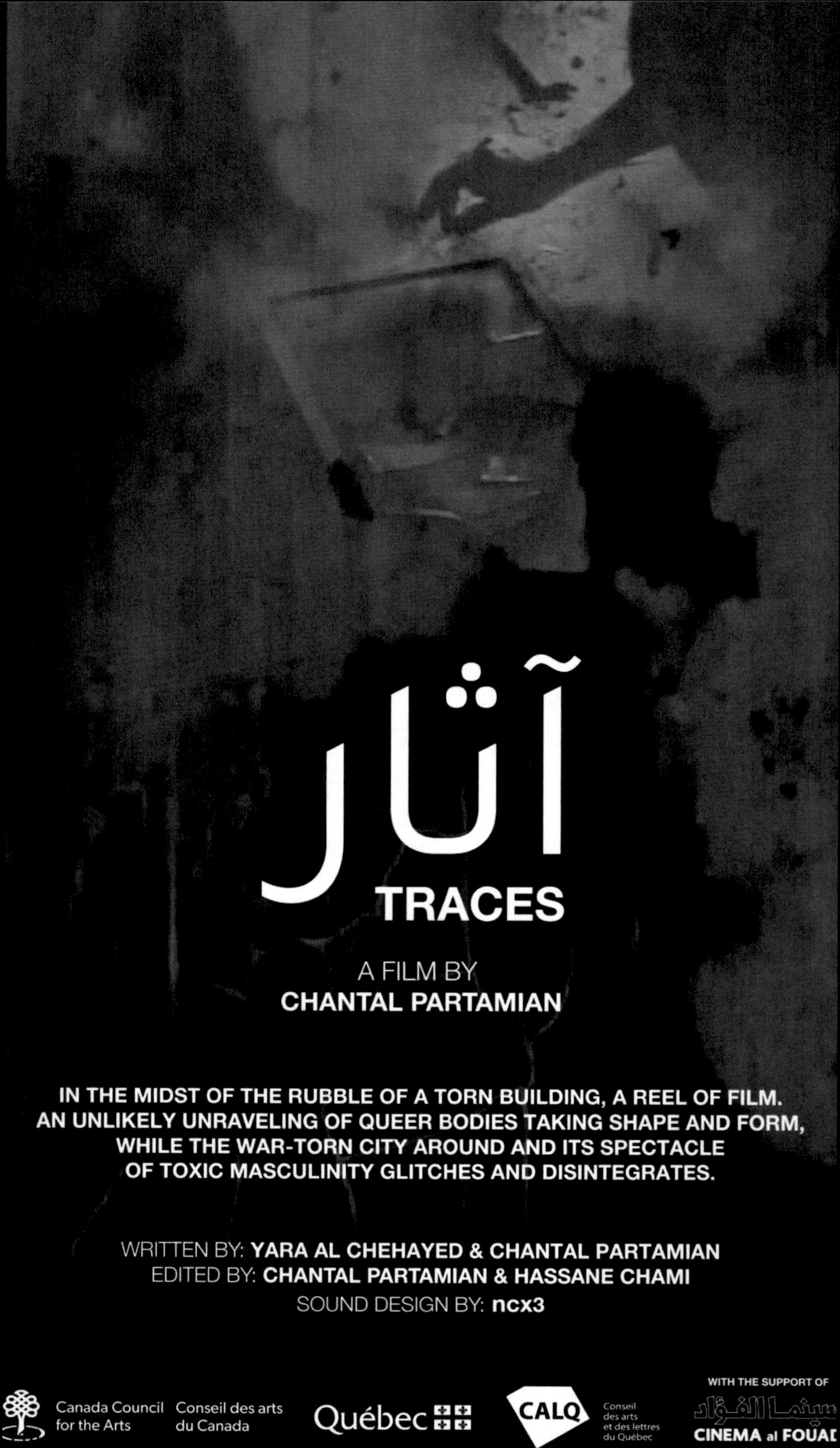

آثر
TRACES

A FILM BY
CHANTAL PARTAMIAN

IN THE MIDST OF THE RUBBLE OF A TORN BUILDING, A REEL OF FILM.
AN UNLIKELY UNRAVELING OF QUEER BODIES TAKING SHAPE AND FORM,
WHILE THE WAR-TORN CITY AROUND AND ITS SPECTACLE
OF TOXIC MASCULINITY GLITCHES AND DISINTEGRATES.

WRITTEN BY: **YARA AL CHEHAYED & CHANTAL PARTAMIAN**
EDITED BY: **CHANTAL PARTAMIAN & HASSANE CHAMI**
SOUND DESIGN BY: **ncx3**

 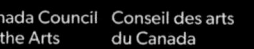 Canada Council Conseil des arts
for the Arts du Canada

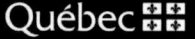 Québec ⊞⊞

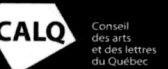 CALQ
Conseil des arts et des lettres du Québec

WITH THE SUPPORT OF
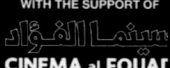 سينما الفؤاد
CINEMA al FOUAD

Traces:
Based on a film project directed by Chantal Partamian. Text written by Yara Al Chehayed and is based on an idea by Partamian.

Amid the rubble of a torn building, a reel of film.

An unlikely unraveling of Queer bodies taking shape and form, while the war-torn city around and its spectacle of masculinities glitches and disintegrates. Alienated does not mean anti-historic.

The film project *Trace* is an attempt to offer a more inclusive version of the history of Beirut, long written and monopolized by those who made, won, and justified the war. The project explores the cinematic gaze towards Queer bodies as well as their constant absence from the recurrent narrative or collective memory.

It started with the discovery of 80s pornographic found footage, and so we asked ourselves: what if this was found in a dilapidated house? What if instead of the process of the image disintegrating, we bring it to life as if the disintegrated lives of Queer women that were meant to stay unseen or disfigured or left to rot slowly come to life and assert their presence within the context of the 80s in Lebanon? A period so overtly represented by war and violence and from which all narrative about personal lives and intimacy is removed.

Beirut, here is a disintegrating city,

declining from being into merely appearing. A representation of a city, an idea, a simulacrum, that has not once existed. The city disintegrates while our narrative rebuilds itself to document the history of those who long existed outside the city's public, collective, and official memories. A city that long overlooked our Queer bodies, can never exist unless in a shape of incomplete representation of itself. As spectacles of toxic masculinity flourished on the ruins of a splintered city, Queers claimed their bodies and desires in the backdrop of the destruction.

Trace relates to our context by being a visual critical analysis on the theoretical work around memory, history, spectacles, and abjection. Through its images, it constructs, deconstructs, and reconstructs the city and its narratives in an indispensable practice to regenerate personal and collective existence.

In a city where all spectacles of toxicity are allowed to be performed, our desires are being created in seclusion from this space, in the backdrop of its destruction. In a city that erases us, dying is pointless. We had to learn how to disappear only to reclaim our existence, our desires, our sexuality in seclusion. Our spectacle is a place for us to be the creators of our own desires, through it we exist, we are present.

Our Gaze constructs, deconstructs, reconstructs the city and its spectacle of victimization, of masculinity and violence, in a practice to regenerate ourselves personally and collectively so our mutual becoming is activated. Through this gaze we are claiming our share of the collective memory, us the virus, the freaks, the slayed children.

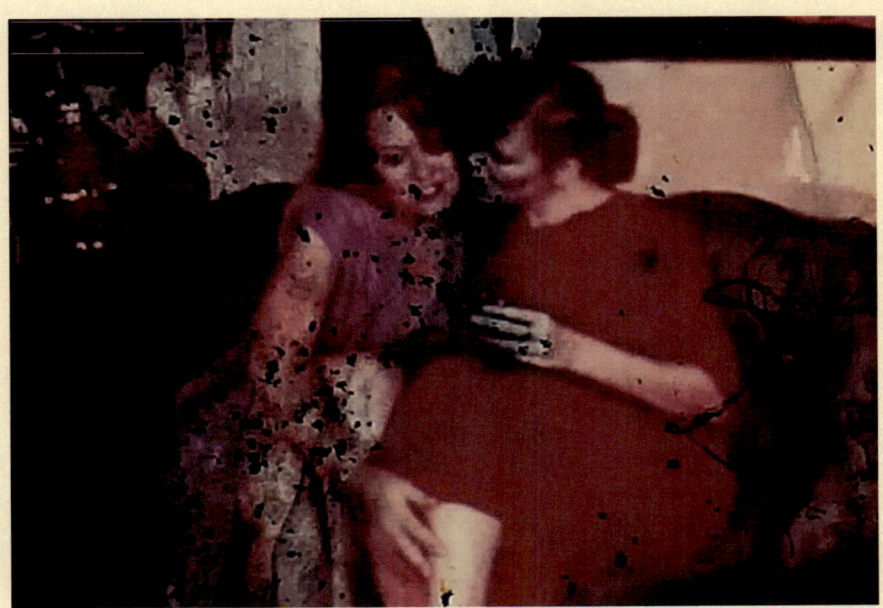

Untitled (Christ on the Cross)

Jamieson Edson

" Throughout history, depictions of Christ have sought to express the dualistic tension between the earthly body and the spiritual. His pained expression of physical agony is equated with transcendent bliss. My favorite erotica hits on a similar note--that which is spiritually significant conjured through the physical body. "

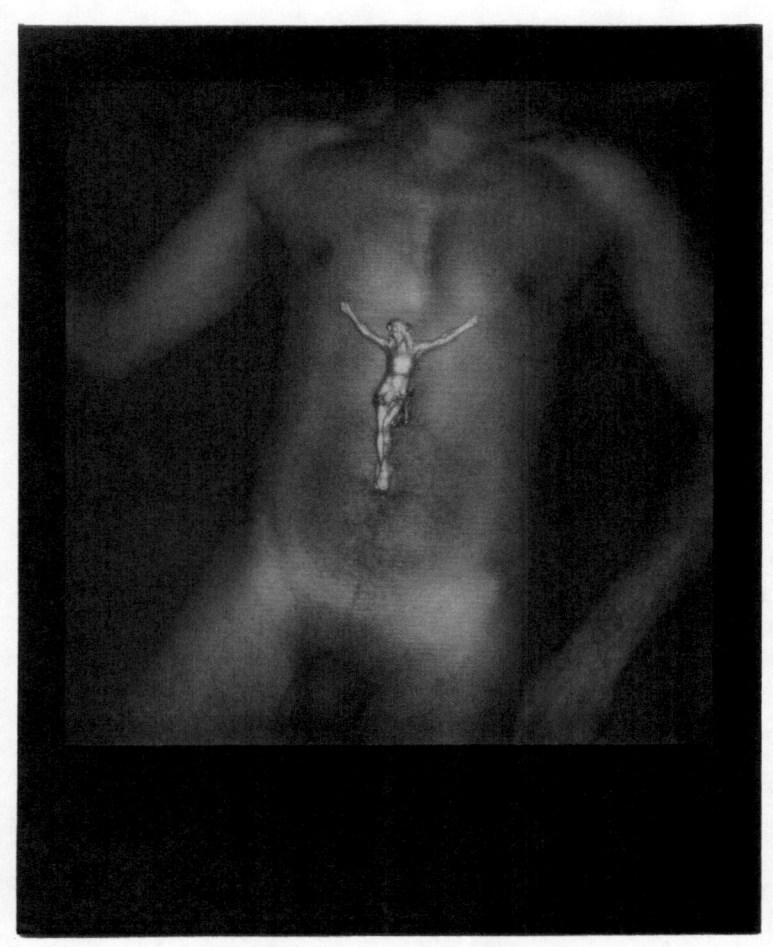

Título 1

This project starts
as an attempt
to condense a
pornographic film into
a three minutes of a
Super8 Tri-X–filming
frame by frame.
The camera is just
another sexual toy
between us.

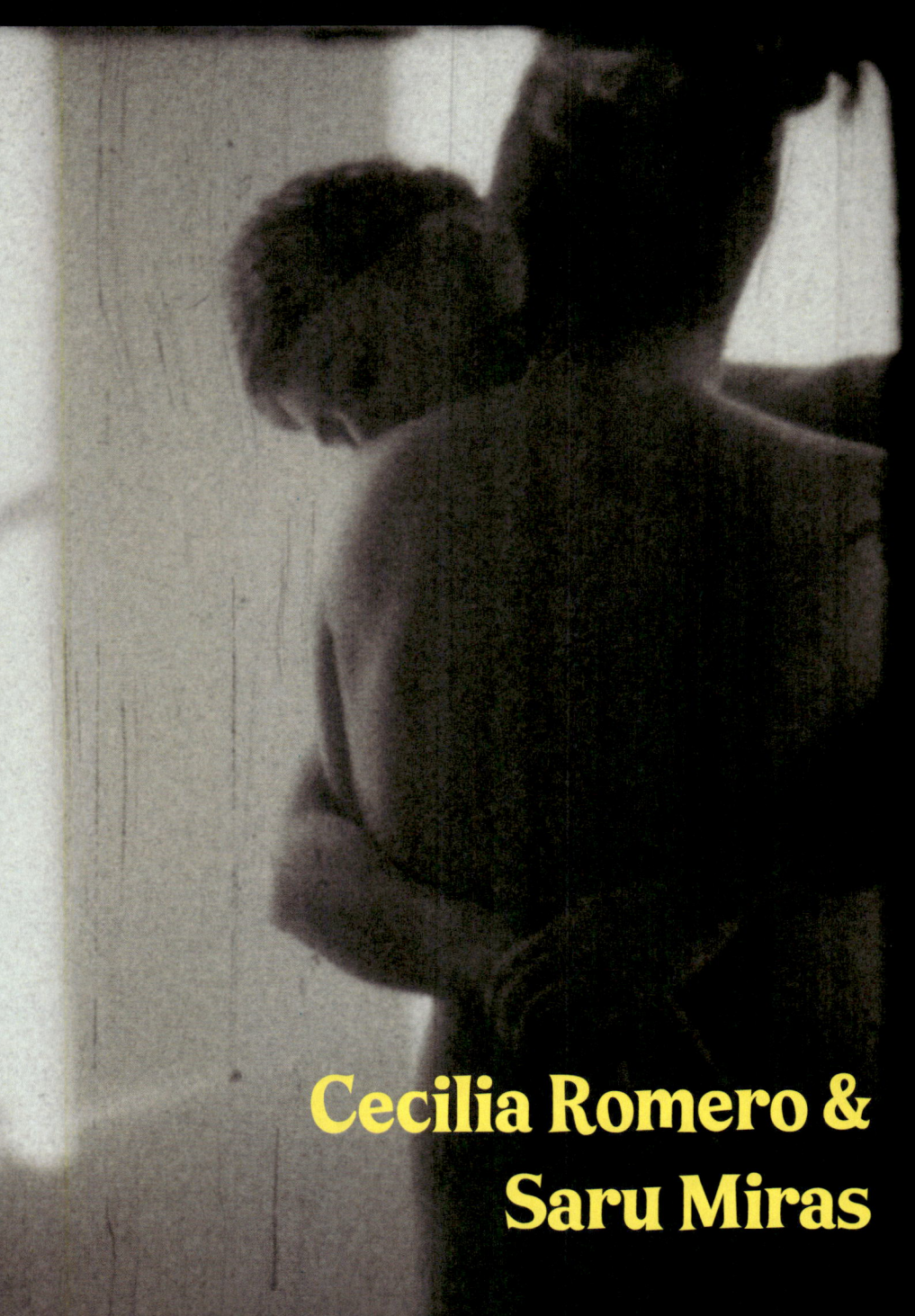

**Cecilia Romero &
Saru Miras**

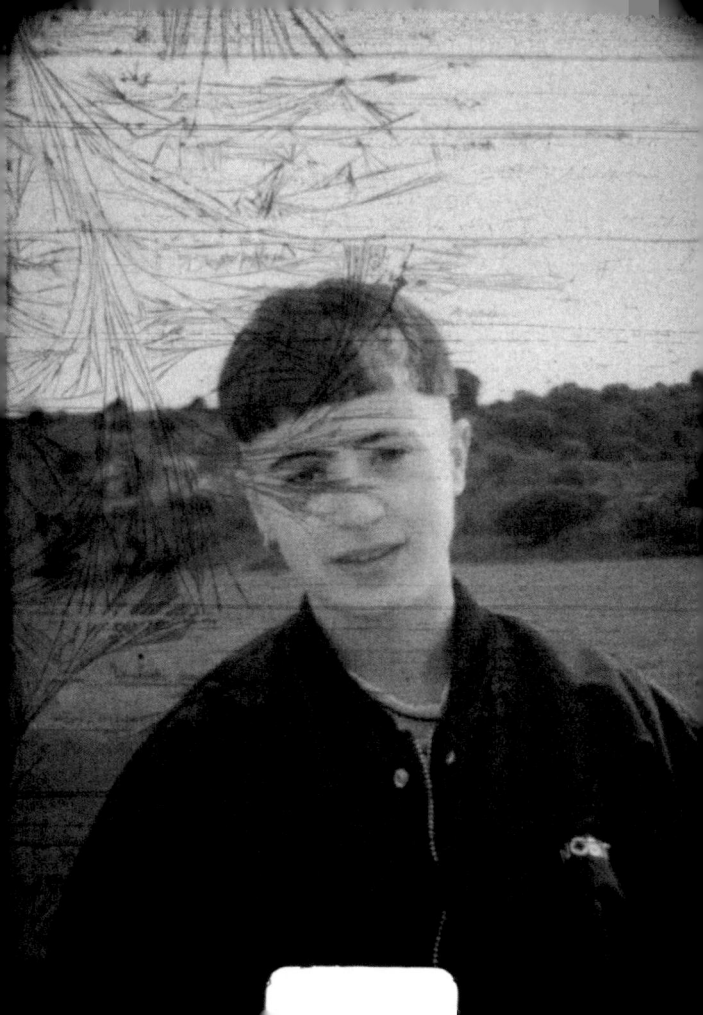

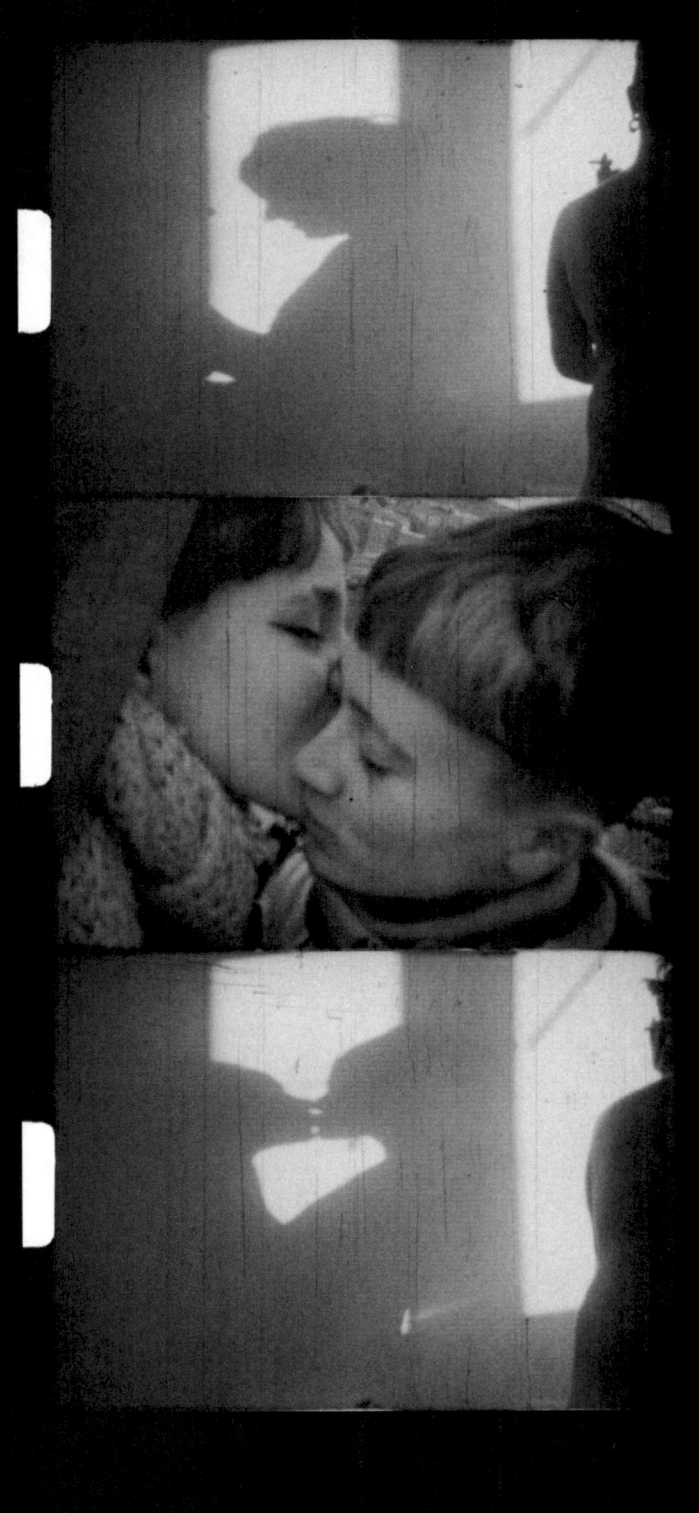

Reimag(in)ing desire, this living film subverts
Hollywood's projections of heteronormativity
by representing the screen kiss as a
performative intervention. The performer
applies lipstick and kisses a 16mm film loop
as it runs through the projector. The lipstick
imprints made onto the surface of the celluloid
are transformed into flickering, abstracted, and
increasingly ecstatic images onscreen.

Screen Kiss

Joanna Byrne

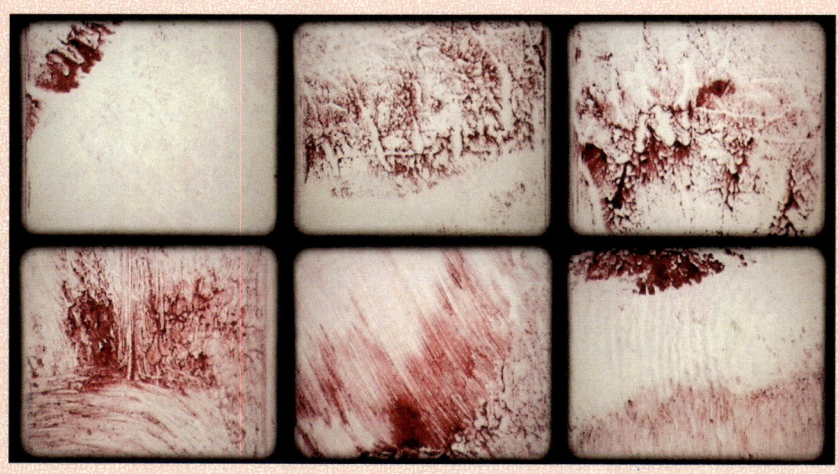

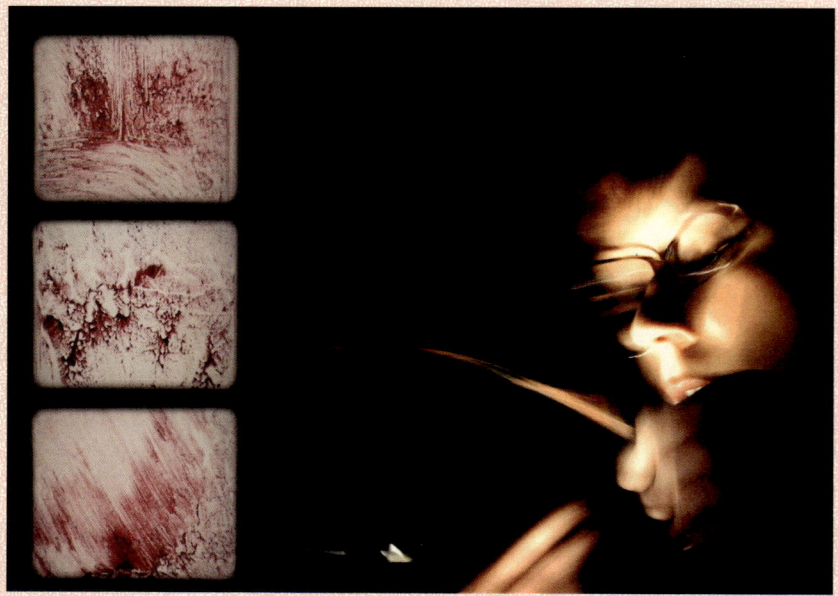

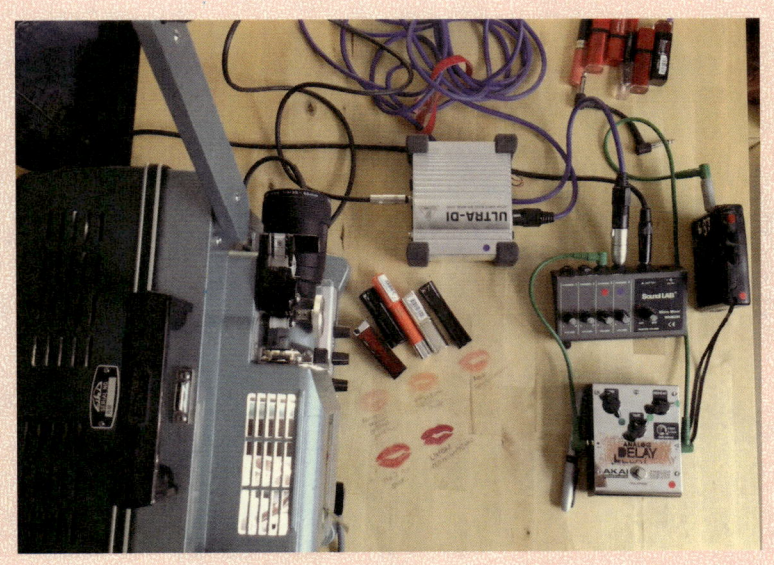

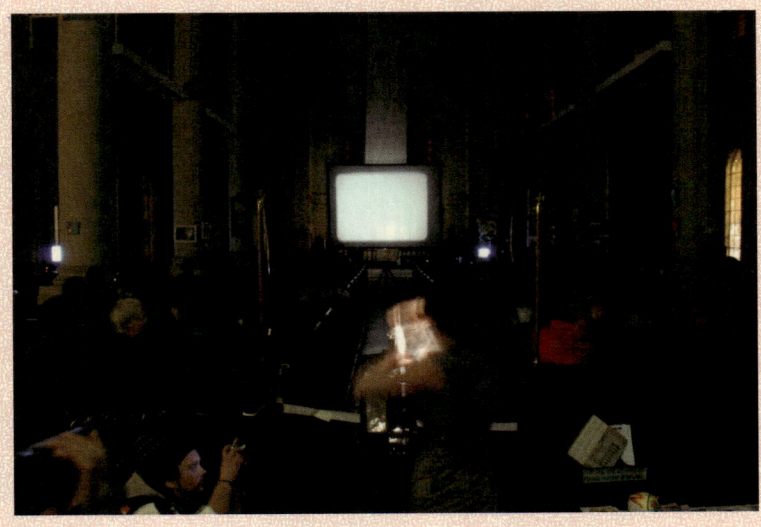

You See in Princess deep shadow

> **"** This series has been created using hand-processed 35mm erotic images of my partner, visual artist Sarah Seené, on a Vision-16 photocamera. The 35mm film emulsion has been hand-painted in order to create a poeticallycosmic vision of this shared moment of intimacy. **"**

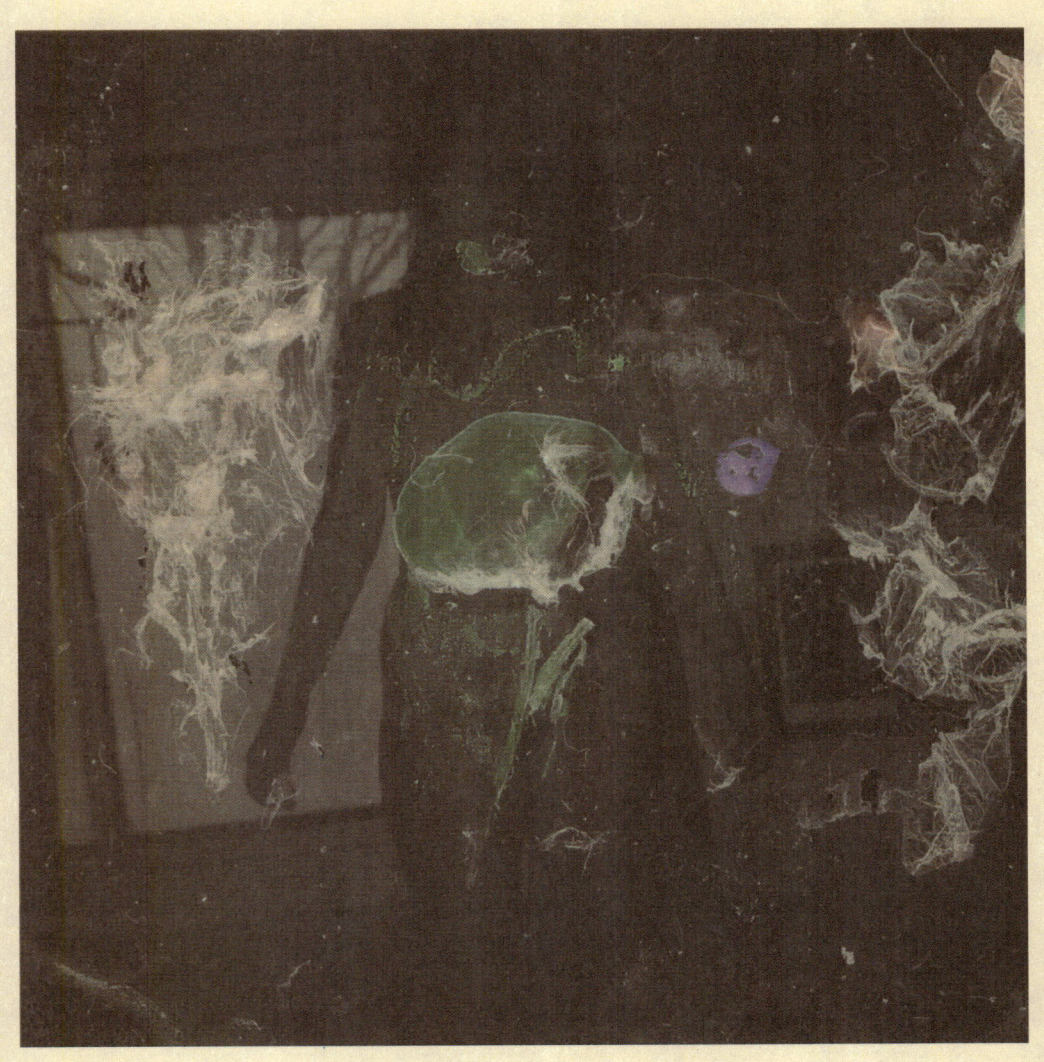

Guillaume Vallée

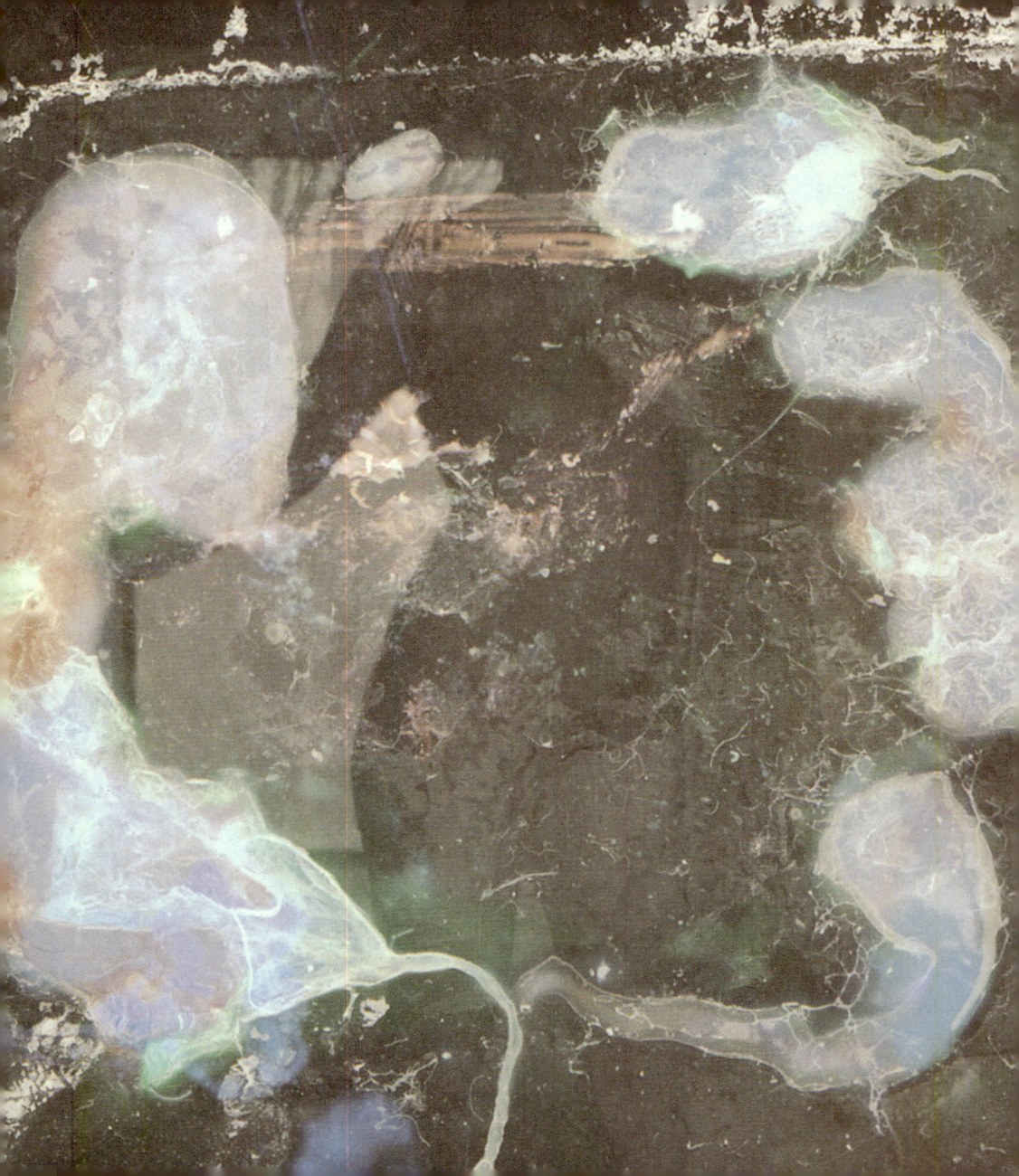

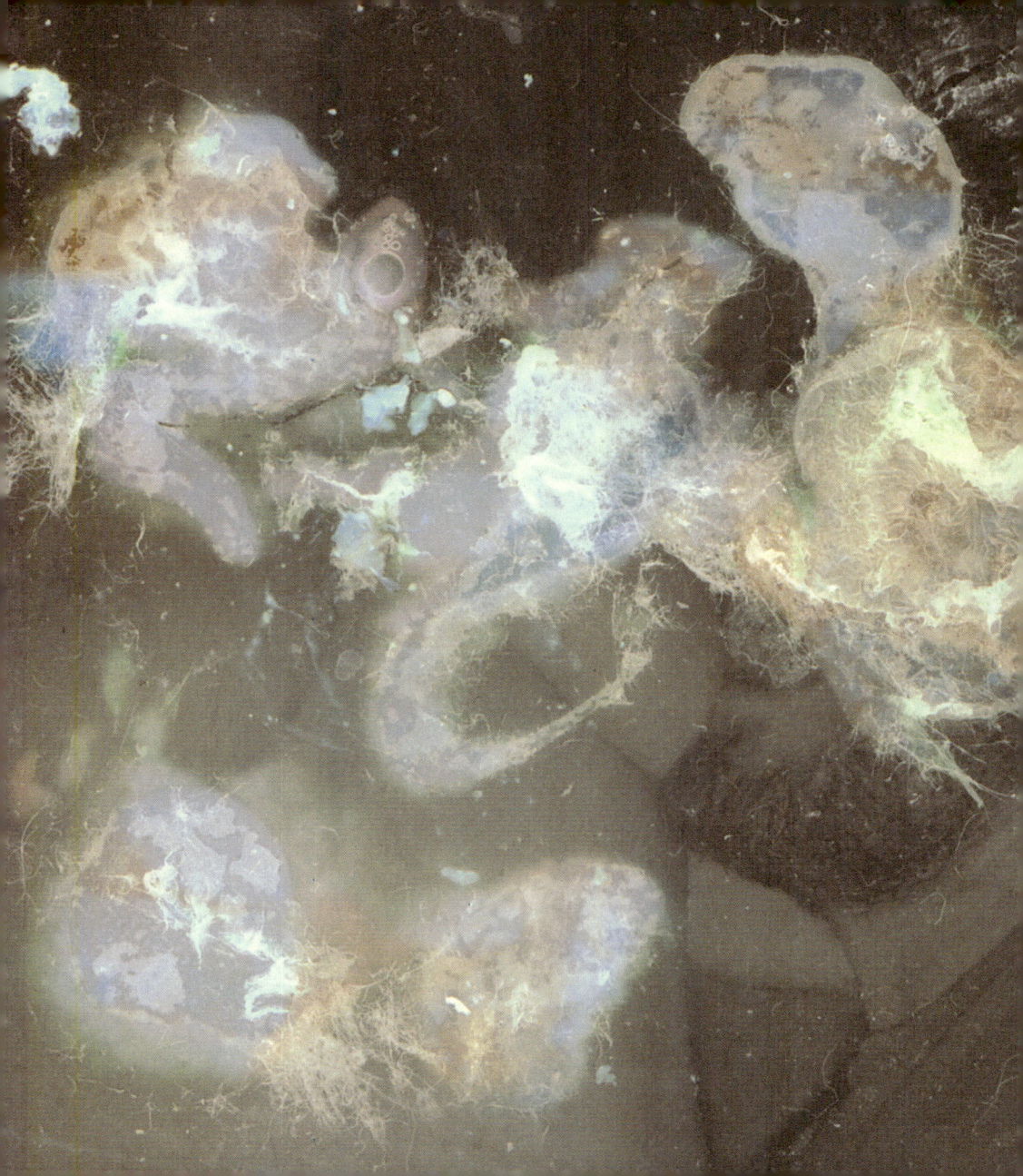

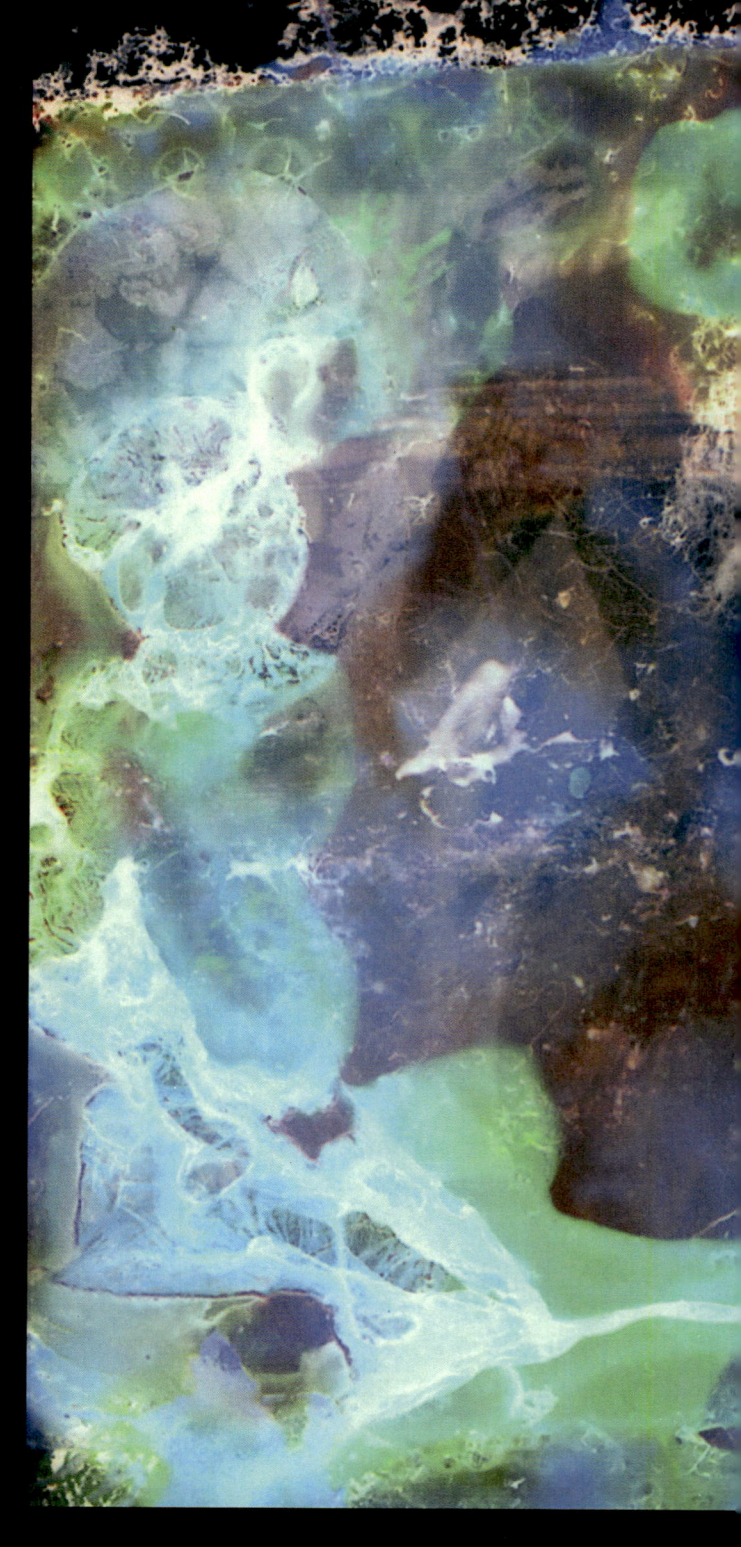

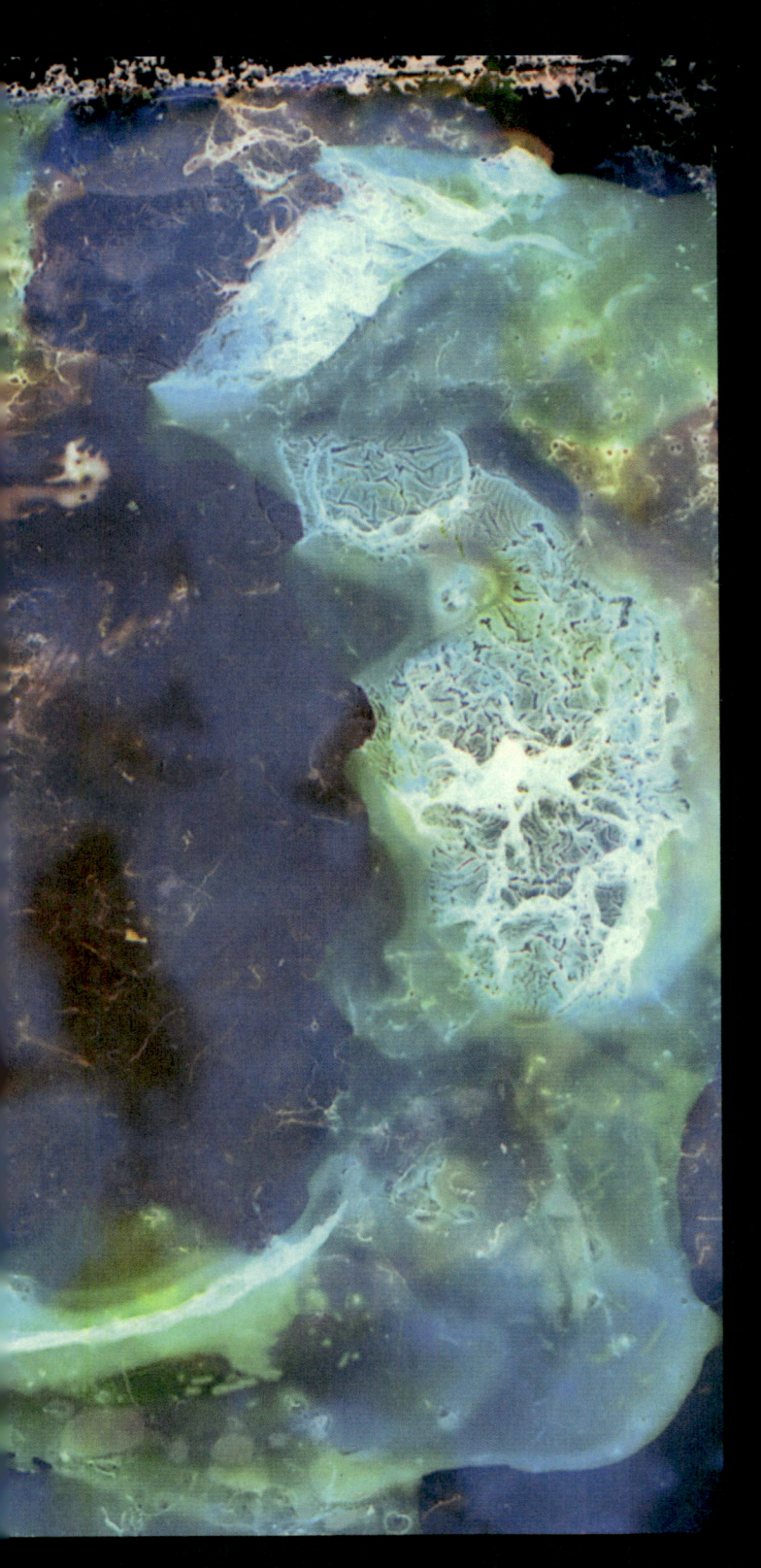

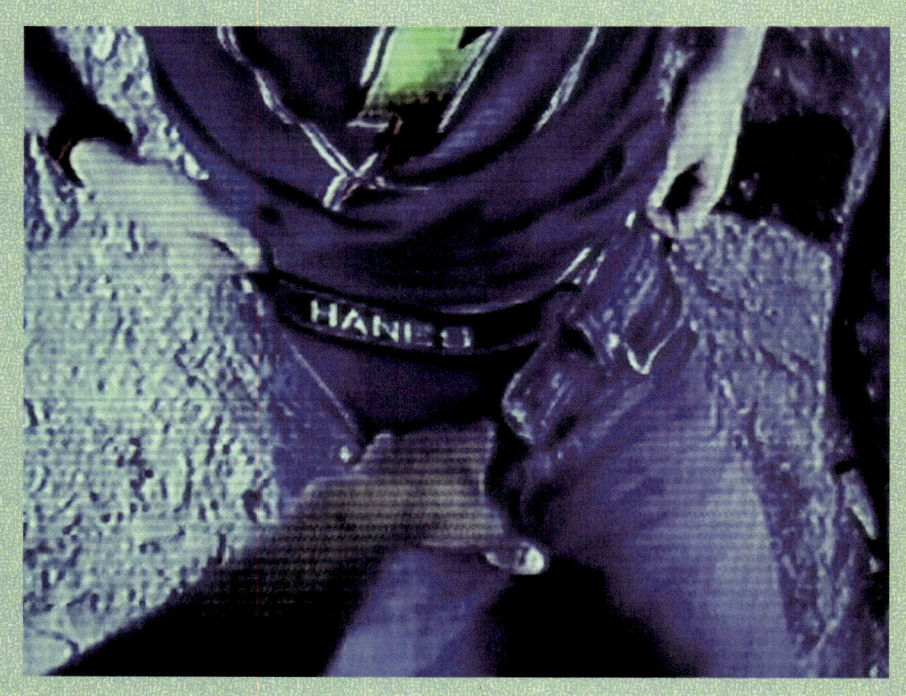

Untitled, Skin Film

Sailor DiNucci-Radley

A transmeditation on the screen & pixel as a splicer of bodies, limbs & mouths. Collected materials from personal archives, online forums, & porn websites are obscured and abstracted through composition & re-imaging, imagining the gendered body as a collective and multiple dream; in some way flickering, like a lamp or light, whose bulb is dead or dying.

Can you explain the process of capturing and translating the anonymized erotic images through clipping audio, DV-tape, and CRT television?

The process itself was mostly simple. I collected various images from a few sources (personal archives, erotic forums, porn sites) and used an old-dv camcorder to record my laptop screen, which I then re-shot on a CRT monitor my friend gave me. I'd had this idea of making a film that could function almost like a snuff film—as a haunted, macabre curio, as something that you could stumble upon while tape-shopping, or at a thrift store or flea market or something—and probing that really ambiguous gaze as a study of desire and the body.

I'm interested in the tension between analog and digital forms, and processing internet images through the acoustic and visual spaces that the microphone or CRT work within. It grants the film a sort of timelessness. It shrouds all of the images and sounds in an illegible fog, and it places the viewer in an interesting relationship to the images on screen. It feels like you're one or two degrees removed from the bodies on screen; you're watching someone watch something they filmed.

Tell us about the theme of stillness in this film and your practice.

I was actually thinking about this the other day! It started out as a practical, formal thing. I like taking big, maximalist, b-movie swings in my work. I also like to follow typical Hollywood narrative structures (intro-rampup-climax-outro), and so I think stillness makes the braver formal moments in films like this more rewarding.

But I've recently started to think about stillness in my work in terms of iteration and looping. I'm a huge fan of noise music—how I think about texture and structure stems from noise stuff I've been listening to since high school. I like to think about stillness in my films as a way to induce trance or transcendence. Like the La Monte Young stuff happening in the 60's, or early ambient electronic music: using repetition and

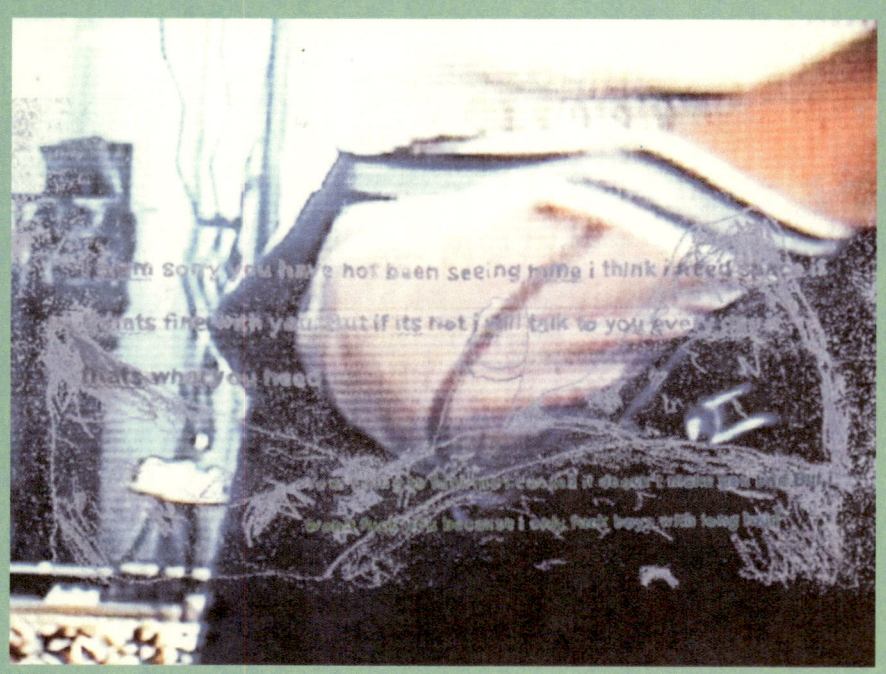

drone to let the sonic space generate its own ecology that evolves and transforms over the duration of the song. The idea that you can uncover hidden truths about a sound or image through repetition is exciting for me.

My undergrad film community at Calarts placed a huge emphasis on duration, and so I think I might've picked some of my durational tendencies up there.

Why are physical materials so important in this work about sculpting transfeminine desire?

For this film, I think I was trying to replicate what dysphoria feels like, which is this crazy dissociative fog that feels vaguely evil and life threatening at all times. I'm still pretty early on in my transition, and this was made when I was even earlier in my transition than I am now. At the time I was thinking a lot about transfemininity and translesbianism as existing in the patriarchy as a sort of "broken" or "failed" cisheterosexuality. I've always waded through my transness through cinema, and I've always been really interested in "bad" equipment and images, so that leap felt natural. I think that the "poor" image of the DV cam and CRT screen feels more curious and complicated than the digital image, where a sharper or cleaner image would've felt solved.

I started off my filmmaking

journey really, REALLY excited about digital cameras. I loved the textures of camcorders and cheap webcams, and how the ISO, noise, or poor framerate of that equipment lives in its own sort of unexplored world. I've always thought about digital filmmaking in analog terms– using the sensor's algorithmic and interpretational relationship to light as its own generative, physical medium. But I always found that equipment really unrewarding to shoot on, because it felt like I was in complete control of it. Shooting with tape or 16mm feels dialectic and relational. I always feel like I'm wrestling with the camera, which is exciting, and for this film, I think it more accurately expresses my relationship to the onscreen bodies and gaze.

There is a tension in using anonymized found film, paired with the sculptural elements of the CRT pixels that both feels foreign and familiar. Could you talk about this tension in your work?

Earlier, we talked about stillness. I think that analog video has the potential to never really be still, just because of the way the CRT scans. Every pixel is being shot out and replacing itself at absurdly fast rates, which creates the moving image and the scanline, and so the CRT image never has the singular stillness of a celluloid film frame. I think that jittery quality, clashed against the slideshow pacing of the stills and the very slight movements of the camera, contributes to some of the tension here. It also provides a very particular feeling of watching, which excites me.

When using found material, there's always an implied process of discovery, curation, and intentional placement. Using the distortion of the screen to disrupt that process scatters the way the images function, and calls their use into question: "why are these bodies arranged this way? Why can't we make out any faces?" I wanted to scrape the aesthetics of what has been labeled as the absolute low-end of image making (porn, home videos, website jpegs, homemade horror movies, etc.) to create a sort of landscape film, a survey or ethnography, about eroticism, the internet, and the screen. I think the relationship between the foundness of the images and the solidness of an analog practice was really important for sculpting the world I wanted the film to live in.

I also think that culturally the CRT image represents this uncanny liminal place for cinema. It's associated with a time before the cinema-image became completely democratized and pilfered by internet or smartphone overload. It feels more intentional and concrete than say, a vlog, but it also doesn't carry the class connotations or spirituality of the celluloid image. It represents an in-between regarding the political standing of the camera image itself. Home movies were shot on it, and so was television, and so were movies, but it's flatter, more ambiguous, and less hallowed than celluloid.

You mentioned the influence of Dennis Cooper's book *The Sluts* and Xiu Xiu's album *Fabulous Muscles*. Could you describe how these works influenced the processes, themes, or techniques used?

I've always been interested in the particular dialects that the internet produces regarding "bad" or disposable language and images, like spam emails and forum posts. Recontextualizing disposable materials into an avant-garde environment is exciting for me. Again, I'd had this vague idea about forum posts and snuff films and porn floating around in my head for a while, and then I read *The Sluts* for the first time and felt like someone had reached into my psyche and pulled out everything I found exciting and terrifying about eroticism, sex, and the internet. Every sentence felt like it was stacking on top of the last, and created this punchy, impossible whirlwind that I really wanted to replicate.

The literary style of Jamie Stewart [Xiu Xiu] is really similar to Cooper's, and *Fabulous Muscles* similarly materializes and accelerates a Queer fascination with melodrama to its most graphic end. A lot of the sound design in this film started off as me trying to make a rip off Xiu Xiu album in my bedroom. The way that album interrupts its own images with fits and spurts of harsh noise and dislodged rhythms–and also the way Stewart plays with acoustic space during the recording process, was really inspiring. I almost think of this film as an adaptation or translation of these works into a cinematic mode.

Can you speak on the sensory and textural audio elements?

I'm mostly interested in audio as a sort of narrative device. I love music, maybe more than I love cinema, and I think noise taps into a raw emotional space more purely than any other artform for me. I think adding highly textural sonic elements that interrupt silence or stillness can create a really immersive, engaging, almost pop song experience if paced correctly. Like, this thing is exciting because it's surprising and fun to watch, and instead of having to engage it intellectually, you can engage it as an experience, and as something self-driving. I also usually make my films in 8-hour fugue states at 6am, hopped up on cigarettes and caffeine and sleep deprivation, which means I have to work in an enclosed time period and usually an enclosed space. I think that grants the soundscapes a certain manic nature and an immediacy. I'm interested in sound as a physical, spatial thing that's interpreted by a microphone, which is why there's a lot of inaudible or clipping audio here. I'm thinking about beauty, like biblical angel stuff, almost– images or sounds that contain too much light or sonic information to be properly captured. This is why there's clipping, inaudible audio, or illegible images that are overexposed. Unknowing as beauty, and textures as secrets that neither me or the audience are being let in on.

Are you working on anything currently expanding on these ideas or techniques?

I'm trying to make my thesis film, which is maybe going to use 16mm and DV footage that I manually scrub through on an editing timeline, clashed against theory excerpts and personal writing and prose. It's in rough stages, and I'm really fickle with a film until I make it, so who knows if that's going to happen. But I think this relationship between secrets and vagueness and watching is something that I'm going to carry on with the rest of my work. I'm still interested in internet textures, and refining my jumbled mess of influences and mediums has been my primary struggle when developing my filmmaking style, but I'm praying that it turns out interesting at least.

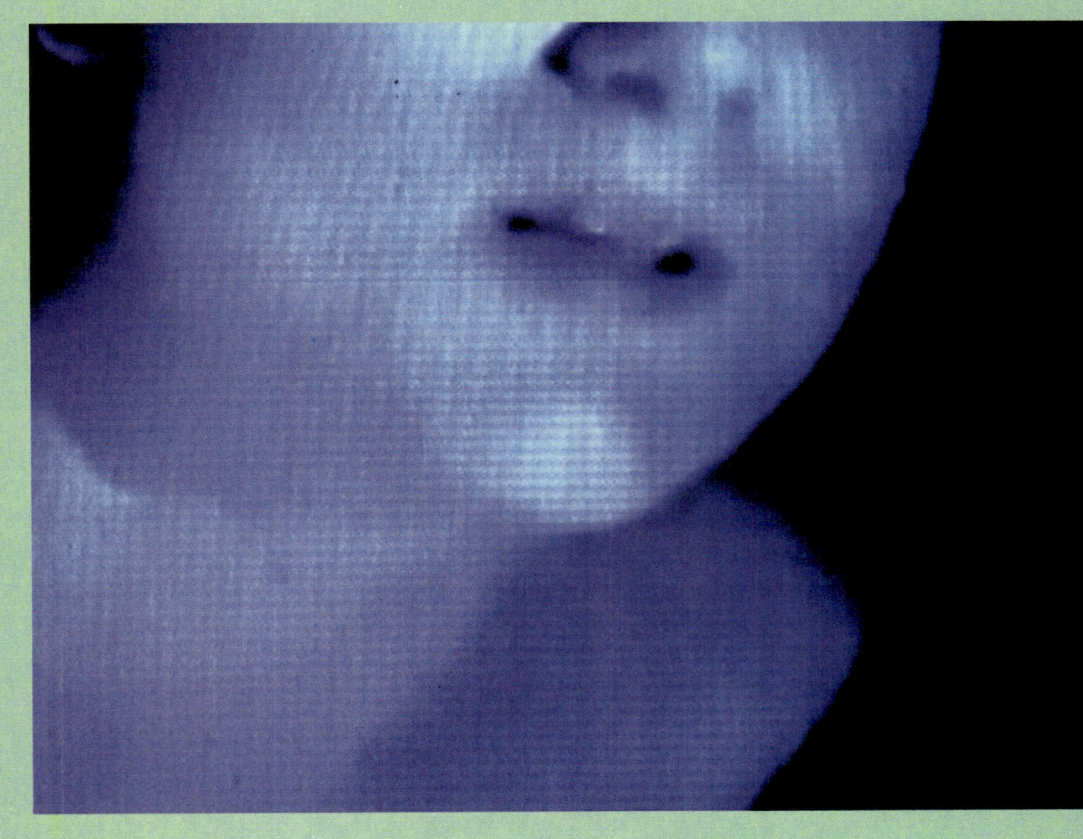

The Perfect Fruit

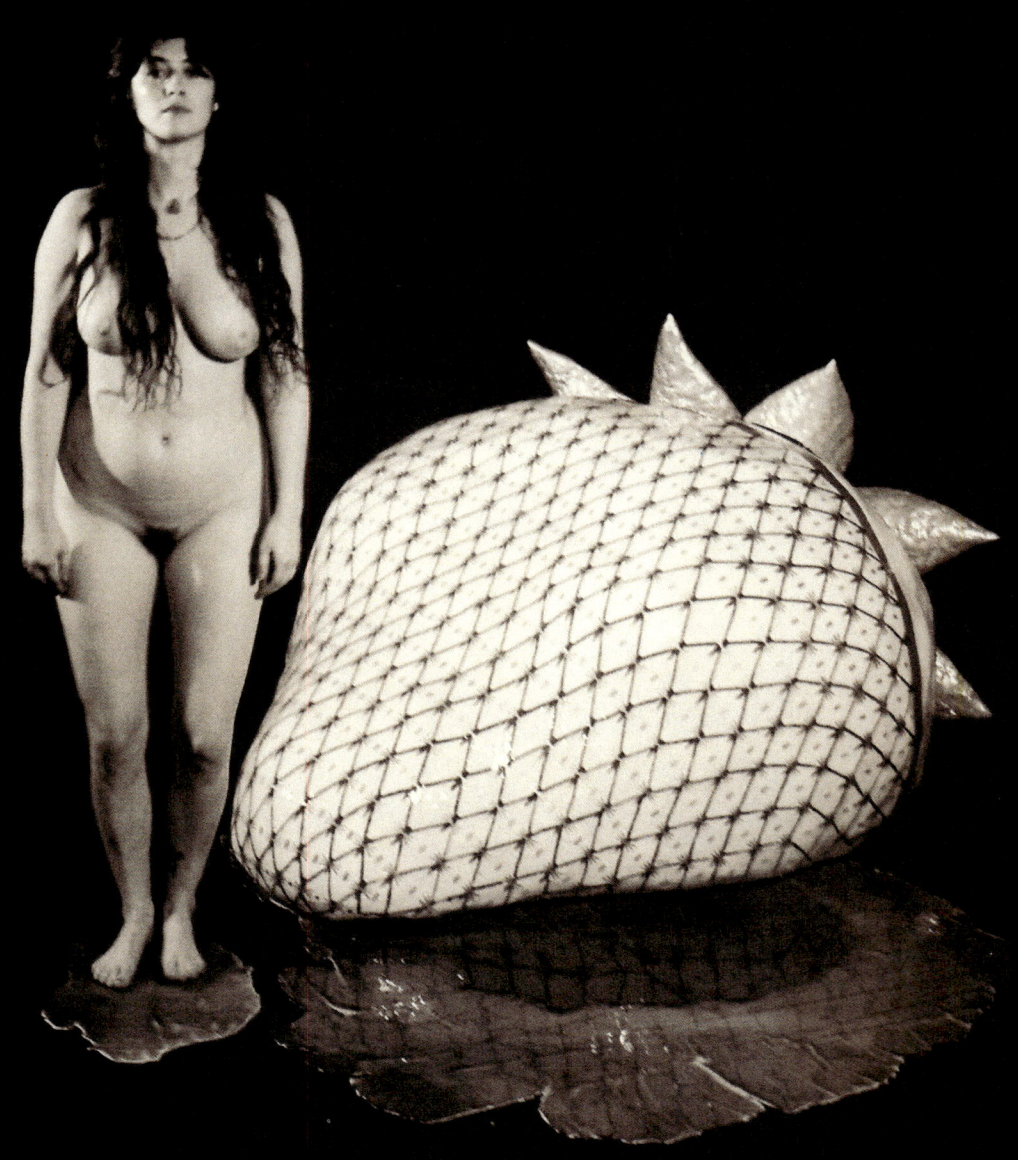

The Perfect Fruit is a combination of a sculpture I made of a strawberry made to look like Russian Porcelain and a photoshoot I took of my friend Sedona. The fruit appears to be rotting underneath the layers of porcelain which is a sort of commentary on Russian society as well as femininity.

Nina Koyfman

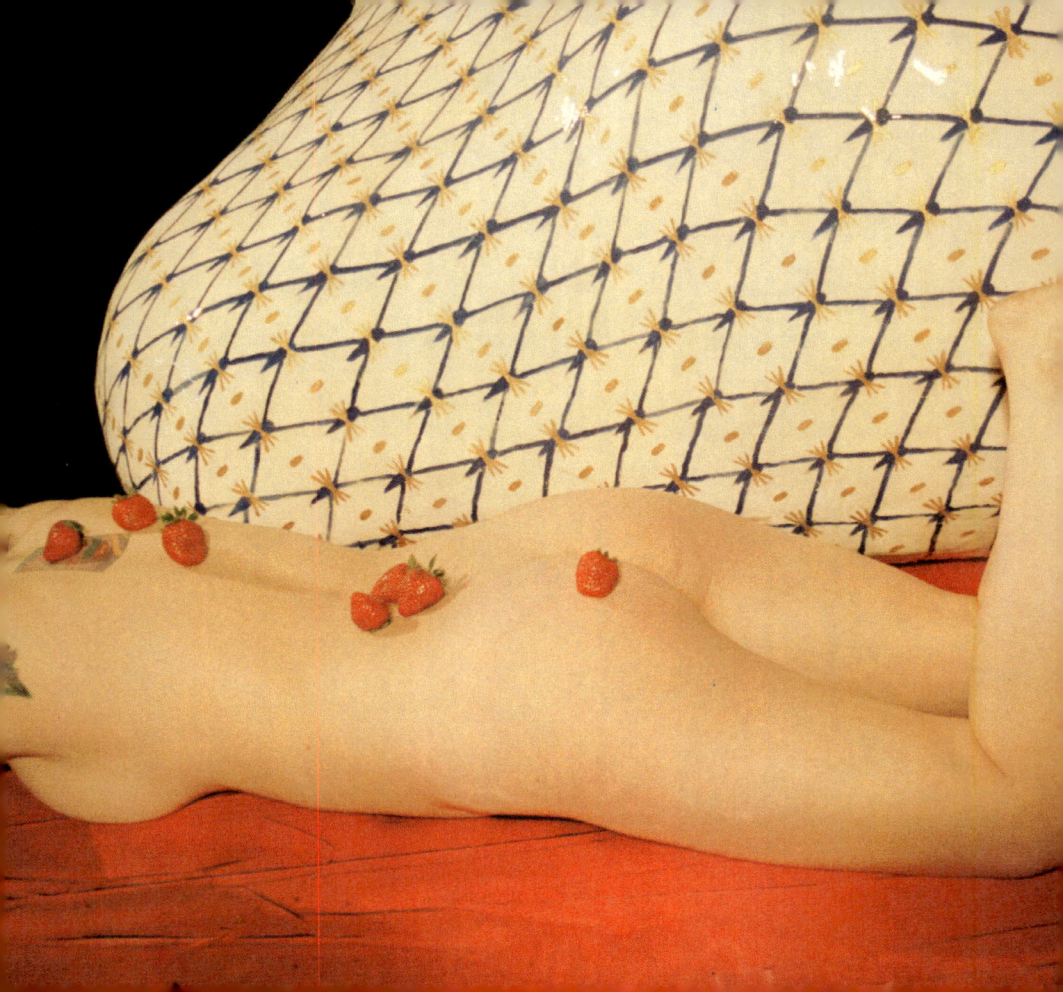

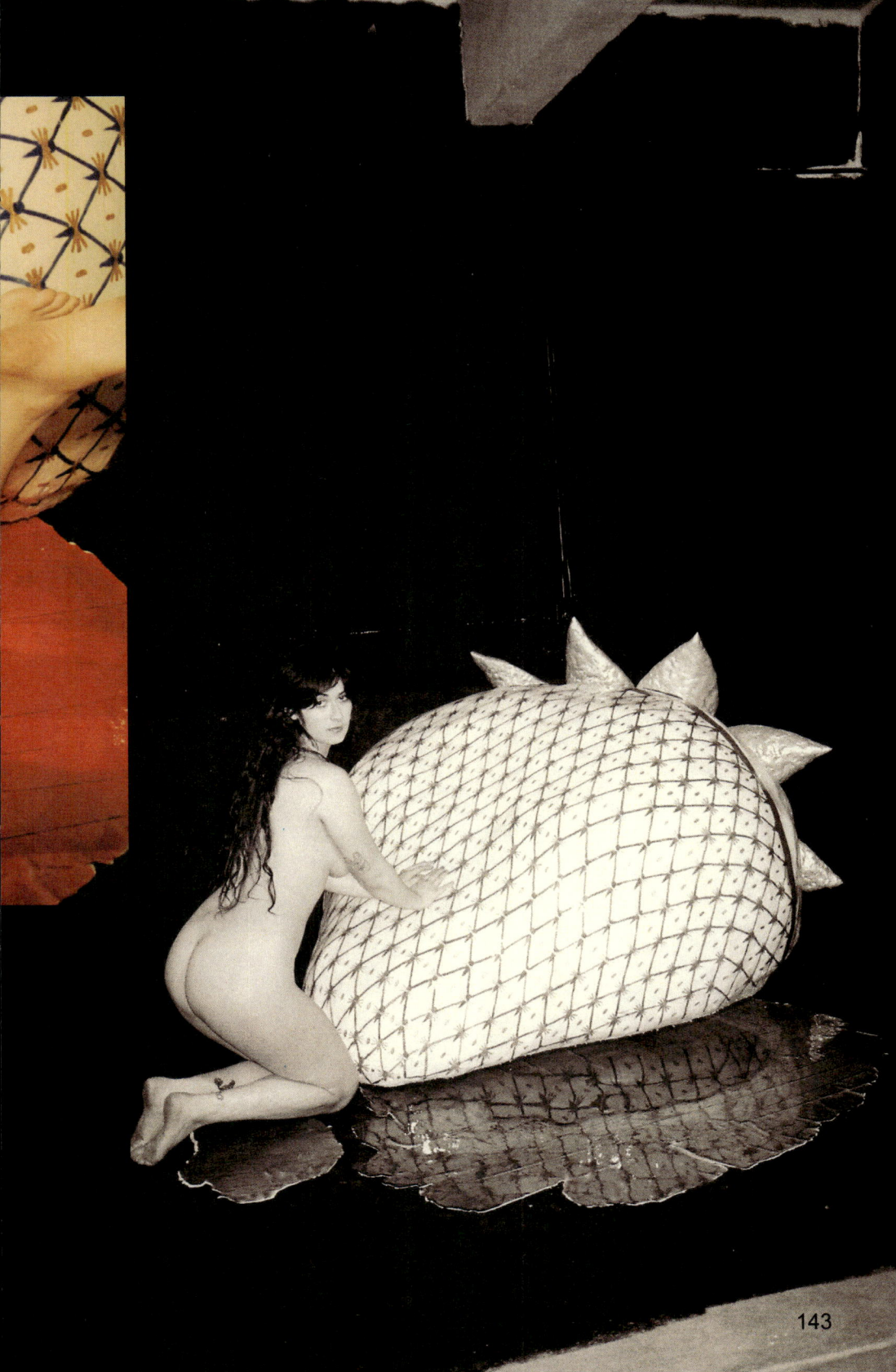

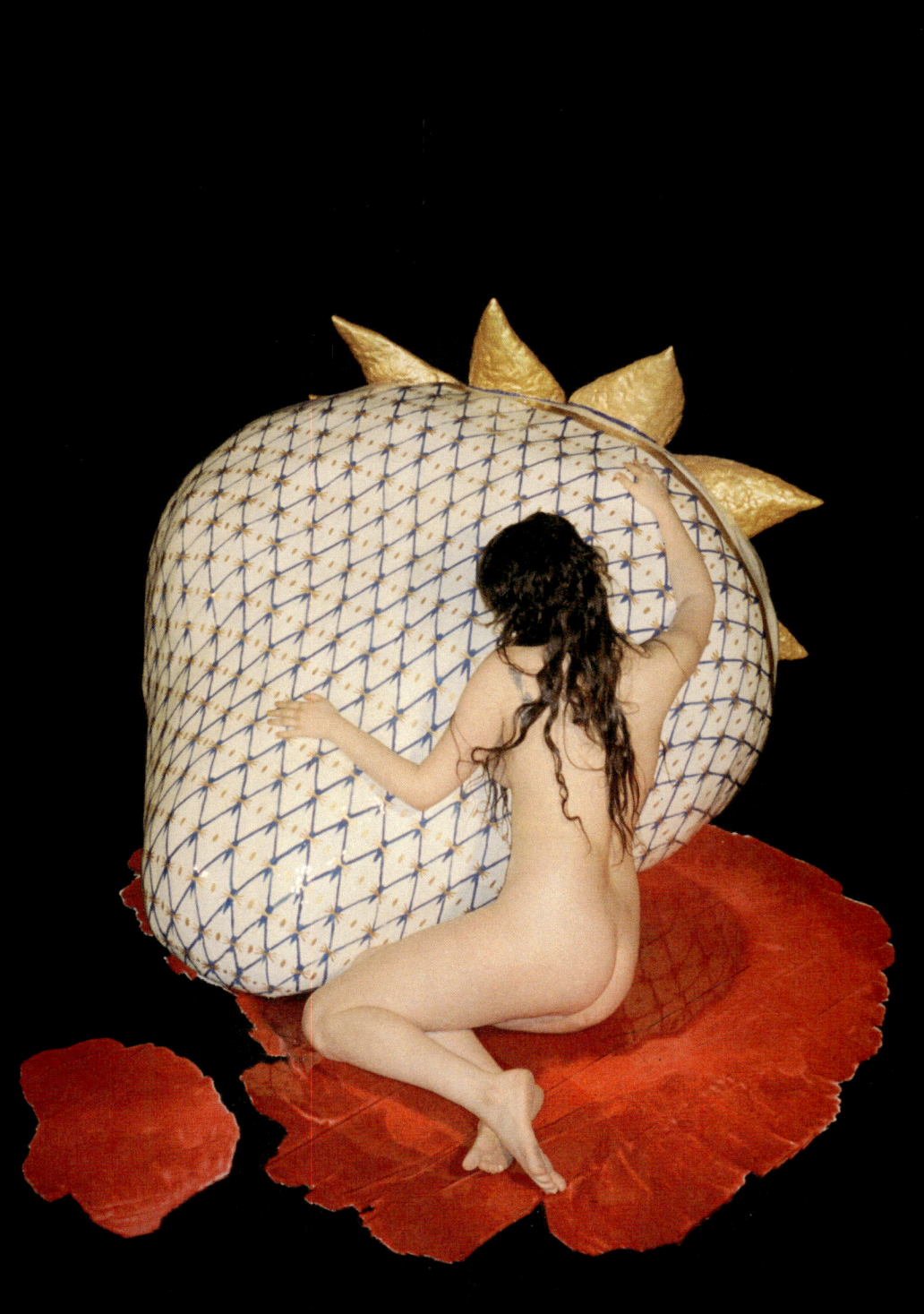

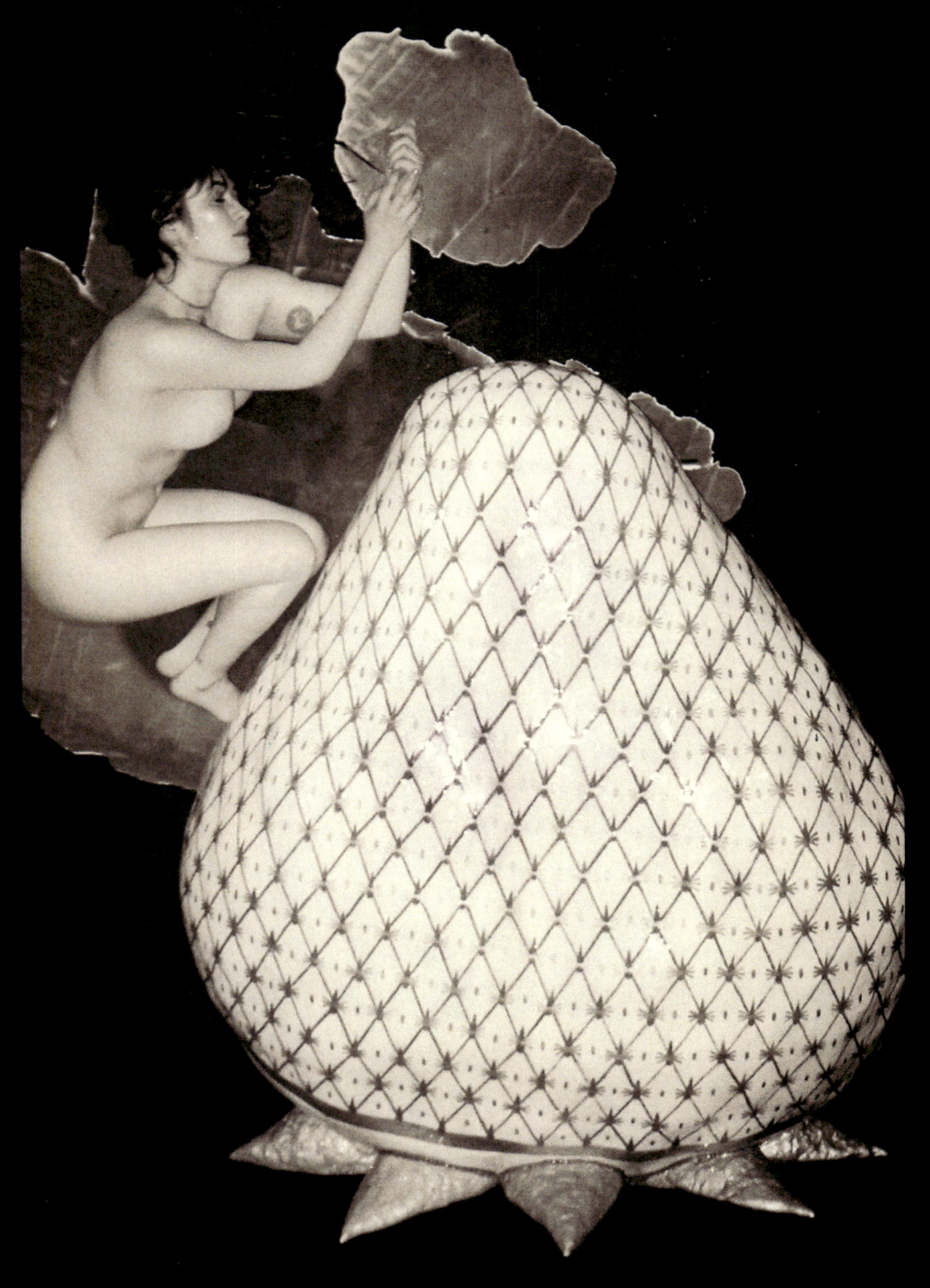

Paris Model

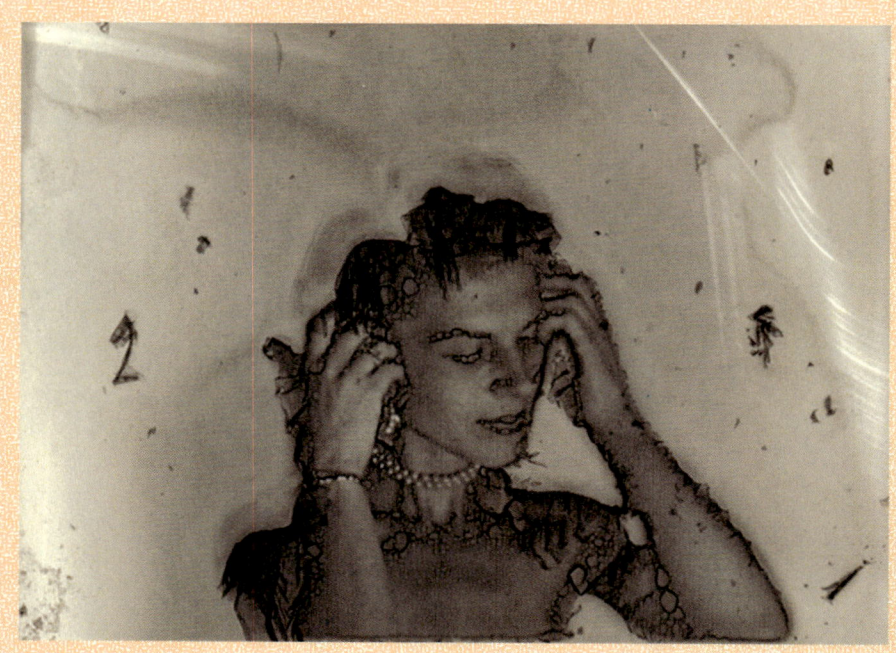

Brittney Appleby

Paris Model was created through the use of found 1940's striptease footage and experimental analog film manipulation techniques mordançage and optical printing. By using a combination of experimental techniques to create a macabre and haunting image, Paris Model asks the audience to contemplate mortality and the temporality of the flesh. The ghostly figure of the model fades in and out of recognition, skin bubbling and dissipating, adding a disturbing yet exciting element to the striptease being performed for the viewer. In addition to this the film also seeks to distort and disrupt the viewer's gaze of feminine bodies and asks the viewer to consider the way in which they view and support sexual autonomy.

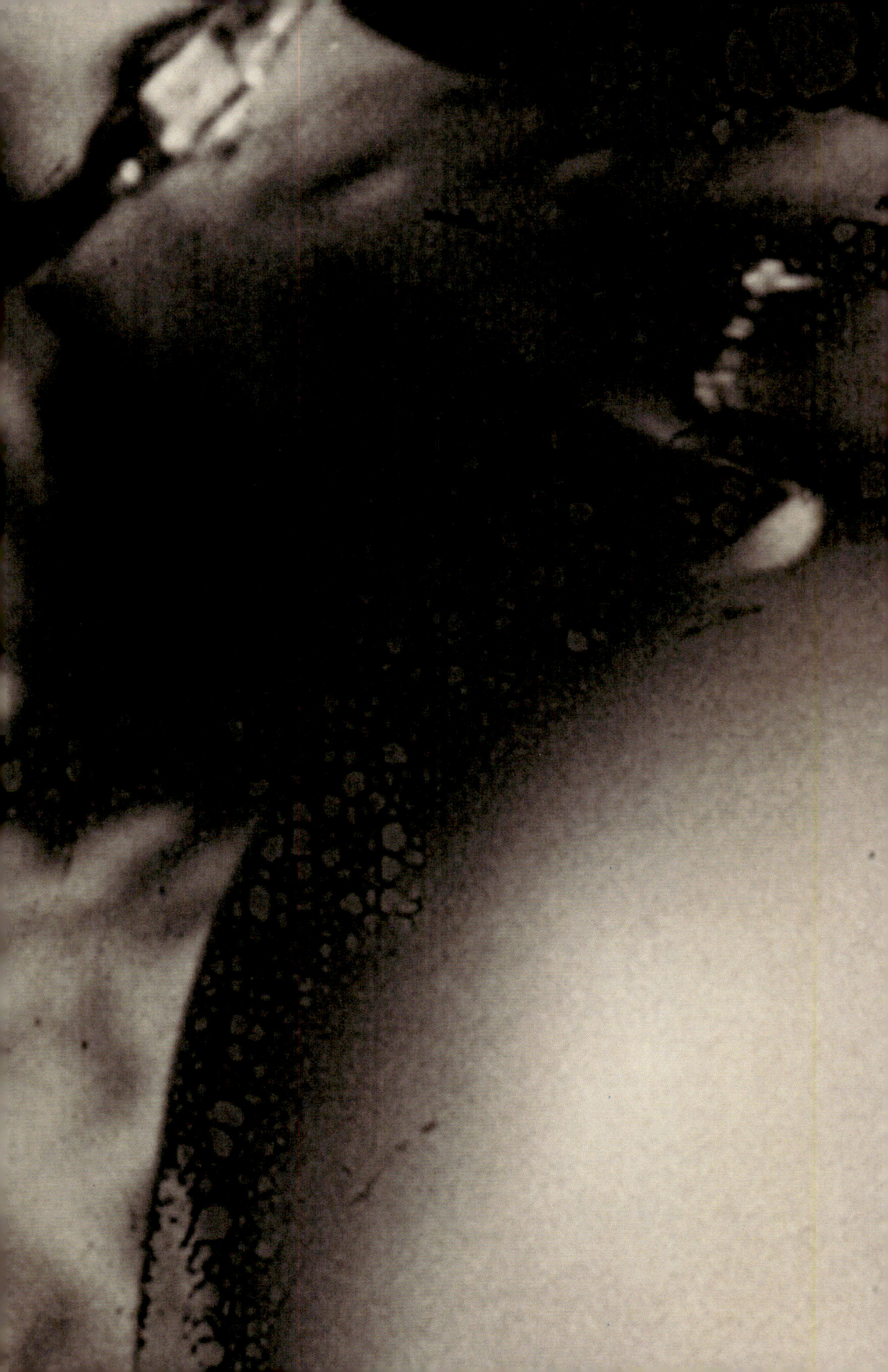

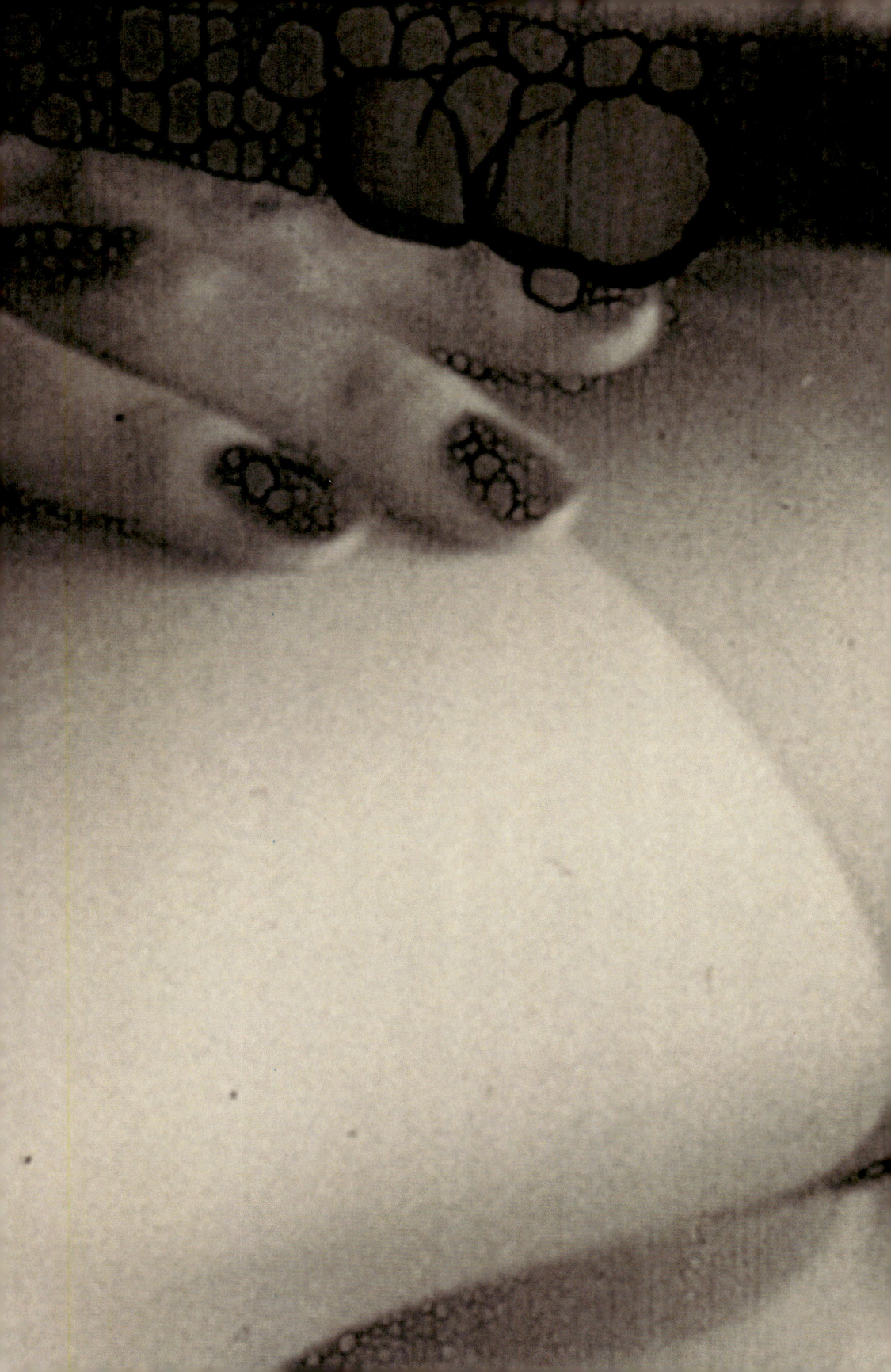

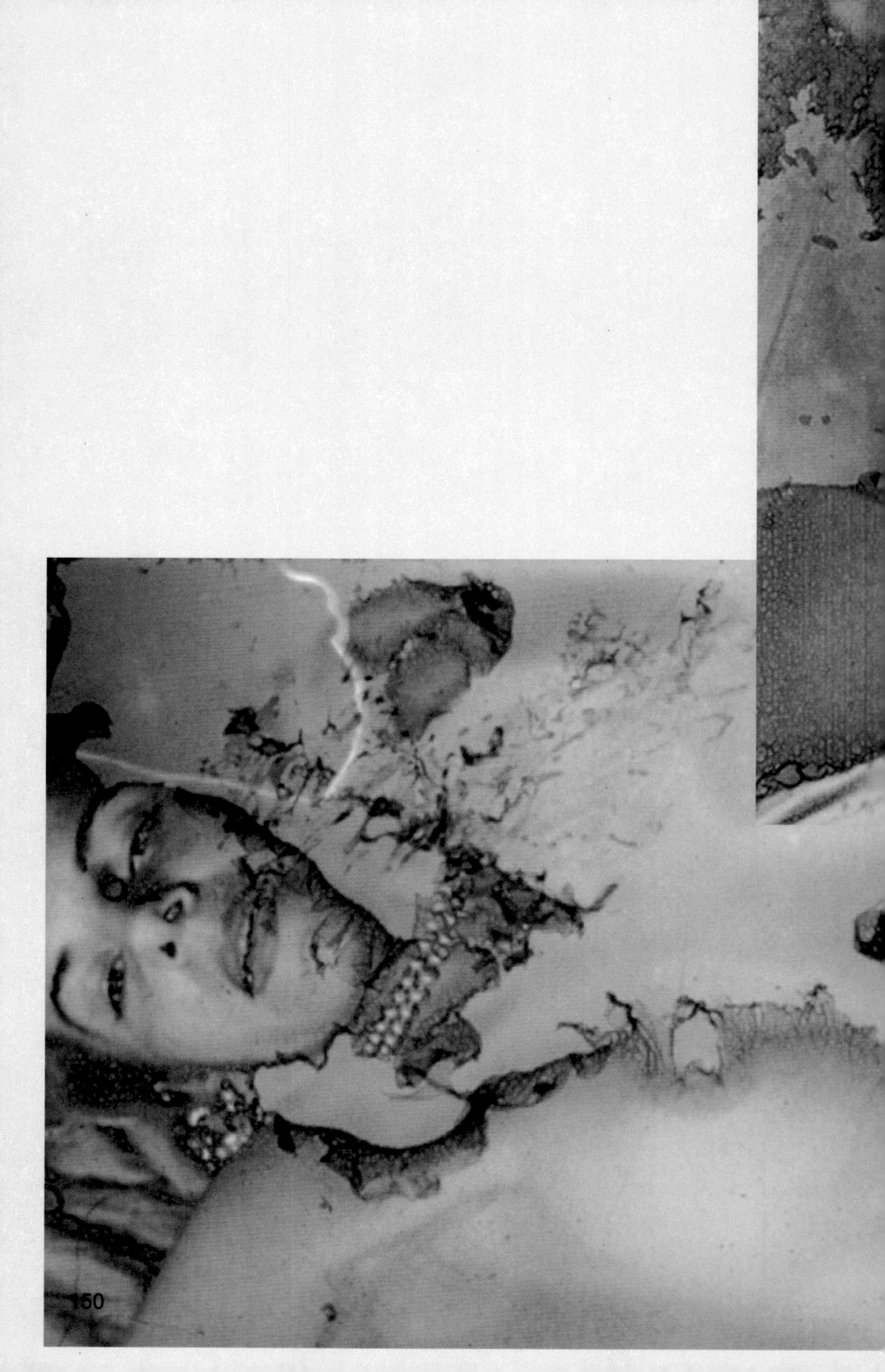

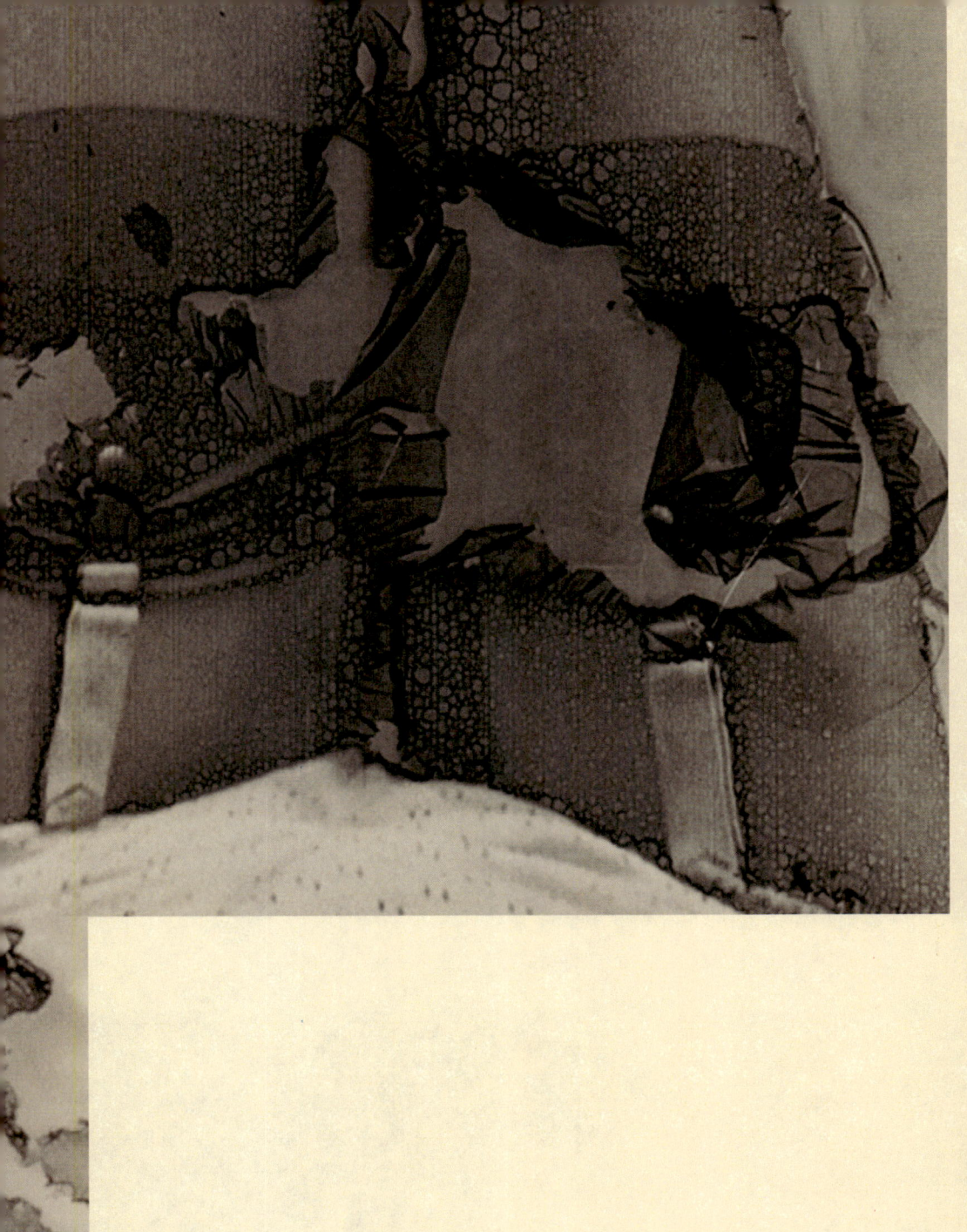

Rotten Love Redux

Program curated by Emily Apter

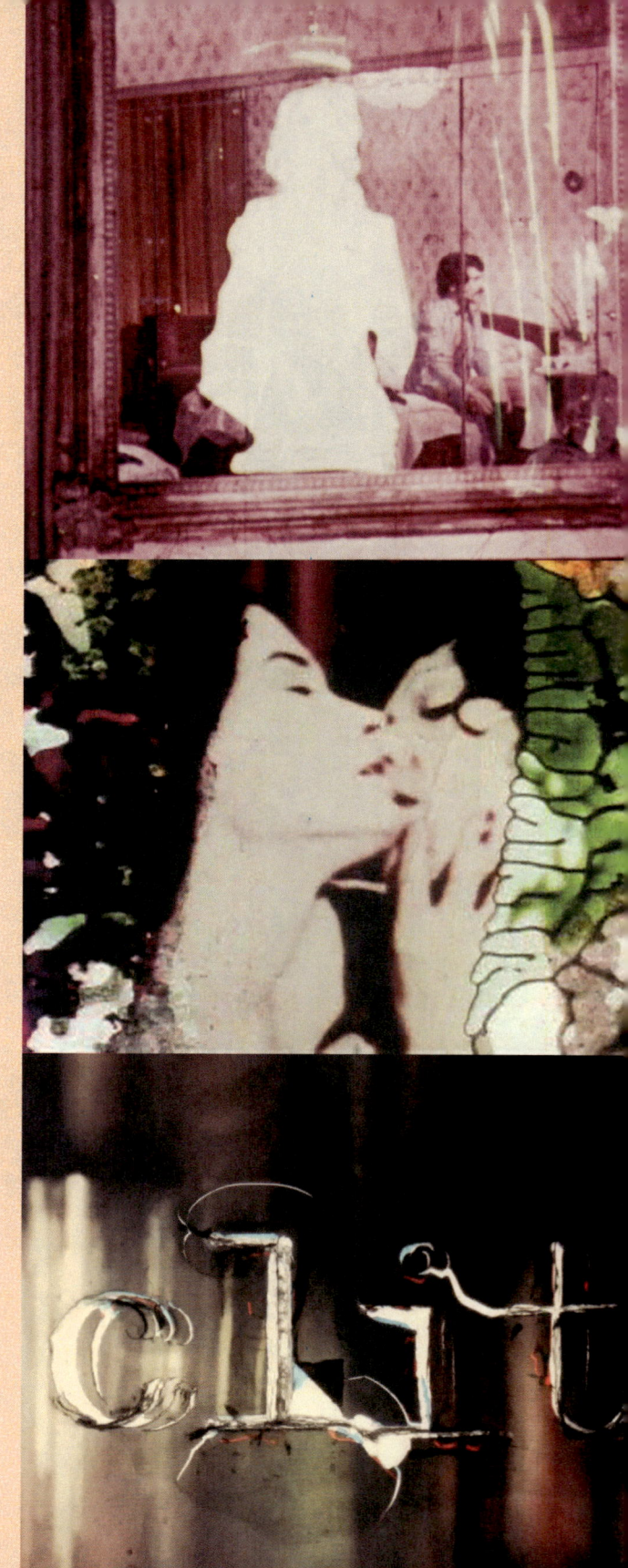

Rotten Love Redux tips its hat to the days of theatrical porn–going with a celebration of tactility, eroticism and utter decay. The program features 16mm porn and erotic films, each which incorporates decomposed or manipulated film stock in its depiction of erotic femme bodies. Working with both found and original footage, the filmmakers in this program employ a wide range of analog techniques–soaking, solarization, painting, scratching, burning, to alter celluloid's chemical make-up and add a material element to the onlooker's gaze. Treating film stock as continuous with the human body, Rotten Love Redux revels in the entangled acts of sex, fetish, and image-making.

What is Rotten Love Redux? Can you tell us a little about the naming of this programming series?

Rotten Love Redux was a program of short 16mm erotic and porn films I put together at Spectacle Theater in February 2022. Each film in the program incorporates decomposed or manipulated film stock–including soaking, solarization, painting, scratching, and burning techniques, as well as the "natural" decay of unpreserved celluloid in its depiction of erotic/eroticized bodies. The program featured stunning, mesmerizing works by Carolee Schneemann, Naomi Uman, Nazlı Dinçel, Peggy Ahwesh, and MM Serra. The aim was to both recreate and subvert the experience of theatrical porn-going, and to revel in the entangled acts of sex, decay, and image-making.

The program at Spectacle was a second, revised iteration of what was initially just called "Rotten Love," an (anti) Valentine's Day screening at the Film-Makers' Cooperative in February 2019. That program was more about love/sex than it was about porn/erotics, though some of the same films appeared in both. The framing was light-hearted, evoking the treacly rotting of teeth and relationships (as much as that of celluloid). The second version is where "redux" came in, a word I added not only to differentiate the two programs, but also to invoke a sense of renewal or revival. The theme of "bringing back to life," which runs through Rotten Love Redux, was directly inspired by the featured filmmakers, whose work with found or damaged materials breathes new life into moving images.

How did you get into programming? As a programmer and curator of erotic experimental work (past and

Images (from top to bottom): *Removed*, Naomi Uman (1999), *The Color of Love*, Peggy Ahwesh (1994), *Solitary Acts #4*, Nazlı Dinçel (2015)

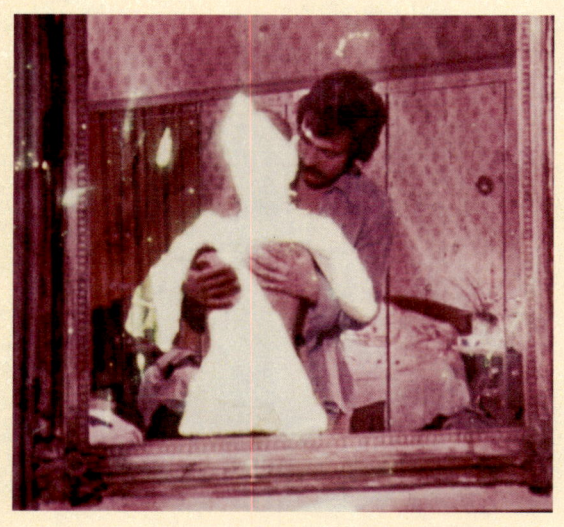

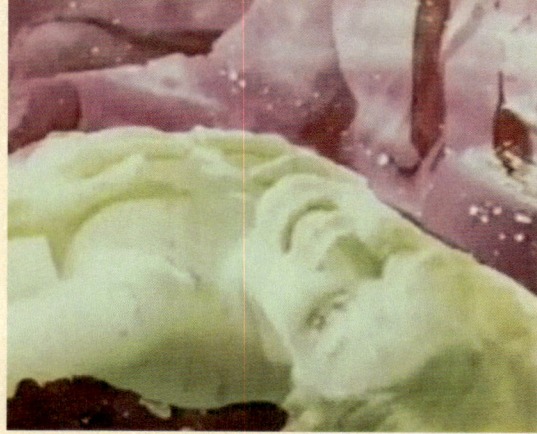

contemporary), how does a curator think about trauma and sensitivities of an audience while not unintentionally erasing important work like you are showing? What is the role of the programmer in how we contextualize the work we show?

When I first moved to NYC directly after college, I had never programmed before. It wasn't even really on my radar yet! I also didn't know that much about documentary and experimental cinema (just narrative). What I did know was that I believed firmly in film's political utility: its ability to increase consciousness, disrupt harmful narratives of history, draw connections between overlapping systems of oppression, circulate political propaganda, and amplify movements or ideologies that threaten the existing social, economic, and racial order. I undeniably believe in and enjoy art for art's sake but in the process of deepening my political commitments (dipping my toes into socialist organizing and engaging in political education) I craved a political home in the film world as well. At that time I was experiencing a pretty strong distaste for the misogynist cinephilic culture I found. There was the sort of obvious boys club flavor to it all, but perhaps more alarmingly what I saw was a pretty politically vacant way of engaging with the history and present of cultural production.

I gravitated toward experimental film and documentary largely because of the crossover of political and artistic interests I found with folks I met there. Curators Jessica Green and Edo Choi two were programming at Maysles Documentary Center at the time I was interning. After I'd stuck around long enough, they gave me the opportunity to put together several screenings as part of a futurist experimental series funded by the Warhol Foundation. I was very intimidated by the prospect. I felt I couldn't possibly know enough about film to make thoughtful, credible, and responsible choices. It was really only with Edo and Jessica's guidance (as well as that of my dear friend, Annie Horner) that I had the chance to try it out.

The first film I chose remains an all-time favorite—Lizzie Borden's *Born In Flames* (1983). Lengthy emails and eventually in person discussions with Lizzie about the film's piece-meal production, necessity-born mixed formal elements, trenchant critique of institutional co-optation/sanitization of social movements, general revolutionary spirit, and eerie prescience in the present day—it all just really hit home what it is that I love about film. During the screening, one of the FTP Coalition rallies marched past our Central Harlem storefront. There were chants from 1980s New York documentary footage Lizzie had shot mixed with "fuck the police, free the people!" just outside our (very much not soundproofed) doors. Lizzie encouraged audience members to join the rally after the discussion.

For me the world of programming really opened up from there. I learned about (and subsequently included in the series) the work of so many others greats—Akosua Adoma Owusu, Cauleen Smith, Barbara Hammer, Lawrence Andrwes, Kevin Jerome Everson, among others, whose films are, individually, mind-blowingly good and, in dialogue, just totally transcendent.

It was then that it hit me. Everything I had previously understood about programming was simply not true. Film programming is

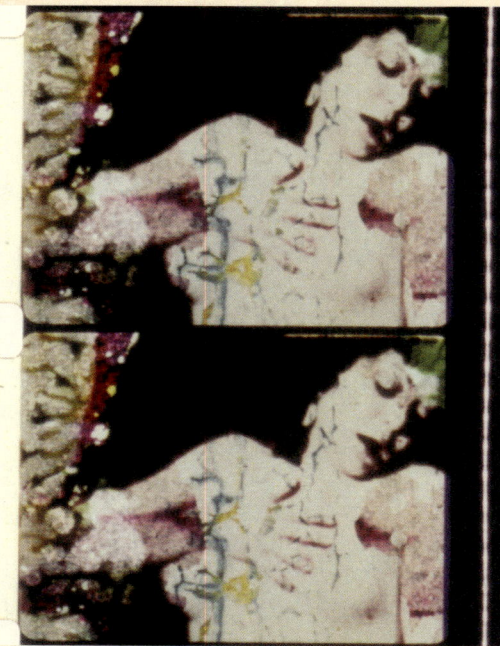

The Color of Love, Peggy Ahwesh (1994)

not the process of reaching into one's pre-existing, encyclopedic knowledge and mining for films you know and love. It's actually quite the opposite. It's about formulating deep and dynamic frameworks, under which films can be platformed, mobilized, shared, enjoyed, discussed, questioned, written about and, at times, acted upon. It requires a thorough research practice to understand and showcase what's been made—as well as what couldn't be made, what's been neglected, or what's been scrubbed from collective memory in service of a liberatory analysis under which the films might be considered.

I like to conceptualize programming this way because it casts it as the process of both gaining and destabilizing knowledge. Since cinema is a movement/time-based medium, I think it's a particularly useful one for shedding light on the invisibilized structures of power that undergird visual archives and cultural production. The joyful, creative, and intellectual rigor of it has to do with understanding the way certain histories are either kept or concealed, and that this is not a naturally occurring process but rather naturalized by the ruling classes. As a result, learning about glaring gaps in the visual archive has been as informative to my curatorial practice as the gleaming discoveries. However indirect, I hope these themes of presence/absence, preservation/erasure, (in)visibility, course through Rotten Love Redux as well.

What got you into the research and study of moving image work that utilizes pornography/erotic imagery?

Peggy Ahwesh's *The Color of Love* (1994) first got me thinking about the relationship between analog media and erotic imagery. Ahwesh optically reprints, re-edits, slows down, and scores a Super8 found porn film from

the 1960s or 70s
of a blood-soaked
threesome. The
kaleidoscopic water
damage stamps
the emulsion with
material evidence
that the film, as well
as perhaps the type
of theater where it
might have screened,
is itself the recycled
waste of cinema's
grittier yesteryear.
Both pleasurable
and extremely
grotesque, *The Color
of Love* (dedicated
to the iconic Doris
Wishman) is a
thematic, material,
and bodily eruption
of tension between
source material,
contemporary
intervention, and the
blooming looming
threat of physical and
cultural erasure.

**Why is erotica and
pornography such
a powerful tool for
the moving image
maker? Especially for
women, Queer, and
enby makers who
you noted you want
to pay close attention
to in your curatorial
work.**

When I think about
erotic analog
work, especially by

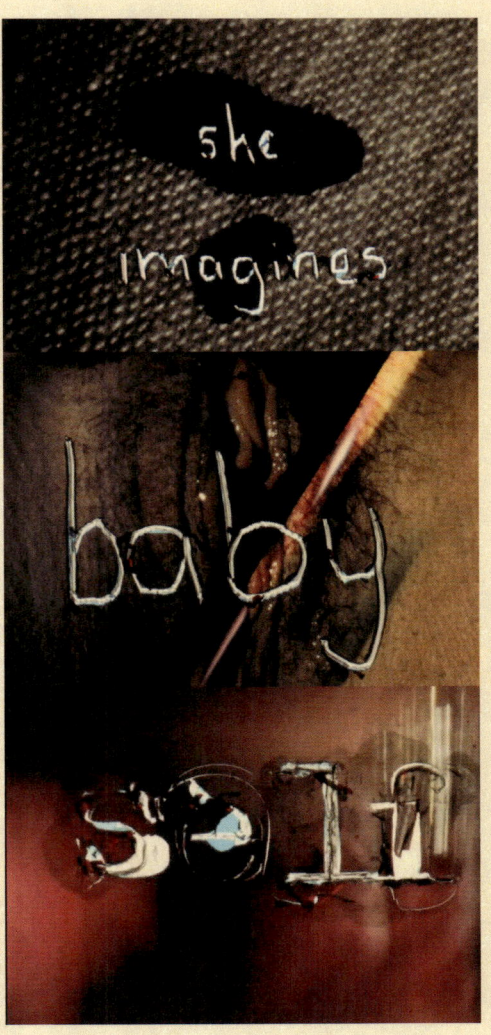

*Solitary Acts #5 (top image), Solitary Acts #4
(bottom two), Nazlı Dinçel (2015)*

women, Queer, and nonbinary makers, I think about celluloid as a continuation of the body. I think it's an especially ripe material for erotic expression because of the way it bridges movement, time, tactility, and looking. As mentioned earlier, the films that made up this particular program specifically utilize celluloid that has been damaged or altered. While, of course, each filmmaker uses these materials in different ways and to different ends. I was struck by the recurrence of these types of analog tactics, especially in erotic work by women, Queer, and nonbinary makers.

I think anyone who's handled 16mm film might agree that it's a highly fetishistic and sensuous experience. And the foregrounding of physical/chemical manipulations, and treating these manipulations as much as content as the photographed images they overlay, lends itself to a more fluid and tactile expression of the erotic. These films can be understood as having unique physical and chemical properties, which alongside the filmmaker and spectator exist in the material world. The very assertion of materiality runs contrary to filmmaking conventions, which typically reify the illusion of a hermetically sealed narrative world. In even the most self-reflexive or hybridized of digital work, the filmmaker/viewer's material reality is more-or-less irrelevant. On the contrary, the films in Rotten Love Redux contain within them the physical sensations of making, exhibiting, and watching.

In cases of damaged celluloid, such as in Ahwesh's *The Color of Love*, the source material is imprinted with the history that produced the conditions of decay in the first place. In other words, what's invoked is the original Super 8mm film's insignificance in the eye of mainstream film culture, as evidenced by its lack of preservation. This context is delivered via the abstract flowery water damage that subsumes what's been photographed—an entire layer of historical meaning conveyed through image and texture.

And lastly, in all of the films included in Rotten Love Redux, the analog tactics render visible the filmmakers' labor of making. I think this charges the work with a sort of fiery insurgency: a refusal to be erased. All of these things-the assertion of existence, exclusion from care systems, (in)visible labor, are extremely relevant when thinking about marginalized genders and sexualities.

What do you see as the role or importance of curating work like this?

As a preserver or canonizer of work that used erotic imagery.
I'm interested in the material forces that surround and underpin the making and watching of movies, in addition to the content of the movies themselves. The history of porn from the mid-century to the present day— beginning theatrically, as in the days of NYC's former 42nd St. sex district, then largely via home video, and then internet, is several histories in one. It includes the exploitation of femme/Queer bodies and labor, the criminalization of Queer sex and sex work, technology and the circulation of moving images, the privatization and destruction of public space.

It's not that these histories are bad or good in a moral sense, but are expressions of the power relations that governed (and continue to govern) what movies and theaters mean socially and culturally. Who makes erotic imagery and who profits off of it? Who gets to experience erotic pleasure and who is endangered or criminalized for doing so? Most broadly, what is possible inside the city's ever-shrinking public spaces? What could a cinema be if we were to transform the social and economic forces of society?

In July 2021, prior to Rotten Love Redux, I put together a virtual film series with my two collaborators Inney Prakash (current Co-Director of Programming at Maysles) and Annie Horner called Cinemas, In Memoriam, which was heavily inspired by Sam Delaney's book *Times Square Red, Times Square Blue*. The series came about at a moment in the pandemic when many critics, distributors, and streaming platforms were hailing the death of movie theaters. Working for a small, perpetually struggling micro-cinema, we were thinking a lot about the forces that govern cultures and conditions of moviegoing that enable the life and death of public space. We had many concerns—the health and safety of our community, the security of our jobs, but our belief in cinema spaces as sites for resilience and resistance was not one of them. Cinemas, In Memoriam was our (cheekily named) declaration of the cinema's renewed life. This sentiment was extremely relevant to my thinking in Rotten Love Redux.

What we long for is not the magic of a big screen and sticky floors alone, but for a people's cinema, able and willing to shift its design and function in alignment with the needs of its community. As ever, we ask ourselves: is there a way in which the resilience of cinema might be bound up with the liberation of humanity?

In *Times Square Red, Times Square Blue* Sam Delaney chronicles the physical and moral demolition of NYC's porn theater district and the complex web of cross-class/race sexual encounters that it enabled (before the development of Giuliani's Times Square). He writes:

[*Times Square Red, Times Square Blue* is not] a plea to reinstate the porn theater that the thoughtless greed running rampant in cities like New York has recently smashed. After all, such greed created those institutions at another moment... My argument's polemic thrust is toward conceiving, organizing, and setting into place new establishments—and even entirely new types of institutions—that would offer the services and fulfill the social functions provided by the porn houses that encouraged sex among the audience. Further, such new institutions should make those services available not only to gay men but to all men and women, gay and straight, over an even wider social range than did the old ones."

Delaney's words really stick with me— not a lament, exactly, but a call to action. I think we could expand his vision slightly to include people of all genders and sexualities, of course, but also to institutions that not only "encourage sex" but connection, intimacy, organizing, agitation, care, erotics, etc. in many forms.

I hope that a theatrical experience of porn films by women, Queer, and nonbinary makers in the present day can serve as both a nod to the bygone days of theatrical porn-going and an entry point for interrogating the exploitative forces that continue to shape the experience of making and going to the movies. I hope that, as Delaney urges, it can be a small part of the fervent and imaginative process of building a just (and therefore more pleasurable) world.

Are you continuing Rotten Love Redux? What other makers would you add to the theme of erotic imagery and physical manipulation to the conversation you started?

I don't have concrete plans to continue this series, though I would with enthusiasm if there is interest! One thematically related project is a written piece I'm working on with Sean Benjamin about the last operating porn theater in NYC, The Fair Theater in East Elmhurst, Queens. We've been frequenting the Fair Theater, as well as two porn theaters in Harford and New Haven, CT over the last year to get a taste of what porn theaters are like in the present

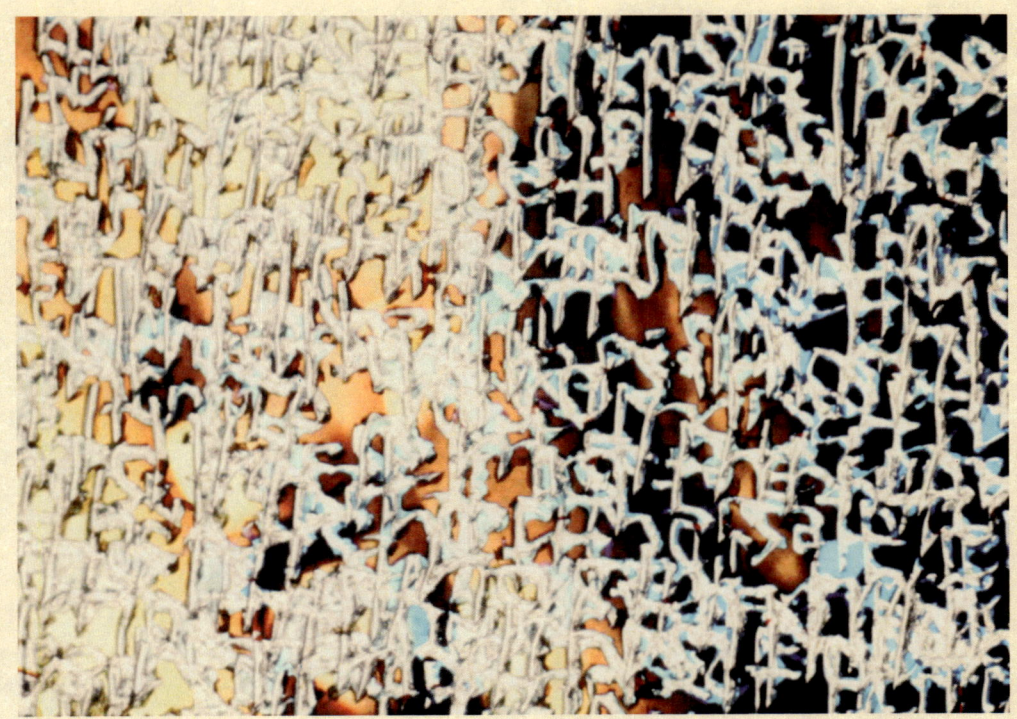

Solitary Acts #5, Nazlı Dinçel (2015)

day.

What else are you currently programming? Or are there any interesting curatorial projects you are in the conceptual stages of?

My current passion project is an ongoing documentary, music, and discussion series, entitled Mir Zaynen Do: Black/Yiddish Struggle In Harlem. It explores the overlapping histories of Black and Yiddish-speaking Jewish organizers and artists in Harlem from the 1930s through the present day. With Paul Robeson's legacy as its starting point who, in addition to being a committed political organizer, learned Yiddish in solidarity with his Jewish comrades, Mir Zaynen Do (meaning "we are here" in Yiddish) probes the myths and realities of "Black/Jewish relations" in Harlem, ultimately, to reinforce our shared imperative against racial and economic oppression today.

The series will likely launch this April, but I'm still looking for a funder who is willing to support programming around anti-fascist, anti-zionist, Black/Jewish communists—no luck yet!

Music

of

Desire

Kristin   Reeves

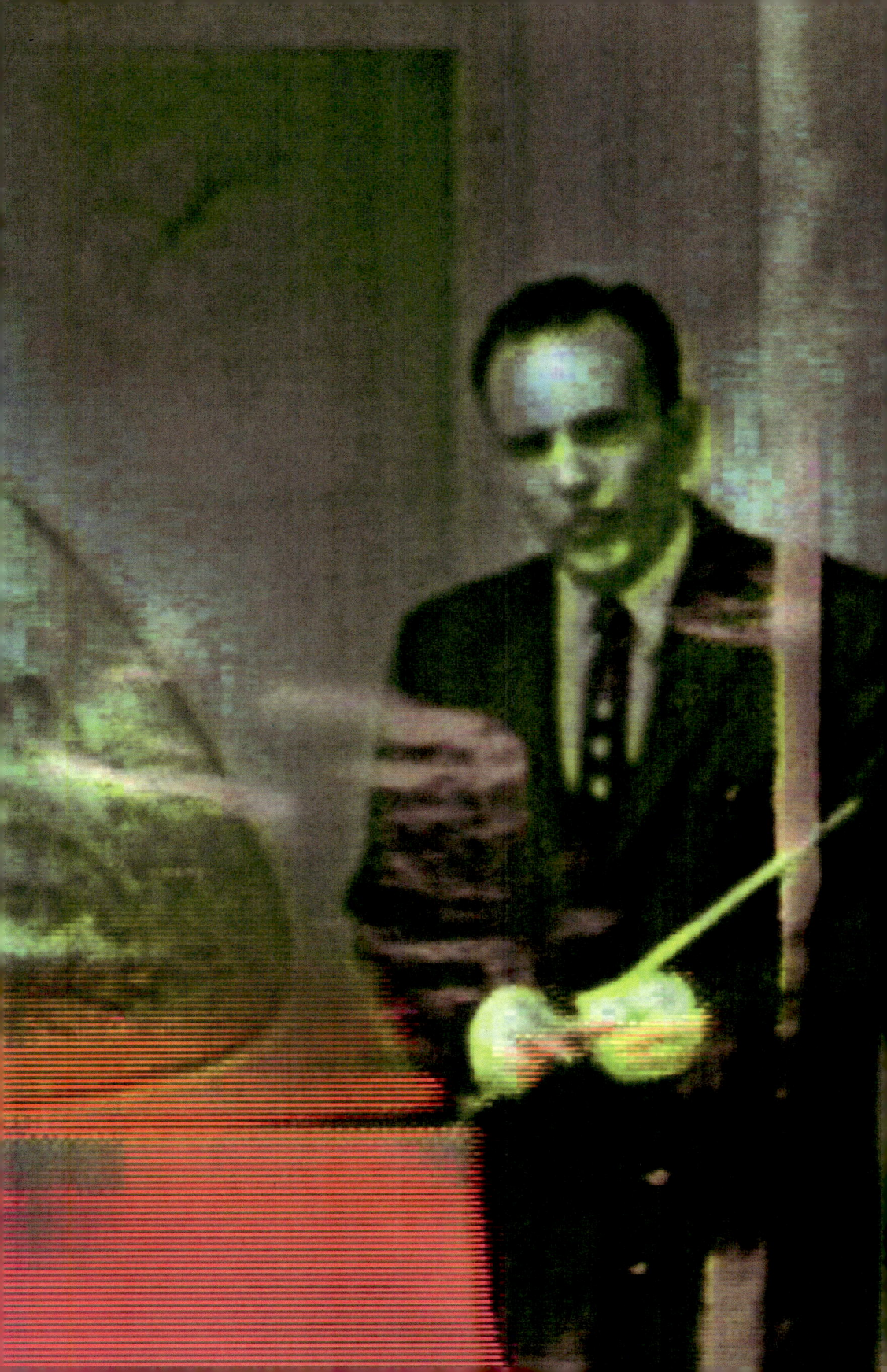

When intimacy couples with dysfunction; feel the sensation of becoming suspended between pleasure and a reverse soundtrack of desire. Produced through a media art residency at Signal Culture using real-time analog video processing tools and found physical media.

Sexual dysfunction and disruptions to pleasure are common symptoms of trauma. High and low-level therapies can include music and body work. I converted the filmic body into a controlling signal, which was then applied back onto itself. The process a model of trauma; the material sources point to the need for therapy, clinical and pop.

What brought you to work with Signal Culture or your desire to work with analog video synthesizers?

I learned of Signal Culture when they had a call for a cookbook of their own. They had a call for media recipes. I developed a workflow using laser cutters/etchers to manipulate film directly through precisely melting vector graphics onto 16mm film. I submitted that recipe for their consideration, and they published that. Then I learned more about their residencies, and so I applied.

I began working with moving image, with analog video editing decks, video toasters, and old-school tools from the nineties. I was at an art school, so we got the castoffs of the materials that the university didn't want. That eventually led me to work with 16mm film because I wanted to get into that analog space again. I love pushing up against the materiality and the process of analog. Signal Culture seemed like a place where I could potentially do that again. I didn't have access to analog video equipment at the time.

My artistic practice is interested in relationships with the body, representation of the body, personal experience, or what it is to be a person through media. I was also interested in the potential of the signal as a way to articulate another form of experience, of lived experience. Physical experience is also the signal and not just the body as meat and bones, but the brain and sensation in that regard, the neurological aspects of the body.

How does concept inform the way you use tools, or how do these tools inform the concept? What is the relationship between the act of making through disrupting/abstracting analog signals and that of the mind/body/signal/sequence phenomenon of trauma? How did one inform the other in how you used these analog synthesizers?

Moving into the residency, I had been researching brainwave signals, body-mind relationship, and, specifically, trauma. The general process of trauma memory as signal overload, as a loop, as not being connected perhaps to linear experience or a linear memory, and that having a real physiological reality.

I knew those things going into it, but I didn't know I would have the outcome of this film, *Music of Desire*. I really thought about *Body Contours*, the educational source film, as in many of my films—I think about them as being research subjects themselves, filmic bodies.

I'm a researcher, but I'm not a scientist, but I play one in the art and my art studio.

In my process– I collect materials, I have ideas and concepts, sometimes I have very specific goals and outcomes, and then other times I just say, "well, what happens if I put that with this?" Then over time, that outcome becomes another finished piece. I finished Music of Desire two years after the residency. But going back to your sort of bigger question of concept and tools, I do definitely work with those together, always thinking about how media, the tool itself, and the process is directly a form of language that I can use as an art-based filmmaker.

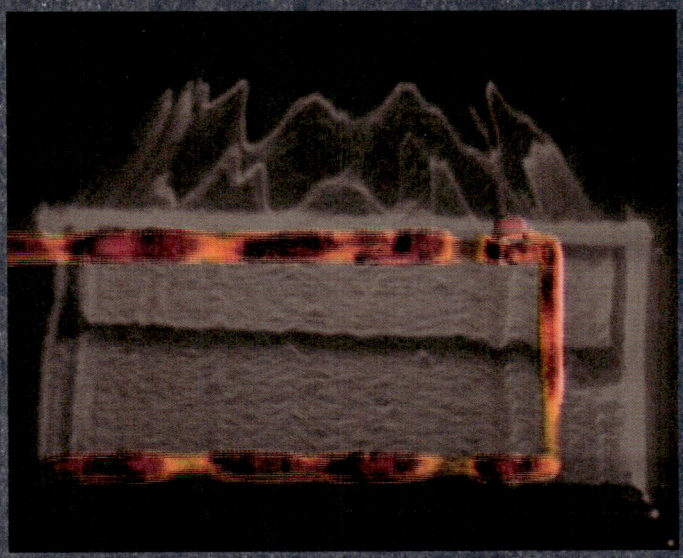

You brought up language. In your statement on *Music of Desire*, you said that sexual dysfunction and trauma needed to be discussed through a new cinematic grammar and syntactical framework like abstraction/collage/signal overloading. What was your approach to creating this new grammar?

In terms of a new grammar for sexual dysfunction and trauma, that came from when I was a screener for the Society of Photographic Education's Women's Film Festival, a film festival within their national conference. I was a screener for one year, which is an open call. There were so many submissions that the subject matter was sexual violence, both in

the form of short narrative films, fictional films, and documentaries. I was watching hours of this, and it was a reaction to that experience that I had to say, "what was not being met in these works? What did I see that there was a need to contribute to this field?" I also want to say I know other people are working in the field of filmmaking and art to explore trauma relationships, so I am not the only one, but it was a direct response to the experience.

At that point, I had the sexological film with the processes that I had discovered through Signal Culture. After the Signal Culture Residency, I started doing more research on trauma, and I was learning about the specific facts of trauma in relation to how they intersect or disrupt intimate relationships and experiences. That is a huge part of living and surviving through such experiences. I felt that was missing in so many of these films was what happens after living with trauma, and also that there are solutions and therapies.

I feel like a lot of films focus on the violence itself or statistics, violence being represented in a way that might make violence a form of entertainment and maybe undermining the seriousness of it, or statistics being important but not holding in the haptics. What are the haptics, what's the sensation, what's that reality? So much of the reality of trauma memories is sensation. It might be unknown to the individual who has had that experience. They might not realize that it's disrupting their intimate lives. They might not have a memory even of what happened.

Something I see being used and especially in narrative films or television, is flashbacks in which you see a series of events that happened in the past. Maybe they're represented in a way that seems negative

with dramatic lighting and different types of visual effects, but I don't think that really represents the reality that is being triggered. And going back to the research in terms of what's physiologically happening in the brain and the body with these forms of memory, is that a traumatic memory can't escape from a loop to go into the part of the brain in which narrative sequence actually exists. Trauma memory and sensation are stuck in this sort of loop, and it could intersect with these other aspects of a linear experience. I felt like I hadn't seen representation and media that shows that. I wanted to create media that could tell the narrative of people experiencing this for both individuals who've experienced it and also for folks that might not have that knowledge.

You talk about this loop and temporal space of trauma that sometimes interacts with linear time but is separate from memory. How did your research inform how you thought about using these synthesizer loops?

The video synthesizers, for folks who aren't familiar, is a system in which there are cables that patch. They're called video

synthesizer patches. Similar to something like a guitar pedal sequence. The order in which you put those patches can actually affect one another, and the video output. The video signal that's going through is affected by each mechanical component, and then it goes into another mechanical component potentially, and then that will have a certain effect based on how the video signal is manipulated.

When I was at Signal Culture, one of the things that I thought was really neat is you can overload by just cranking up the "volume" of the synthesizer. There are waveforms that manipulate and create images and signals, and you can crank up how fast that signal is repeating and looping within itself. You're creating this physical system with the tools and I was thinking about that in relation to the tools to the neurological system and that it's going through a different kind of poetic interpretation. Filters of memory or experience and those are intersecting, and one contributes to another, like these video synthesizers.

What was exciting at Signal Culture, I remember one of the last days I decided to stay up all night, running

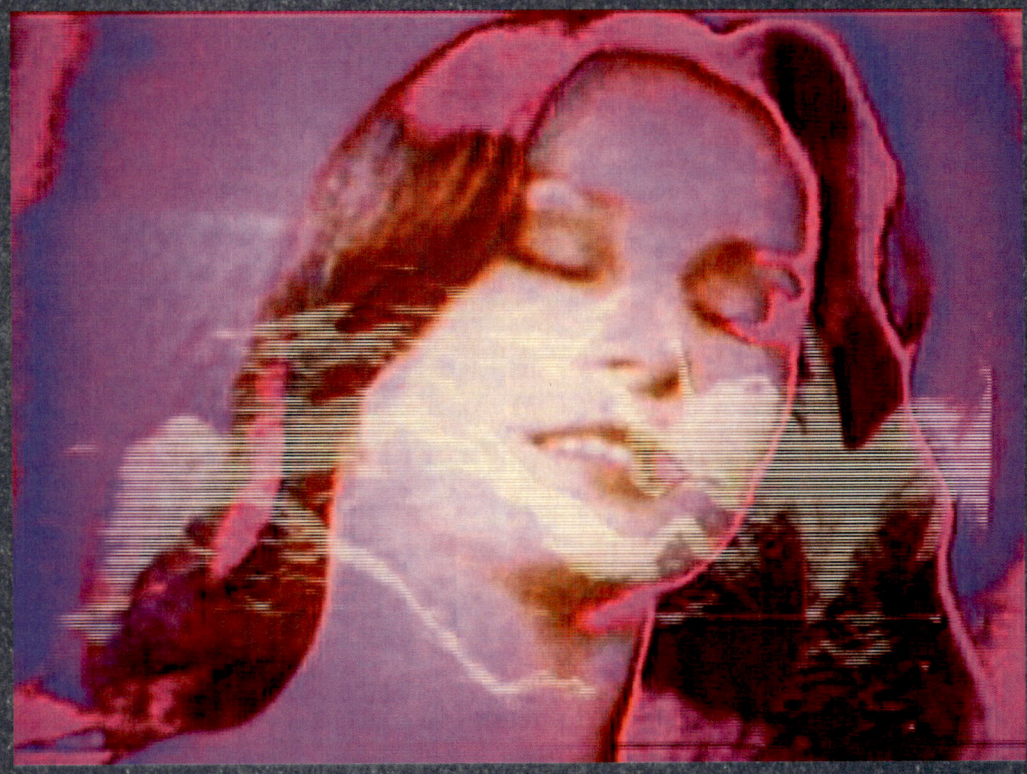

these machines, and I didn't want to stop, because I was enjoying how the patches were working after running them for a long time. I was talking to Debora Bernagozzi from Signal Culture, and she told me that it made sense because when the machine gets hot if it's used a lot, it'll actually work differently. These physical machines' constant use and the heat they produce can actually contribute to the output image.

This process reflected the idea of overload, brainwave overload, and trauma memory. The tools did that, and I can have the idea that I want to conduct and work with these concepts, but the tools themselves are the things that are articulating them. The tools, therefore, are the meaning.

Another thing I learned at Signal Culture is I could actually take the image itself, and the image could be turned into a signal. So what I did was I then took the image as a pure signal and then applied that signal onto itself. There's a specific tool called the Dave Jones Raster Manipulator, and it's this one-of-a-kind machine at Signal Culture, and works very similar to an older tool, the Rutt/Etra scan processor by Steve Rutt and Bill Etra. Normally, the way those machines would work, was you would have an image that would be affected by various wave signals and forms to manipulate how it looks. In this case, it was that, but the signal was of itself on itself. And so I was thinking about that in relationship to trauma, memory, and experience in terms of this constant loop of a sensation kind of echoing and echoing, and looping back on to the

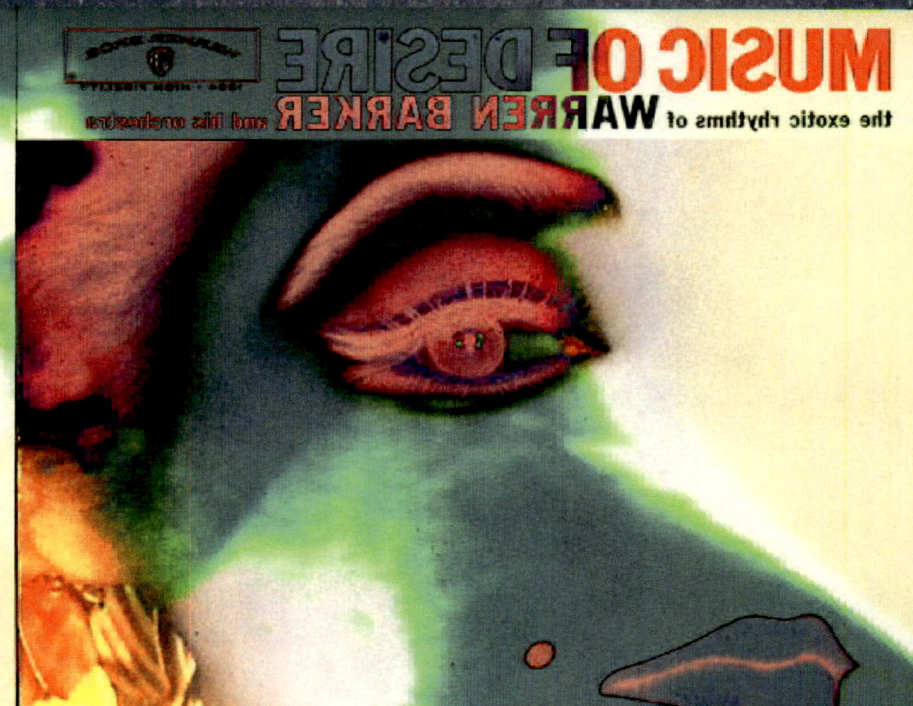

body and creating a kind of overload, and going back to the kind of thinking about how patches are structured together physically within the machine, but also within our neurological system. That repetition loop isn't necessarily where a signal or experience ends or begins, but they start to overlap and echo.

I've been learning these techniques and processes, and now I can apply that to these media bodies. And I think about the media films, and especially found films, as being a body that I find that has its own life and

agency, and then I can place those sort of digital or analog manipulative processes as a researcher onto those bodies to see how they perform and react. That reaction can be an outcome that can be negative, challenging, an obstacle, but it also can be a visualization tool. As a media maker, I also think, what could be a solution or a remedy? I think about making visible, diagnosing it, seeing it, confronting it, acknowledging it, sharing that experience, and then also at the same time, thinking about ways and opportunities for therapies or solutions. I want to

empower that filmic body to maybe have an outcome in which they could take control again.

It seems your previous experiences being photographed for medical journals have influenced the way you see and interact with film, almost from a medical or research perspective, and even in the way you see the film as a body or cadaver. How does this perspective inform the way you use 16mm work or archival images?

I had a unique experience

where I was photographed for some medical research when I was a child, but it wasn't really clear at the time that that's what the photographs were going to be used for, you know? I have a kind of unique medical issue where my body doesn't process phosphorus correctly. But at the time, they didn't have a diagnosis for that. Long story short, it just put me where I had a lot of experience in the medical world growing up really young and going to different hospitals and different kinds of researchers to try to discover what was going on with me. One of those things I had to do was be photographed. And then, in one case, I found photographs of myself unexpectedly when I was still a kid. It was really shocking because I remembered the experience of being photographed, but the way I was photographed didn't represent the me that I think about as myself. This was at a time when I was getting photographed for school, and I remember the experiences with the medical photographers were similar, where I was having some fun banter with them. I think it seemed really cool, and I'm in the studio space. I mean, at that time in my life, I didn't know I'd become a media artist, but I'm sure all those things kind of were like ticks and boxes.

But, I found these images where focus isn't on me but on an issue that I was having like physically with my body. So, they cut me out as the person. We see this in medical photography all the time. It focuses on whatever the condition is, and cuts out, or blacks out, the human in the photo. There are lots of reasons for that, and through my research, there are also issues of things like wanting to dehumanize the body so that you're not traumatizing potentially like surgeons, for example, who are cutting into bodies. Removing the idea that it's a person, that creates some of these aesthetical choices, these formal choices. I was confronted with this very young, I didn't have that sort of language or understanding of representation. It was just a shock to be represented as a dysfunctional body issue, but I am this other person. Now I can explore these concepts with my own power as a media artist, a media researcher or scholar, I can then use my own experience to kind of unpack what that was like a firsthand kind of haptics.

One thing that took me a really long time to realize was my experience as a clinical photography subject is very personal, and I think about it in a personal way, and I know that other people share that similar experience. It's designed not to be personal. That friction is really interesting to me, and it's something that I push up against with my own work. I push into that dehumanizing aspect, I'm intentionally really aggressive at times with the media. How far do I push this process and am I being exploitative to the point where I can make that exploitation or dehumanization visible? Then again, go back to what would be a remedy for that exploitation. The analogy I like to use is you poison your lab rat so that you can then cure the lab rat, and you hope in that process you don't kill the lab rat, and maybe it's for the greater good. I'm not saying that that's for the greater good, but I'm bringing up some ethical issues, like classical ethical dilemmas and ethical debates in the medical field, bioethics, biopower, and biopolitics. I think about those relationships of power and control, thinking about what's in the greater good for the individual or society versus the potential dangers.

I think what is interesting about some of my

experiences contributing to my work and research was a real sense of our bodies have this other life. I remember thinking about other kids when I was at research hospitals, like the Mayo Clinic or Riley Hospital for Children in Indianapolis. I'd be in waiting rooms with other kids, and I was thinking, who are all these kids? Are they being photographed? I just remember thinking of this sense of like our bodies were not just in the present space of like where I am right now in the waiting room. But our bodies have this other life. And thinking about that other life in the form of media. I couldn't articulate it then, but that's definitely thinking about how we live our lives, not just in our lived bodies, but through media bodies and our media body's experiences.

Those bodies, our media bodies, are being distributed and used in ways in which you might not have control. I had this sense of anxiety about it when I was younger too, that how is my body being used? Would I find it? Would I recognize myself? It was outside of my control or knowledge, and that having a real sense of anxiety or worry that led me into looking through medical catalogs, and wondering if I

would find myself or find my history visually.

What I had found of myself in those pictures was this abstract image of myself? The abstract was personal for me and political. These experiences definitely led me to unpack my own experience and think about both sides of the ethical debate.

In your found footage works, you're also playing with that idea. By abstracting, you do see the figures, they are recognizable, but then we sort of lose them in this loop, this echoing. They're sometimes recognizable, sometimes not. Found footage often has an interesting play of familiarity and foreignness or distance. How do you see the physical decay and previous context of these films as speaking silently through their materiality?

I love all these questions. So one of the things that led me to work was with educational films specifically, and found footage, is I was making some previous work where I was being critical of the manufacturing of research subjects in and of itself. Thinking about regardless of the need or the outcome or

good or bad, right or wrong, or how much it positively impacted the world, that just being a subject in and of itself was transformative. I made a piece dealing with that, but with live action original footage. I felt like if I really get down to the bottom of this argument, could I be critical? How can I be critical of others or unpack this, if I'm making my own research subjects, even if it is for art. But what if I move to found footage? Here we have, especially educational, films in which people are already performing as subjects. I'm kind of recycling their use, so maybe I'm not making new subjects; I'm using past subjects to talk about this. Initially, I thought it was kind of a loophole out of my own ethics, and now I can not be accountable for this or critiqued on this. The 16mm educational film itself is like this interesting genre of film. These are bodies that don't have their own like agency, right? No one cares about them anymore. So I kept kind of pushing further into my logic, and started to see them as really vulnerable bodies, you know, and the fact that they're like a cadaver.

When you have a cadaver, you have to be really mindful of how you're using it. It needs to be respected, because it can't act on its own behalf. I started thinking then further over time as to how to allow the educational film, rather than bend to my will and perform for me, I wanted it to also have aspects of what is its life, both pre mortem, so to speak, before its death as a useful media object.

For example, the source film *Body Contours*, I spoke to a little bit about how I started working through the tools that Signal Culture. It was called an "educational film" that I found on eBay. It's a woman, a nude figure, and she's spinning on this giant Lazy Susan. There was this text at the beginning of the film that said it was for "educational purposes" for drawing students who could not afford to pay for a model. But it really seemed like it was probably made in the 1950s as softcore pornography, as a way to distribute it legally. The subject in that film at some point makes eye contact with the camera and she seems like she's trapped in this continuous loop. So in that case, I was just kind of thinking like, here is this media body that's perpetually in this state of being subjectified, or used in a way that wasn't really

for its own benefit. I started thinking more about the life of these subjects within the film, the life of the film, and how I could then apply some of my techniques and methods to them to see how they perform together. So over time, giving them more agency, and wanting to show that former life with its current use and kind of bring it back- to, in a way, reanimate the cadaver.

I also had an experience where I handled human cadavers for a brief while, as an art student at the University of Florida. A MA candidate in Art History there, knew of the history of cadavers being used in art, so they arranged with the medical school that graduate students from the art department could then draw the cadavers in, then like a similar fashion that folks would have in the past with Art History. I was interested in that history. I volunteered to go along and do this.

For about a few months every Friday, we would have access to these cadavers after they had gone through their two years of service. So normally, a human cadaver, if you donate your body to science, it's used and then it goes back to a final resting space. And so these were at the end of that. Being able

to have firsthand experience with these cadavers, I could see on their bodies scars that would have been from whatever happened in their life, but also all of these marks from their use in research held in the history of their body. And I thought that was really interesting in relationship to some of the things I was thinking about in terms of media and filmic bodies as human bodies and where those relationships were. The experience of handling the human cadavers, there were a lot of conversations that came up between myself, researchers at the university, and my other peers about the efficacy of using the human cadavers and how we were representing them through drawings and art.

This thinking influenced the way I saw and used educational films. How much I show and how much I don't show really goes back and forth between those experiences. I want to make work that speaks to how it was used in the past, what its life was, and then also how we could continue to see that use or misuse per se in the future, or in its relationship to our current culture.

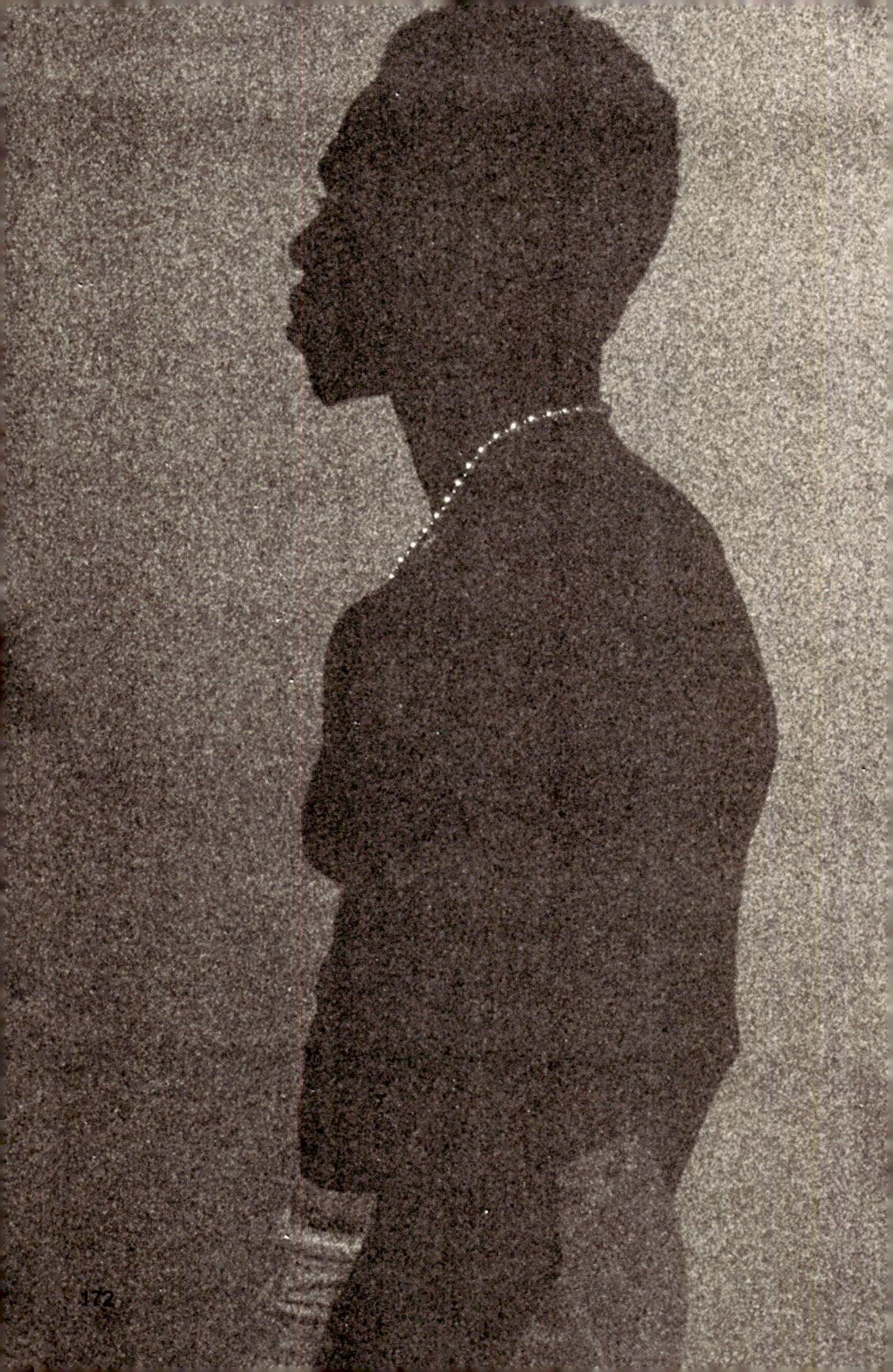

Nadia Bedj

What does erotic mean to you in terms of art making?

The erotic itself is a very powerful force that drives people to feel, act, and create. Not reading into the usual connotation of eroticism that involves nudity, I consider it more as the aesthetics of the inner desire, a psychological force driving you towards something and giving you that impulse for the art making. Therefore erotic is very symbolic for me: a moment, a detail like hair on the face, or a lens flare from the sun, hands touching, or a photo of a phone screen with a text message on it. It all can bring up the feeling of intimacy and sensuality.

Your subjects seem very comfortable with you. How do you go about creating a safe and trusting space when you photograph people?

It's just my innocent face! Hahaha.

I like to spend time with my subjects prior to the shoot, either models or actors—it is important for me to get to know their personalities. I often shoot people who I already know. There is already an established connection between us. I love "street casting" non-actors in movies who already have the right personality for the project. I like when filming mixes with an observation of a character, when there is enough room for improvisation and when the relationship between the camera and the subject is transparent, trustworthy, and honest.

I like to create a comfortable space not just for the subject, but for myself as well. It is hard for me to pretend and give cliché directions. Unfortunately, it happens often on commercial and fashion shoots. For my personal projects, I avoid this approach–the image is not going to work, and the "moment" will be absent.

How does shooting on film change your work? What do you like about it?

I love shooting on film. Who doesn't? The film has a specific aesthetic and texture, and the time you spend on it makes it even more valuable. You actually think about each frame and care about it. It offers a different shooting process and methodology, forcing you to get fully absorbed in photographing and development, rather than digital post-production.

Besides film photography, I've been exploring 35mm film for many years. I recently directed my first motion project, a short film, shot on 16mm film. The director of photography is my talented friend Walt Mzengi. My narrative work from before was shot mostly digitally, or with some Super 8 film. This time it was a much more careful and thoughtful process with each frame. There were fewer takes of each shot, and actually, all the takes looked great. With shooting motion on film you definitely learn and grow as a visual storyteller, it helps to define your language and style. You know what coverage you need. I also like to leave room for spontaneous magic, because it always happens on set. For this reason, shooting digitally is easier, but with film, this magic becomes even more phenomenal.

What draws you to a subject?

Something that is hard to name. It is some kind of a sense of talent or sense of a person's energy that correlates with mine. Personality plays a huge role, and I'm often looking for someone we can collaborate with beyond just depicting an image.

As an introvert, growing up in an oppressive country with no actual freedom of speech and where modesty should prevail in person, especially in women, I am used to being careful in expressing myself verbally. Therefore, the camera helps me a lot to find subjects and connect with them. If it works, there are no borders left between my lens and the subject, and creating a project together becomes an extraordinary fulfillment that the audience feels.

You are also an

accomplished filmmaker. What stories do you want to tell, or are you already telling? How does the medium affect or shape those stories?

I directed a few short films and a feature film *Beware of Dog* that premiered at the Slamdance film festival in 2020. I am also in the NYU Grad Film program that is really helping to expand my voice further.

The themes I raise in my narrative work include coming-of-age self-exploration in an oppressive society, search for identity and belonging, dealing with anxiety and mental health issues while surrounded by misunderstanding, and lack of self-worth in the digital generation.
The visual aspect plays a huge role in developing a story. When I write–I see. And photography often helps me, as more of a therapeutic way of thinking about the story I write, thinking with my eyes. Working within the same style and exploring similar motifs, photography often serves my screenwriting and helps with casting–I meet new faces and explore them through my lens.

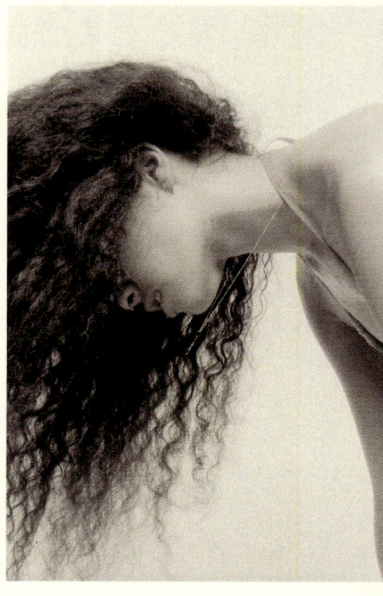

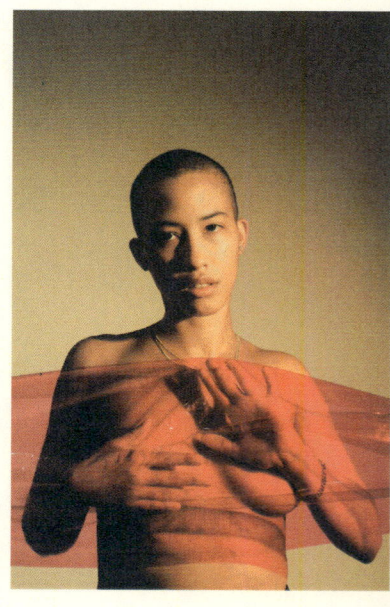

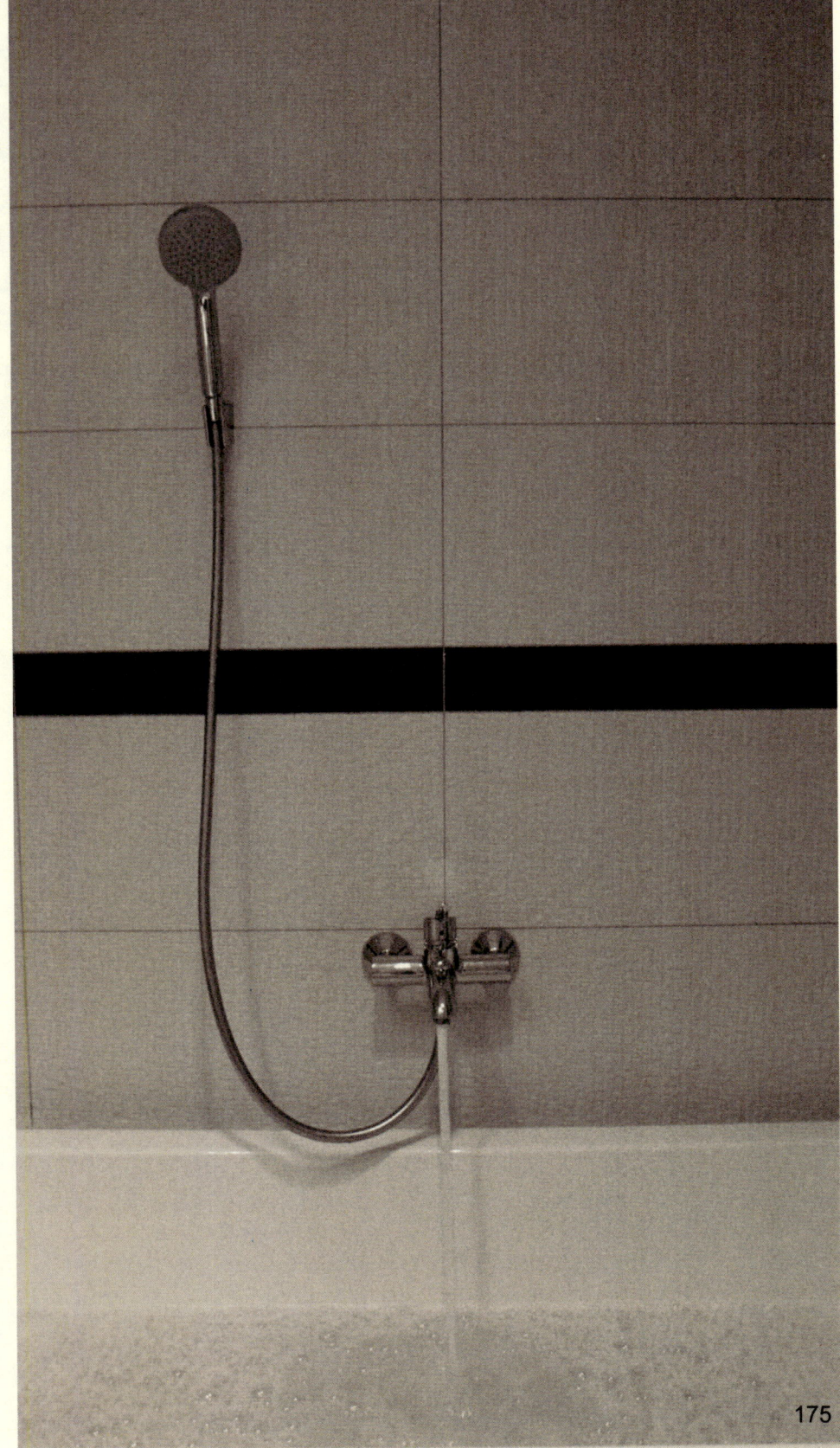

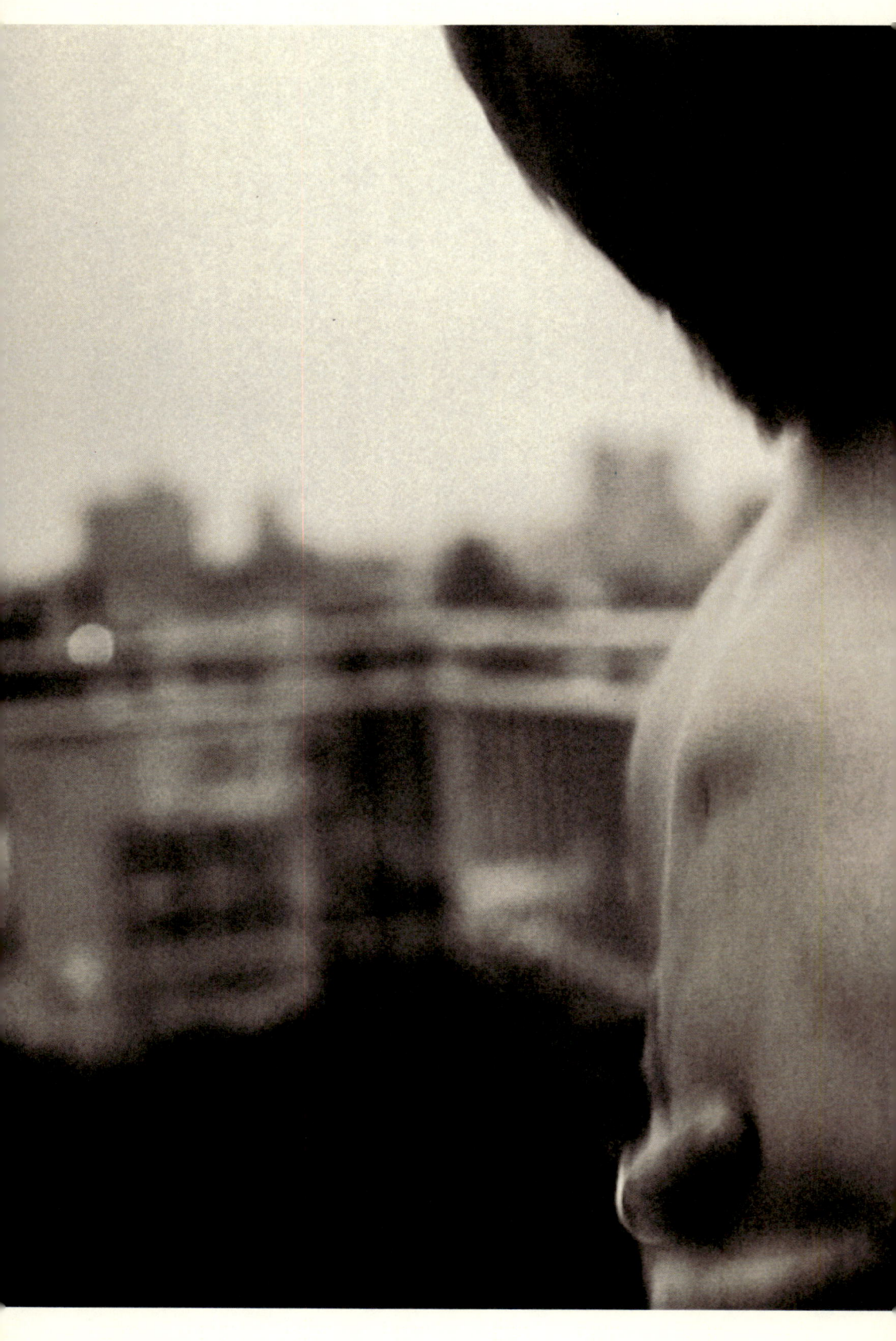

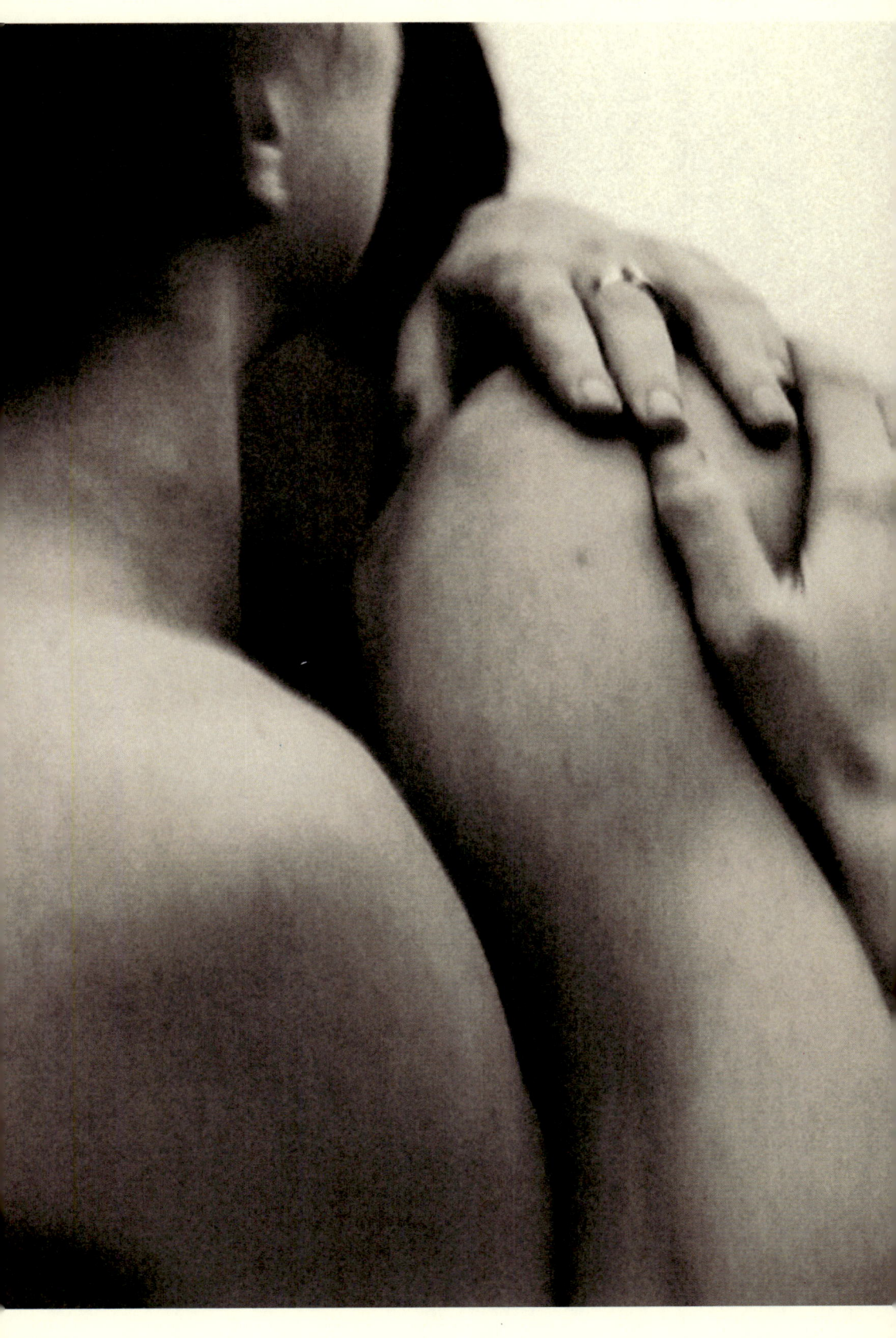

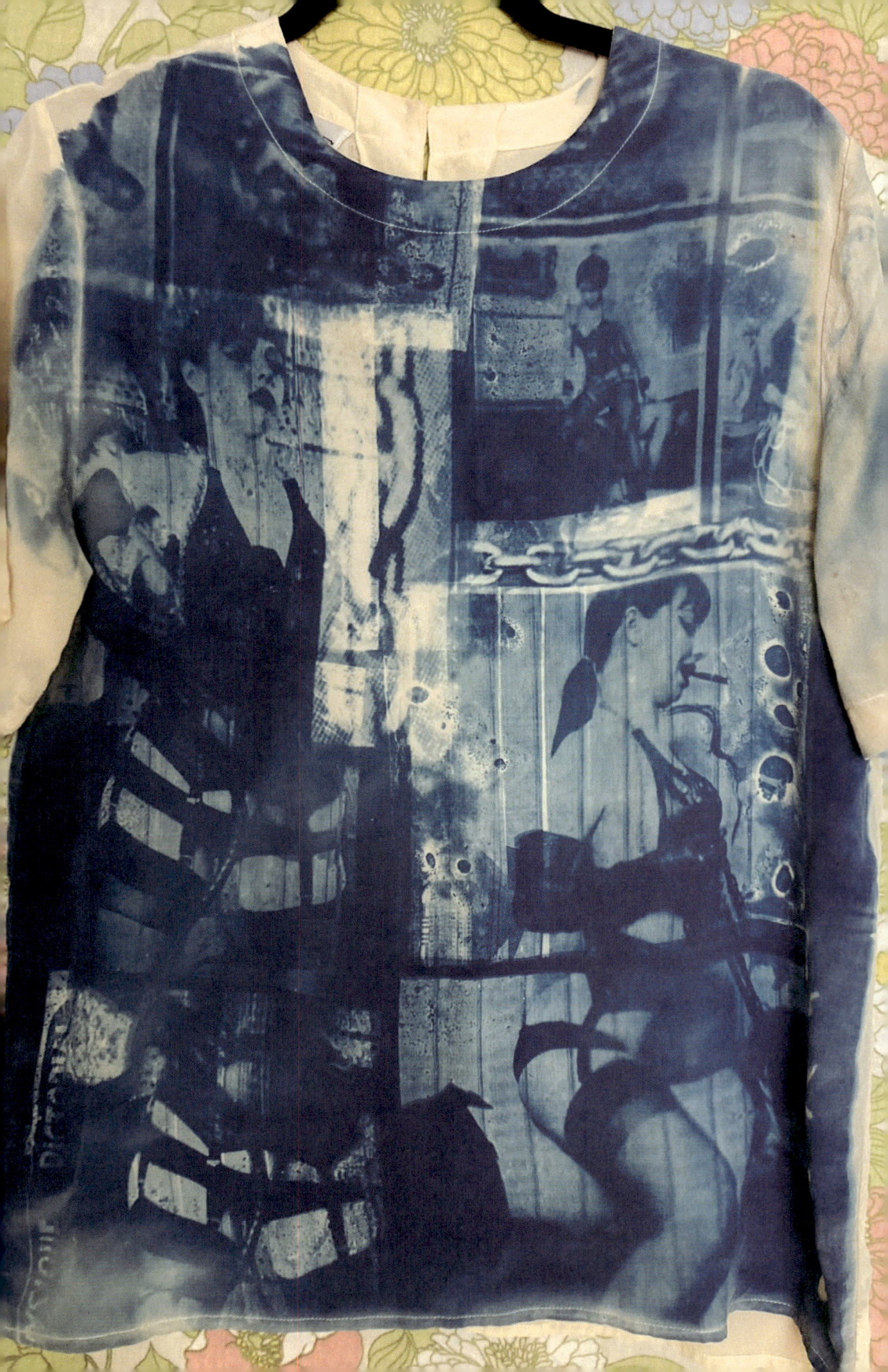

Softcore Print Shop

Sunprints on recycled materials using found pornography

Hannah Helton

Softcore Print Shop is a departure from your work as a multimedia artist. What inspired you to make the shift from fine art to Softcore Print Shop?

I started playing with cyanotypes because they're so straightforward and accessible while still being a place to explore texture and composition. I can get too in my head with my fine art and needed a process I couldn't overthink. I am not a photographer by any means and going blind into a new medium is really freeing.

How did Softcore Print Shop start? Why pornography and how do you source the pornography for your pieces?

On my first date with my girlfriend four years ago she told me her parents bought a house that came with trunks of gay and BDSM porn from the 1940s-90s. I've always loved vintage cheesecake art and photography, probably because I feel so alienated from most contemporary sexual imagery. I was also raised so conservative and repressed that it's a little thrill for the rebellious baptist kid in me. A lot of it is just so sweet to me–the models look like people you'd know in real life but maybe aren't considered marketably attractive by today's standards, and they're just having fun dressing up. Most of the other collage elements are from books on satanism or public domain reviews.

How do you choose the text for your prints?

I just scan and warp stuff I like from writers like Kathy Acker, Frank Bidart, my friend Stone Irvin's poetry. I think writing is better at creating a mood than visual art.

How does thrifting play a role in Softcore?

Everything I print onto is thrifted or sourced by vintage seller friends. It's exciting when I find a great piece that has a wine stain or something and I can give it a new life. Everyone now is scouring thrift stores looking for like, a Stone Cold Steve Austin shirt from 1998 to flip for $100, but it's a fun challenge to transform a weird frumpy nightgown into something really special. When I source clothing I like to open up all these possibilities for myself beyond what's considered fashionable.

Resourcefulness inevitably gives interesting results. I wouldn't call the process sustainable necessarily, but it's nice to know I'm not creating clothing where there was nothing before.

What's your process for creating the cyanotypes in your work? Are there any tips you have for folks working with cyanotypes on fabrics for the first time?

I just invert an image to print on

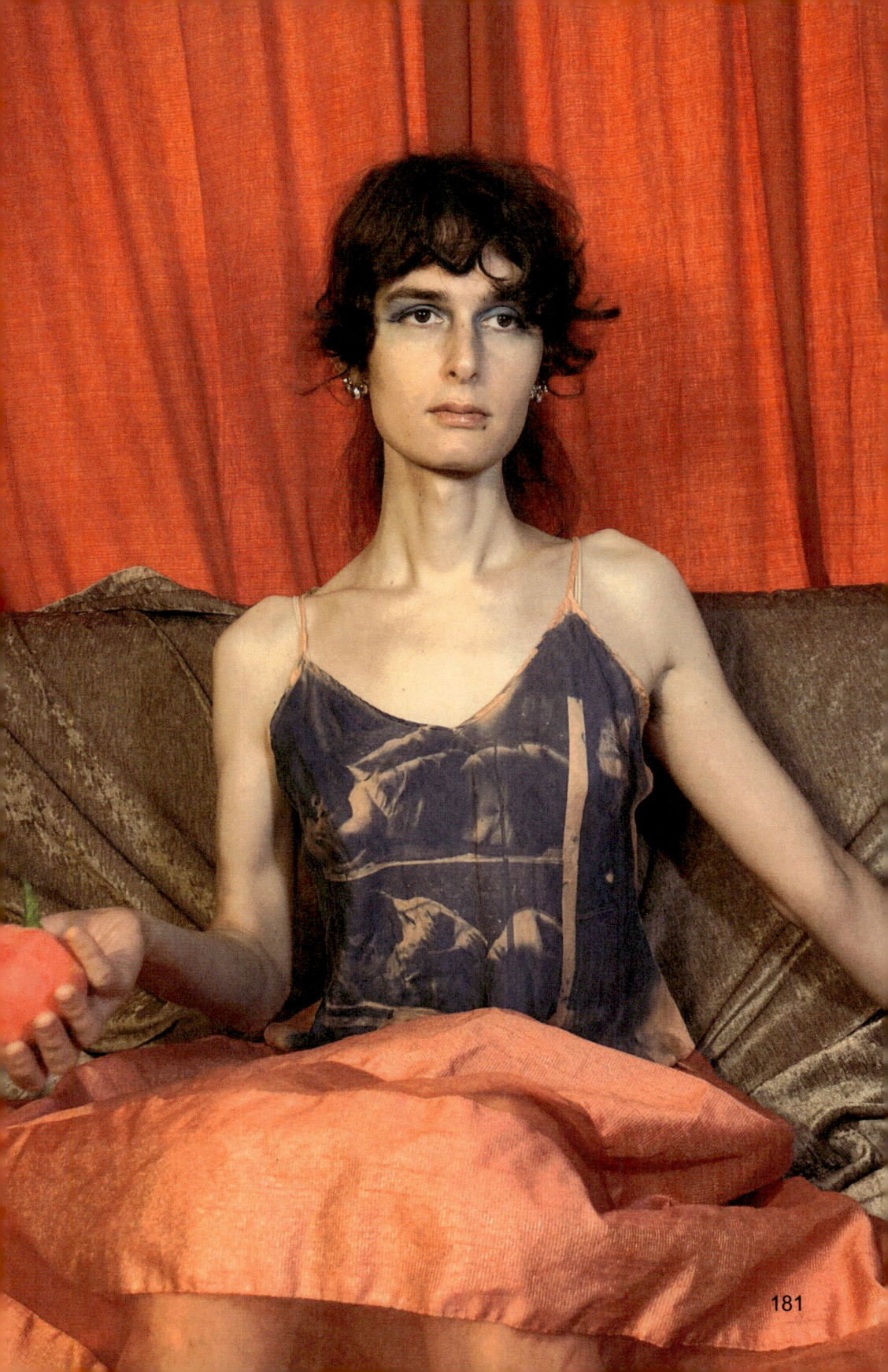

transparencies then collage those elements on my material. It's embarrassingly simple. The internet is your friend! Google anything and everything! I just cobbled together a process from the dozens of guides online and found what worked best with what I had around. Just experiment without trying to be good-challenge yourself to fuck it up and make bad work. My favorite pieces come from asking "I wonder what this thing would do with this other thing or what if I add this," etc.

How do you create the different textures and layers in these prints?

My favorite texture is from the scrap transparencies that I spray water onto and mush together to move the ink around. It kind of looks like burnt celluloid. Also window screen, tortured cheesecloth, and netting covered in liquid rubber. Sometimes I throw soda ash on the finished image for subtractive texture.

What has been your favorite print you've created so far?

Lately I'm really into scans of busted up ancient statues and end-of-times biblical texts.

What's next for Softcore?

I'm playing with sewing and reworking recycled clothing. I also have some collaborations in the works with talented friends who do embroidery, beading, and quilting.

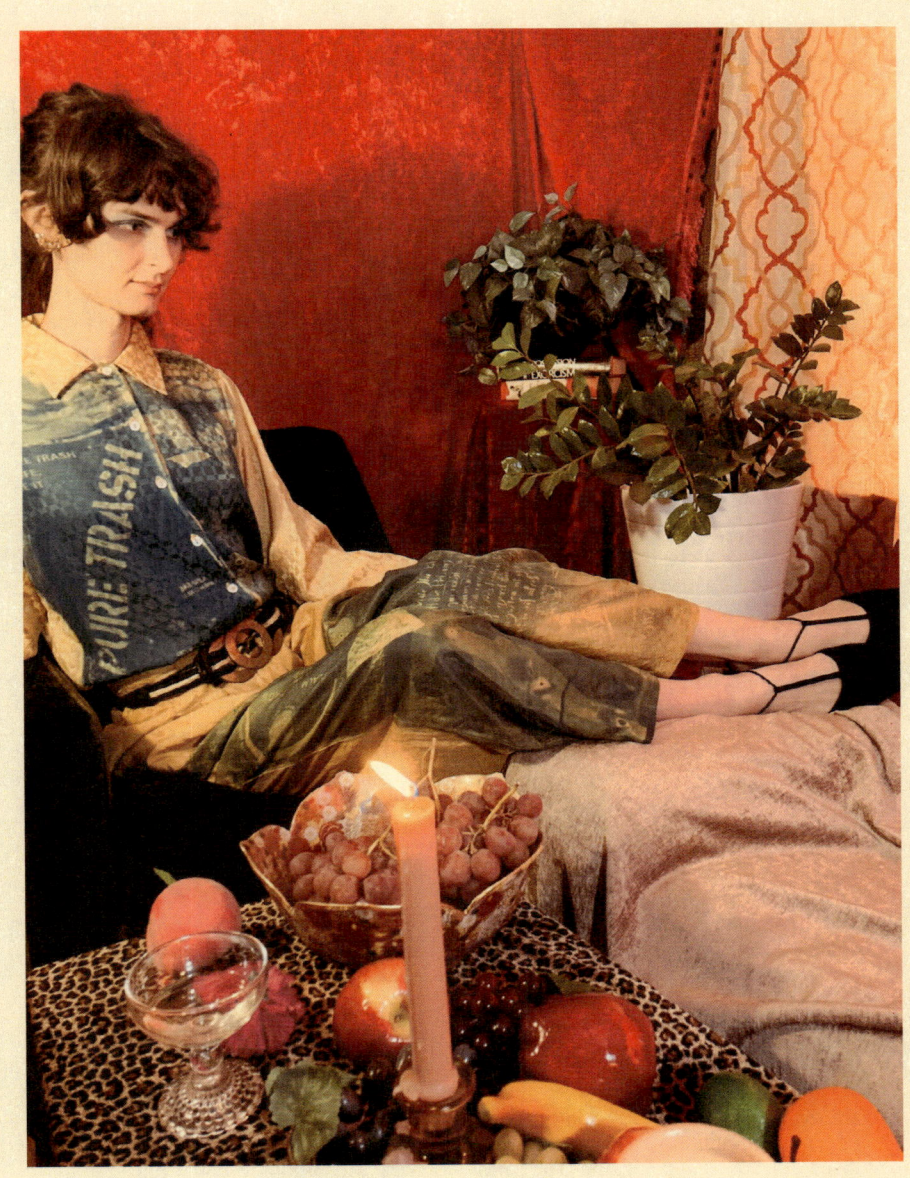

On Knowing (What I Like)

The first thing that comes to mind when I hear the word "erotica," is Madonna's 1992 album and title track of the same name. Not because it held any significance for me at the time it was released, but because against all odds it is still in steady rotation at the strip club I work in.

Customers always ask me what I do for "real work," because although they all want to pay for sex, no one wants to pay a sex worker. When I tell them I'm an artist, they gesture to my undulating, overly-coiffed, chronically-ill and pained body and say, "of course you're an artist!" as if they are being generous about this job. No, sir, I am quite literally an artist. And, no, I don't need a euphemism for my work. I've found happiness and fulfillment in many flavors of sex work, and yet I'd be hard pressed to say I find any of it erotic. My earning potential hinges on my ability to create that experience for someone else, though, and so I think about it a lot.

What makes something erotic? What makes something erotic art? When I Google erotic artwork, I largely find nudity and penetration. When I ask my friends what makes something erotic, they tell me that eroticism lies in our secrets and in our shadows.

Let me tell you some stories about nudity and penetration. Let me tell you some stories about eroticism. Spoiler alert: they are not the same stories.

I am laying on the most uncomfortable bed. The man standing over me asks how I'm feeling. I'm feeling bad, but I say I'm fine and politely ask how he is. He ignores me. He opens my shirt and touches me without asking. The door opens, and someone pops their head in. They have a whole conversation with each other over my body, shirtless and supine. Then, in front of our audience, he tells me there's nothing wrong with me and my symptoms might be psychosomatic.

Two weeks later, another doctor. He asks if three people can watch. Students. I say okay. One asks me if she can try the procedure and I agree. She pulls my gown open to listen to my breathing, and a room full of men see my breasts. You've probably gathered this by now, but this is not unusual for me. I'm just usually in control of it. She penetrates my nose with a scope. It pushes all the way back and down my throat. She tells me to breathe through my mouth, but I gag anyway as it rotates and surveys my insides. It makes me cry. I leave with fewer answers than I came with and a lot more discomfort.

Afterwards, I see a client. He asks if I'll do anal. I won't, and I say that. He says that's fine. He asks if I'll give him a blow job. I tell him I can, but he can't push my head down because I don't like to gag. He says of course. He touches me, and when he does so, he repeatedly tells me that he knows how I like to be fucked. I fake it (expertly, if I do say so myself). If eroticism lies in our secrets, I must be erotic as fuck because my secret is that I don't like him at all. I leave with enough money to pay my Brooklyn-sized bills for a week.

The next morning, I get a call from a friend. There's a video of me on a porn website that I didn't know was taken. She sends me a screenshot, and I immediately recognize a client's home from years prior. His whole channel is this - voyeuristic videos, taken of various providers, over a series of months. I use the contact form on the porn company's website. They delete all of the videos in record time.

I've always resented the way we talk about photography. What do we mean when we say "taking" a photo? When someone is staring down the barrel of my lens, am I taking anything that is not freely given? I know that I'm not – I know no one would, but now I know it can be done. My image was taken from me, and given away. And given away. And given away.

Years later, I lay nestled into my partner in bed. She laughs when my eyelashes tickle her neck just below her ear. My eyes won't

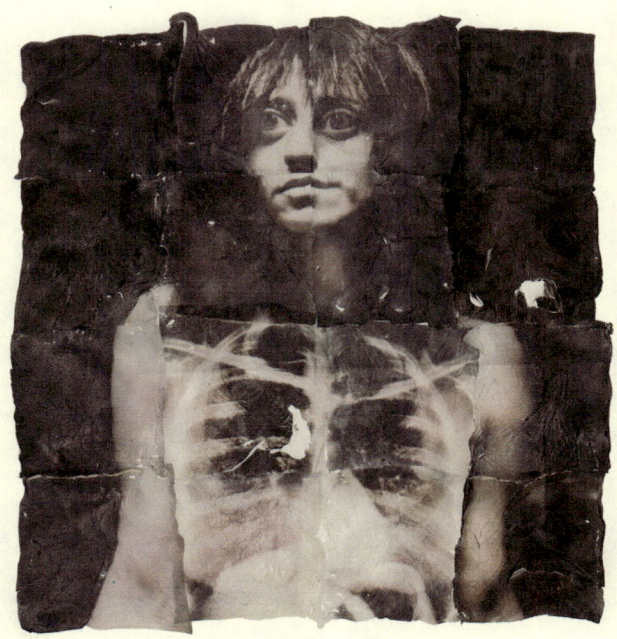

focus, but I can't stop looking at her. I ache, and I ache. We don't have sex. We can't, because my body is stuck in cruise control. We can't because I don't know myself. How do you tell someone that you don't know yourself anymore because so many other people think that they know you?

If eroticism is in our shadows – if it's in the deepest stirrings of ourselves – I feel it in our shared healing. I feel it when she breathes into my hand instead of flinching when I rest it over her heart. I feel it every time I tell her all the things I am afraid of. My whole body is electric when she fights my hopeless, wild hair with her fingers, and in every moment our mouths are close enough to share the same air. I ache, and yet this is so much more than enough.

Every other time I feel it, I'm in my studio. I spend time self-imaging. I scour prints of my x-rays looking for something to tell me what I like. I document my body. I project my body onto my body and document it again. I stare down the barrel of my own lens and I give everything I have – a gift for my future self. I make images. I take nothing.

My future self develops those images. I use noxious liquid and a very light touch. Perhaps a bit on the nose, but I spend hours peeling away layers of emulsion to reveal what's on the celluloid underneath. I pry Polaroids apart. Sometimes they come apart like a dream, and other times the emulsion rips, and flecks of myself are divided between the two halves. It feels good, sometimes, to be shredded.

When I brush the chemicals from each piece of emulsion, it's the most careful anyone has been with my body. It's the most gentle I've ever been with myself. I let my body float in water, weightless and unencumbered. I spend hours pushing those slides around, arranging them just so. I manipulate my body and my skin. I put myself back together. The most erotic I've ever felt is in this work. In crafting my own image. In making it the way that I like. In knowing what I like at all.

-Andi Avery

FREYTAG'S PYRAMID OF CLIMACTIC LIGHT

By taking TRI-X black & white reversal 16mm film and capturing 900 different stills from NC-17 rated films through a 35mm photo camera and projecting the images at the standard cinematic frame rate of 24 frames per second, *Freytag's Pyramid of Climactic Light* interrogates the relationship between the individual film frame and the audience's perception of ideology projected from the relationship between each frame. The images that I selected were bodies of individuals in non-violent and sentimental acts of love and friendship. By using a cropped frame, the bodies extend beyond the frame and onto the sprockets, allowing the subject to devour cinematic space and time that has been dissolved and satiated through censorship. The images synchronize with sound snippets from critically-acclaimed films from 1968 to 2017 that have been rated PG-13 by the Motion Picture Association. The violence of the sound is reflected in the pattern of light emitted from the flickering images, which is chronologically representative of the five acts of Freytag's Pyramid.

Freytag's Pyramid is a dramatic structure based on Aristotle's Poetics and consists of five acts: exposition, rising action, climax, falling action, and denouement (Freytag). The five-act structure is used as the framework for most mainstream films.

Mainstream audiences often consume images without considering the censored ideology that shapes their viewing pleasure. The MPAA has been curating mainstream audience appetites through censorship since 1968 with ratings from G (General Audience) to NC-17 (Adults Only) (Motion). Many theaters refuse to exhibit NC-17 material. The MPAA rating system often treats LGBTQIA+ material more harshly than heterosexual and violent material (Pollard). My goal for this piece is to disrupt the audience's complacency about their consumption of images to expand the possibilities of narrative storytelling in mainstream cinema. This project began as a short experimental film and has expanded into a 5-channel video installation.

Randy Schildmeyer, Kyler Bruner, and Ross Clarke helped me design, build, and install this installation in Studio A of the Becker Communication Building on the University of Iowa's campus.

Randy and Kyler standing at the center of the installation where the audience is positioned to sit.

The installation with the five images rear-projected.

Kai Swanson

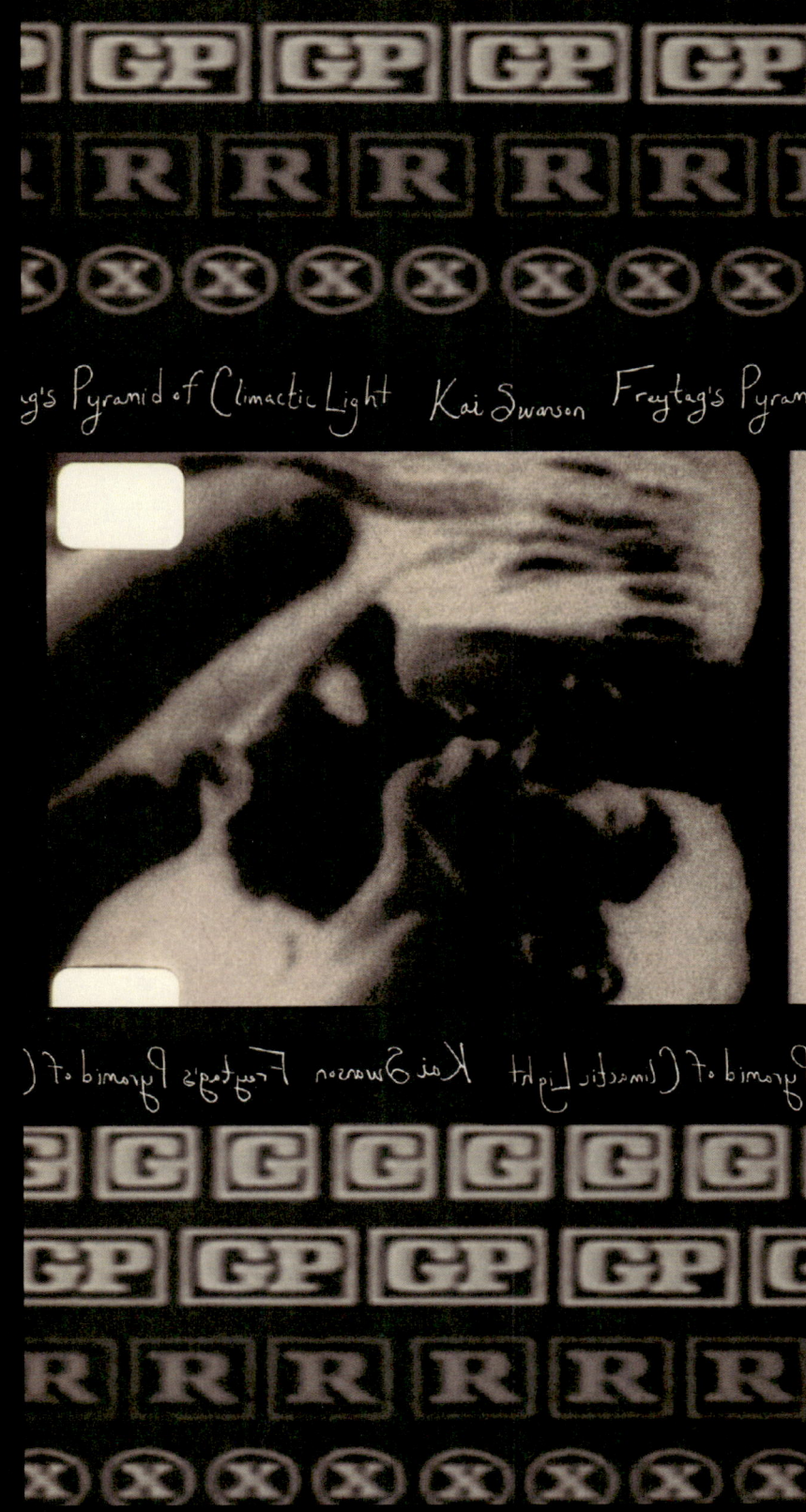

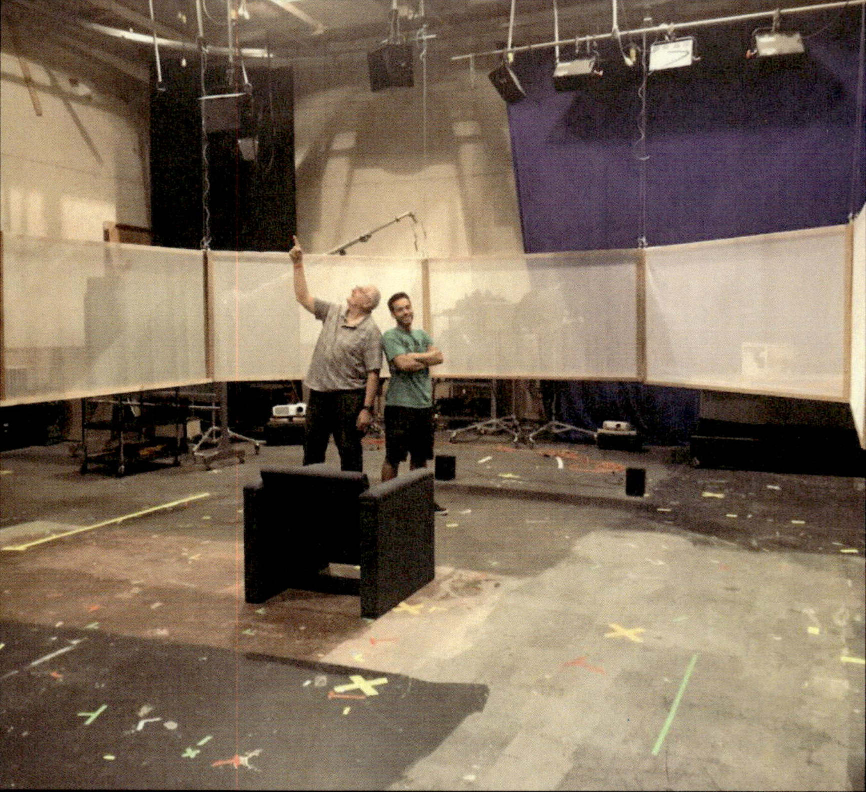

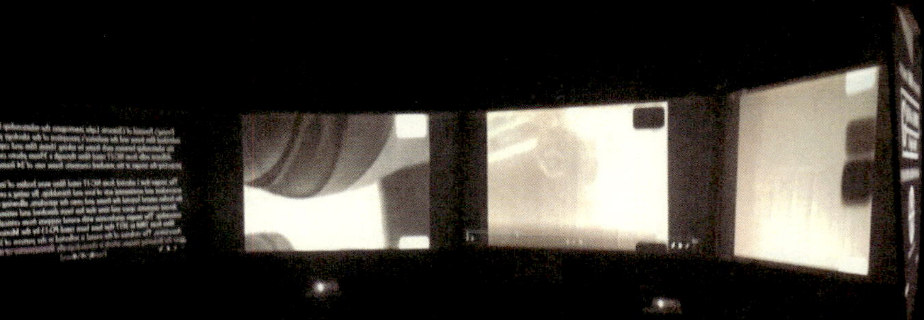

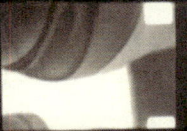
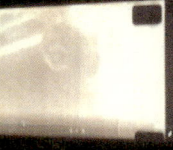

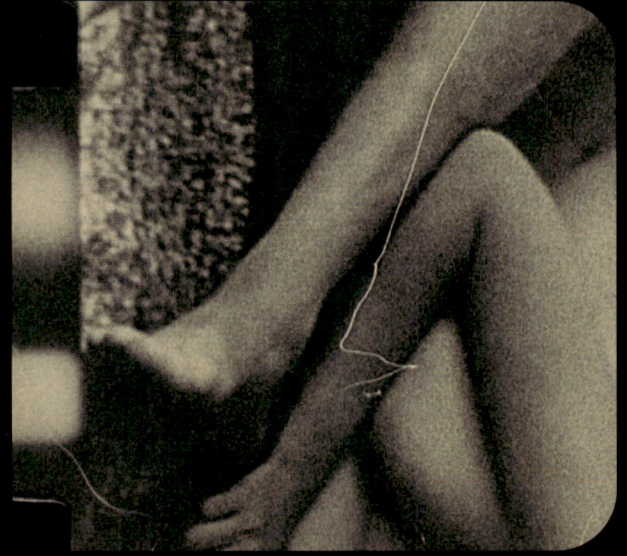

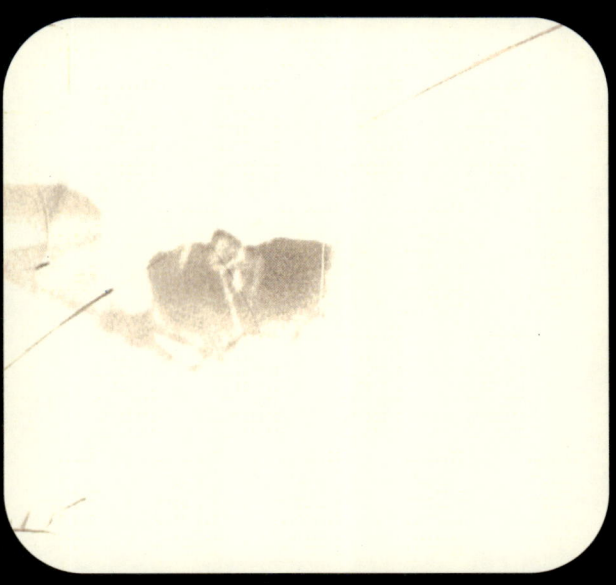

Work Cited:
Freytag, Gustav, and Elias J. MacEwan. Freytag's Technique of the Drama: An Exposition of Dramatic Composition and Art. Johnson Reprint Company, 1894.
Motion Picture Association of America, Inc. "Film Ratings." mpaa.org, Motion Picture Association of America, Inc, 2018, http://www.mpaa.org/film-ratings/.
Pollard, Leslie Thomas. "Sex and Violence: The Hollywood Censorship Wars." Sex and Violence: The Hollywood Censorship Wars, Paradigm Publishers, 2009, p. 135.
Special thank you to Eli Boonin-Vail, Kyler Bruner, Chris Butner, Ross Clarke, Mike Gibisser, Christopher Harris, Traci Hercher, Tom Jackson, Brian James, Sam Kessie, Angie Looney, Tim Looney, Randy Schildmeyer, and Matthew Schlimgen.